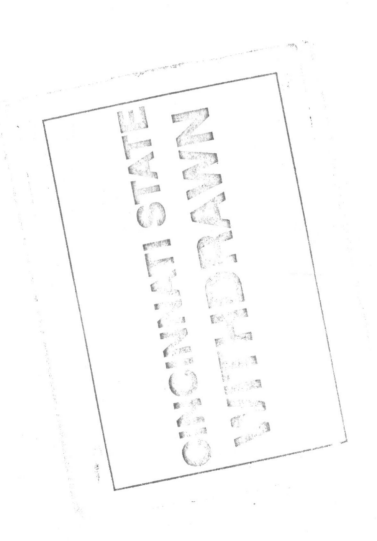

interview

interview

Claudia Dreifus

Foreword by Clyde Haberman

Seven Stories Press
New York

Library of Congress Cataloging-in-Publication Data
Dreifus, Claudia
Interview / by Claudia Dreifus. — 1st ed.
p. cm.
ISBN 1-888363-42-8 (alk. paper)
1. Interviews. I. Title.
PN4874.D74I58 1997
081—dc21   96-37549
                                        CIP
10 9 8 7 6 5 4 3 2 1
Seven Stories Press, 632 Broadway, 7th fl., New York, N.Y. 10012
In Canada: Seven Stories Press /Hushion House, 36 Northline Road, Toronto,
Ontario M4B 3E2, Canada.
In England: Seven Stories Press/Turnaround Publisher Services, Ltd. Unit 3,
Olympia Trading Estate, Coburg Road, Wood Green, London N22 6TZ, U.K.
Book design by Adam Simon
Printed in the U.S.A.

To Beatrice Dreifus, whose love and steady
example have made so much possible.

Contents

Foreword

The interview is the DNA of journalism, the nucleus from which all life flows. Newspaper and magazine writers draw vital information, and sometimes inspiration, from government documents or corporate memos. These days, many journalists are chained to their computers, surfing the Internet for material. But it's all lifeless data without an interview, without going out to learn what real people think. Even if the reporter does nothing more than put a quick clarifying question to an expert on the phone, he is conducting an interview. And how he has thought out that question and worded it can spell the difference between producing something people will want to read or toss aside.

Imagine then how much more delicate, and demanding, an interview is when the goal is a searching probe of a celebrated figure. The task seems deceptively straightforward. Many Americans have misguided views of what an interview should be from having watched too much television. On TV, reporters often delude themselves into thinking that they are at least as interesting as their subjects. The result is an insufferable amount of on-air preening and pomposity, with questions that are either excessively combative or totally inane.

"Tell us, Mr. Mayor," the TV reporter says with feigned sincerity. "Is this the most difficult decision you've ever had to make?"

"Bob," the Mayor responds with on-cue earnestness, "this is the most difficult decision I've ever had to make."

Numbing.

In this collection of interviews, which were conducted for *The New York Times Magazine* and other publications, Claudia Dreifus shows us how the job is supposed to be done. Of course, most readers will be interested primarily in what the subjects themselves have to say. But in this book they also get important lessons in how a skilled journalist climbs inside another person's skin. It is by being well-prepared and asking the right questions; by knowing when to be quiet and let the subject rattle on; by knowing, too, when a topic has been exhausted and it is time to move on; by truly listening and asking follow-up questions.

An interesting interview is a collaborative effort, between a willing subject and an artful questioner. If either one falls short, forget it. Even the most fascinating person will come across as dull if the questions are not sharp. And not only does Dreifus ask good questions, but she also goes about her work so subtly that the reader may not notice. Which is how it should be.

Take her conversation with Andrew Young, the former American Ambassador to the United Nations and a man Dreifus classifies under the heading of "Saints." Young recalled how once, during his days as Ambassador, he was at the Waldorf-Astoria, where a guest handed him his car keys, believing out of knee-jerk racism that this black man had to be the parking attendant.

I cannot begin to count the number of reporters, including many held in high regard, who would have expressed dismay and said all the politically right things—and then switched subjects. Dreifus, instead, asked a question that was wondrous in its simplicity: "What did you do?" It produced an intriguing response. Young said that he took the keys and carried them to the fellow who did park cars.

"Does it ever bother you?" Dreifus asked. That's another question many journalists would not have troubled themselves with. Isn't it obvious he would be bothered by this insulting behavior? Well, maybe it is obvious. But by not asking the question, they would have lost an intriguing insight into Andy Young. "My parents raised me to treat racism as a sickness," he said. "And you don't get upset at sick people."

I first met Dreifus in Jerusalem a few years ago, when I was the *New York Times* correspondent there. She had come to interview Hanan Ashrawi, whose many TV appearances made her the most recognizable Palestinian figure besides Yasir Arafat. By then, I had spoken with Ashrawi quite a few times myself. Yet I was amazed how Dreifus, fresh off the plane, already knew more about this woman than I did. Plain and simple, she had done exhaustive research, the basic building block of a successful interview. Without knowing your subject going in, how will you ever know what to ask?

Unfortunately, preparation alone does not always do the trick. As in any other field, successful interviewers need good timing, and sometimes a dash of moxie. Dreifus showed this when she went to Rangoon in 1995 to interview Daw Aung San Suu Kyi, the Burmese pro-democracy leader. Aung San Suu Kyi was newly released from years of house arrest and testing the limits of her freedom. It was the perfect moment for a Western reporter to show up. Dreifus did. But Aung San Suu Kyi's aides said that she would have only half an hour with "The Lady," not nearly enough time for a serious interview. So Dreifus pleaded and wheedled, prying two hours loose and tenaciously coming almost every day to ask for still more time—and then get it. No one ever said this is always a lofty enterprise, journalism. Raw talent is essential. But so is raw nerve.

With each of the interviews in this collection, Dreifus takes us backstage, and she is a candid guide. She admits to having cried after a session with the Dalai Lama went badly. She is not shy about pursuing subjects who initially agreed to interviews and then said no, like Benazir Bhutto and Richard Dreyfuss. In both those cases, she eventually got her way.

But she doesn't always. Arafat and Fidel Castro are two interviews that Dreifus sought and never got. Just as well, some would say. Both men are notoriously uninteresting in Q-and-A formats, latching onto almost any question as an excuse to speechify rather than illuminate. Still, as Dreifus said to me at one point, "one hates to fail."

Clearly, that doesn't happen to her too often. Dreifus has a knack for persuading remarkable people to sit down with her and open up. And she also knows how to take care of herself.

After that interview with Hanan Ashrawi, she made copies of her many tapes and asked me to keep them safe in my Jerusalem office. She was going on to Jordan across the Allenby Bridge, which is controlled on the West Bank side by Israeli forces. Who knows what might happen, she said. Just in case the soldiers confiscated the tapes, for whatever reason, she wanted there to be a duplicate set.

In the end, her worrying was for naught. The Israelis didn't even bother looking at her bags. But I admired how she had planned ahead. It was a helpful reminder—especially to someone like me, whose tape recorder often dies because he's forgotten to put in fresh batteries—that being ready for any contingency is essential.

Still, being clever about the mechanics of the job is hardly enough. The simple fact is that Claudia Dreifus is exceptionally skilled in her subtle craft. That's because she is keenly interested in people, all sorts of people. I mentioned to her once that she really seemed to like the folks she'd interviewed. "I do look for the better side of human behavior," she agreed.

"I prefer such people." But don't mistake her for a Pollyanna. "I assure you," she said, "that I've also interviewed plenty of the other kind."

Clyde Haberman
New York, February 1997

Acknowledgments

Front and center, great thanks to Jack Rosenthal, Adam Moss, Gerald Mazarotti, Micheala Williams, Harvey Shapiro, and the editors of *The New York Times Sunday Magazine*, whose foresight, creativity and commitment have permitted me to experiment with the interview form these past years. These editors make work a joy and provide me with endless opportunities to learn and to perfect my craft. Thanks also to the entire crew at *The New York Times Magazine*—story editors, picture editors, researchers, secretarial staff—they are some of the smartest, best-natured, and hardest working journalists in the news business.

Special thanks to Alan Burdick, until recently a story editor at the *Times Magazine*, and the official supervisor of my work. Burdick's special combination of wit, kindness, and patience nurtured many a difficult story. Elvis Burgos, a *Times* researcher, has been the source of much excellent information at a moment's notice.

My thanks to David Anderson for much useful advice. And to Clyde Haberman for his good words and forebearance.

More gratitude to G. Barry Golson, formerly executive editor of *Playboy* and *TV Guide*, and currently editor in chief of *Yahoo! Internet Life!!!*, for many opportunities and also nearly two decades worth of lessons in the art of the interview.

Thanks to J. Henry Fenwick, editor, and John Wood, articles editor of *Modern Maturity*, both great appreciators of the interview form who have brought a regular interview feature into their extremely popular magazine. John was particularly kind to share his thoughts on the art of interviewing with me.

Warmest appreciation also to my literary agents Ellen Levine and Diana Finch, a source of support and good counsel over the years. Their associates Louise Quayle, Jay Rogers, and Deborah Clifford were so helpful in sorting through the details that had to be covered if this book was to happen.

There is love to Celine, Arlene, Betsy, and Rosalie for their fortitude—and gratitude for so many kindnesses. I am also tremendously grateful to Ernest Thorington, a talented artist who puts in two tough days each week as my personal assistant and whose efforts on this book were critical.

There are sad remembrances of the late Erwin Knoll, editor of *The Progressive*, a kind of substitute father figure who in one of his non-crumudgeonly moments suggested that I put together a collection something like this one. It is impossible to express how much Erwin, with his spikey, angry, funny polemic, is missed. The only comfort is that Matthew Rothschild has taken over *The Progressive* and has successfully reinvented it.

Deep thanks to my students in the Graduate Creative Writing Program of the City College of New York. Their varied life experiences, their fellowship, and their astonishing stories constantly inspire me. Wednesday is always my favorite day of my week.

Finally, there is special gratitude for Dan Simon, the publisher and founder of Seven Stories Press and a unique figure in the publishing world. This is a man who cares about books and ideas with such passion that he transforms work into love. It's not for nothing that the French recently made him a Chevalier: he was one before he was knighted. Dan's Seven Stories crew—Jon Gilbert, Moyra Davey, Carolina Garcia, and Mika De Roo—are the definition of the term, "young, gifted, and smart."

Introduction

Some years ago, I happened to be sitting next to Ringo Starr—perhaps the wittiest and least appreciated of the Beatles—and we found ourselves chatting about his percussionist's craft. Starr believed himself to be one of the best drummers in all the rock and roll universe. Yet few pop historians agreed with him.

"It was always thought that I was in the background with those 'funny fills,' as the press used to call them," he complained sweetly. "Well, those 'funny fills' are my art! No one can play them like I do. A fill is when a drummer goes dud-dud-dud-dud, when you're filling in the gaps. I had this weird style of playing them, and it confused a lot of people. . .Do you understand what I'm talking about?"

"Interviewing is something like drumming," I told Starr. "You stay in the background and people think you haven't done much."

"Id-jets," he returned, in perfect Liverpudlian.

More than a decade later, I found myself sharing a speeding New York taxi with a journalist of enormous reputation and accomplishment, an elegant woman in her eighties who'd witnessed firsthand some of the major events of this century. I had just begun publishing Q and A-style interviews for *The New York Times Magazine* and my work was eliciting a lot of comment.

"You know, Claudia, people wonder what it is that you actually do at the *Times*," this legend commented, as our taxi lurched from one lane into another. "Just the other day, someone asked me, 'What's so special about asking questions and printing the answers? Anyone can do it.'"

"Oh, can they?" I asked frostily, adding: "There's a craft to those questions and answers."

"Of course there is," she allowed, not convincingly.

"Id-jet," I thought to myself.

There's something about interviewing—it may be the visual simplicity of the work, those deceptively uncomplicated Q's and A's—that results in the form being the abused and underappreciated stepchild of

American journalism. Yet, for those of us who earn our daily bread as print interviewers—Studs Terkel, Lawrence Grobel, Robert Sheer, Oriana Fallaci—the interview is an elegant form, a showcase for ideas, personality and language—clean, unobtrusive, minimalist. And such fun.

"Good interviews read a little like great dramas," asserts John Wood, articles editor at *Modern Maturity*, which prints a lengthy Q and A with a different history-maker in every issue. "They have a beginning, a middle, and an end—and catharsis. In a good interview, subject and journalist are antagonists, and then come together, and it's all spontaneous."

The interviewer, in fact, creates a mini-play. The use of playwriting techniques is key to producing a readable product. Every exchange should be motivated, one line of questioning should lead to another logically, the story has to have internal integrity. In other words, there has to be a narrative to all these questions and answers. The ending ideally should have some connection to the lead. A reader hopefully should feel they've been on a journey that made sense.

I always tell myself: kid, you're writing a two-character play, and you're the minor one. The interview-subject is, of course, the lead. The interviewer is the supporting player who moves the story forward with an intelligent line of questioning. The interviewer can also be seen as the voice of the reader, making those ultra-logical queries a reader might make, were he/she in the room.

G. Barry Golson, who for twelve years as executive editor was the guiding force behind the *Playboy* Interview (and who now edits *Yahoo! Internet Life!!!*), agrees, and adds, "Instead of theater's many contributors, the Q and A depends on two people: the subject, of course, and the interviewer, who must be journalist, researcher, interrogator, actor, diplomat, playwright, editor. I always found it harder to hire good interviewers than good writers."

The pieces collected in *Interview* are the end product of that extraordinary job description. I've tried to provide some interesting revelations by some of this decade's history-makers, and also a guide-by-example for journalism students. (My students in the Graduate Creative Writing Program of the City College of New York have long urged me to create a text for them on interviewing.) All the interviews included here were produced in the 1990s, and most appeared originally in *The New York Times Magazine*, the rest in *TV Guide, Modern Maturity, Premiere* and *The Progressive*. For the book, I've restored portions of many of the interviews that were left out of the magazine versions, since there is a bit more room in a book to roam and graze.

If there's a theme to the twenty-one pieces collected in this volume, it is my personal interest in the way power works, in the ways individuals affect history, in how history changes character. I grew up in a family of refugees from Nazi Germany, people deeply scarred by their encounters with dictatorship, war and immigration. In my own time, I've seen the civil rights movement, the women's movement, human rights campaigns, space exploration, and computer technology transform everything we know. And all this is tucked into my tote bag—along with my tape recorders, file cards and notes when I enter a room to begin an interview. "How have you changed the world—how has the world changed you?" I'm always asking. I deeply want to know.

Perhaps because it is such an intimate business, interviewing requires curiosity, empathy, a touch of charisma, and something that the Germans call *menshlichkeit*—humaneness.

But the great interviewers are also seducers. I remember Q and A-ing the Italian interviewer, Oriana Fallaci, and feeling that her skill was probably less in her well-advertised confrontations with subjects, and more in her charm—which was considerable, and burned like a Klieg on anyone in her presence.

Oriana Fallaci once told me she had loathed interviewing renowned North Vietnamese strategist General Vo Nguyen Giap in 1969—because the general out-maneuvered her. "I couldn't function as I usually do," Fallaci complained of the victor of Dien Bien Phu and Tet. "I had very little time. Then Giap, he dominated me, though we had time to make a fight. At a certain moment, we were shouting at each other. And when [Henry] Kissinger said he would see me because of that interview, I could not believe my ears. The Kissinger interview [was] even uglier... because it was so short, because he didn't open up. I need time to make an interview. And I need complicity. And I had neither."

Though she probably didn't mean it in the Giap context, Fallaci's comment points to one of the great secrets of the Q and A, its unspoken sexual element. Like love-making, interviewing requires attention, involvement, time—a willingness on the part of both subject and the interviewer to go with the moment.

One of my favorite interviews was with the Mexican novelist Carlos Fuentes in Chicago in February 1985. Our topic was revolution and literature in Latin America and Eastern Europe. There was a blizzard outside, so we sat around the Drake Hotel for two solid days drinking red wine and telling each other stories. The piece ultimately had the dreamy feel of a tryst, and it was that tone that carried the text along.

Here's Lawrence Grobel, one of the best in the *Playboy* stable, talking shop in *Writer's Digest*: "I sold encyclopedias for a short period of time and it probably taught me more about interviewing than anything I've ever done. . . . When you walk in, look around. See if they have paintings on the wall, something you recognize—a particular book, piece of furniture, anything you can relate to." Grobel describes coming into the room and immediately moving a piece of furniture or sitting on a certain chair that the subject hadn't intended for him. That's his way of signaling, "I'm not going to let you confine me." Grobel believes that interviews are always a power struggle between interviewer and subject. He's probably right. Every time you turn on the tape recorder, the bell sounds for another battle of wills. Who will control this encounter? Who will win this game? Lawrence Grobel has his little tricks. We all do.

I began with a degree from New York University in theater, and only later became a journalist. Originally, I'd hoped to be an actress. Or a playwright. Yet, by the time I'd finished school in 1966, the higher drama of 1960s politics overtook me and my first jobs as an adult were in the political realm—writing speeches, press releases, organizing things.

The problem was that politics interested me intellectually, but didn't suit me temperamentally. I hated the everyday lies that were endemic to the business, "the spin," as they call it now. I despised the manipulation, the falseness, the bad deeds rationalized by the dream of the good end. And so, at the age of twenty-three, I embarked on yet another career—reporting.

From the first, journalism was a great fit. As a writer, I could observe the political world, without being of it. I would witness, rather than exhort, which was fine. Like Chauncey Gardner in Jerzy Kozinski's, *Being There*, I preferred "to watch."

And interviewing, that unique sub-specialty of journalism, particularly suited me. It used all I knew. Interviewing was the only area in print-reporting with a serious performance element to it. Even now, when

I write up my Q's and A's, I constantly ask myself acting-type questions. Is the dialogue motivated? Does this sound real? Was I really "listening" to the interview subject?

Probably the most important decision an interviewer will have to make is in the choice of subject. This may sound terribly obvious, but I try to choose interesting people with something to say.

As such I scan the Sunday morning television news shows for signs of politicians who talk in something other than sound bites. I also read *The New York Times*, *The Washington Post* and more obscure publications like *World Press Review* and *Hollywood Reporter* for ideas. If I am interested in the president of Sri Lanka or the Mayor of Ankara or Demi Moore, I might look up their clipping file on the database Nexis to see what sorts of interviews the potential subject has already given.

I also rely on my editors, who often have even wider experiences and interests than mine, to find the eclectically interesting. The notion of interviewing Alvin and Heidi Toffler and Art Caplan came from the ever-catholic mind of Jack Rosenthal, editor of *The New York Times Magazine*.

What I look for in my subjects is an openness, a fluidity of language and honesty. With Q and A, because one has less room for interpretation, one either has to run with the piece—or kill the story. The interviewer has to be pretty certain that the subject is truthful. I once spiked a *Playboy* interview I'd spent much time on because I thought the actor in question might be using me to libel an actress he was feuding with. There was no way to prove or disprove some of his juicy assertions and I did not want to be party to anything so potentially shady.

Sometimes, my preliminary research will undo an assignment. Recently, a publication asked me to do a Q and A with ex-Watergate figure and now radio talk-show host G. Gordon Liddy. At first, I thought he might be fun. I mean, the guy is so edgy in his extremities and the fact that a former Watergate plumber is winning First Amendment awards is interesting. But when I read his autobiography, *Will*, and saw a recent *Playboy* "20 Questions" with him, I decided to bail out. To me, he seemed humorless, wooden, unreflective. The usually light and playful "20 Questions" feature dragged. I sensed this was an assignment that wouldn't work. At least not for me.

If, after a few pitches, a potential subject is truly and totally negative about an interview, I'll drop my pursuit of them. No point. If someone is going to act like you're dragging them to the Spanish Inquisition, they won't help you create the kind of material that will read well.

On the other hand, here's former *Playboy* editor Murray Fischer in *Alex Haley: The* Playboy *Interviews* describing how Alex Haley got Dr. Martin Luther King to sit down for a 1965 *Playboy* interview: "After a frustrating series of cancellations and three trips to Atlanta, he still hadn't met the man, and most interviewers would have given up. But Alex had taken pains to befriend King's secretary, and he finally threw himself on her mercy. He couldn't face his editor empty handed again, he told her and she sent him to a church barbeque King was attending. 'Let him see you there, but don't press,' she advised. He did what he was told, sitting there with a plate of chicken and potato salad till King finally took pity on him and came over to say hello, suggesting that they might talk for a few minutes over in his office. Their little chat stretched late into the night."

The second most important decision an interviewer must make is to commit to preparation. You should go into a session as prepared as any trial lawyer before a jury. Thus the interviewer should know the answer to any question he or she might as, or at least have a vague idea of what the answer might be and have alternative follow-up strategies ready.

At the same time, the interviewer must be willing to be astonished. It is useful to come in with a line of questions and a rehearsed plan but it is important not to hold rigidly to it. If this is a play, it is an improvisational one. And just like in acting, the interviewer must be able to listen, to go with what is heard, to change course mid-interview.

Whether or not the interview will succeed will very much depend on the chemistry between the subject and the interviewer. That, in turn, depends on the level of preparation. An actor needs to know his lines, understand the motivation of his and the other characters. An interviewer needs to know all that is possible about the interviewee—through Nexis, books, clips, interviews with friends and relatives—before he or she ever turns on the tape recorder. Whenever I feel anxious about a particular interview, I combat my fears with aerobic research.

Even the toughest subjects will respond warmly to a well-prepared interviewer. The fact that I have confidence in my material makes me a strong questioner. Interviewing can be a bit like an intellectual boxing match. One had better enter the ring in top shape. As Oriana Fallaci, a more combative practitioner than I, once told me about her state of mind when she begins interviewing, "My insides are the insides of a soldier who begins to storm a hill."

Fallaci fights her fear with aggression. I control mine with tenacity and preparation.

Of course, the actual interview—the face to face—is the really vital part of the process. If the journalist doesn't get good material on tape, there's little that can be done to improve the story later on. As in documentary filmmaking, "If you don't have it on film, you don't have it."

Now, not all journalists think highly of tape recorders. Gay Talese, in his preface to *The Norton Book of Interviews*, rails against interviewers using the machine. "A tape recorder is to fine interviewing what fast food is to fine cooking," he suggests. "It permits the journalist to spend a minimum amount of time with the subject while following the question and answer path that leads to the undistinguished kind of article-writing that prevails today. The plastic rolls of tape record the first-draft drift of people's responses, and I think it has inspired laziness on the part of young journalists, and deafened them to the subtle nuances inherent in all exchanges between communicating people. What is being lost, in my opinion, is the art of listening. . ."

Gay Talese may be a nonfiction genius, but he's wrong on this. The very thing the tape recorder permits a journalist to do is listen. There are no taking-notes type distractions, no pens to run out of ink. Just you and the subject, interacting. I think this enhances listening. Now, there are journalists who are just lunkheaded and don't know how to listen, but that's not the technology's fault.

What is the technology's fault is how unreliable, regardless of price, most tape recorders have become. There was a time when I'd buy a machine and it would last two years. Two months now is lucky. I always bring two to an interview, just in case one fails, and frankly, one usually does. I've solved the tinny machine problem by buying my equipment with a service contract from Radio Shack—when the machine breaks down after five or fifty uses, I take it to the mall in whatever town I'm in and trade it in for a free new one. I always go into interviews with fresh, fresh batteries and pre-tested tape.

(One final note on mundane matters: I use ninety-minute premium brand tapes. That's because the interviewer wants long tapes, but the two hour kind tear too easily. Anything less than the ninety-minute kind gives your subject too many breaks in the Q and A, too many opportunities to get off track.)

The first question an interviewer puts forward is key to the success of the interview. I spend hours developing my lead question. (Dan Rather once spent a whole month constructing a really good one for Richard Nixon.) It sets the mood. It also shows the subject, right off, that I've spent a great deal of time thinking about them, trying to understand what they do. And subjects, unless they are total fools, will respect a reporter for doing her homework.

I try to transcribe the tapes myself. Besides reminding me of what actually happened and giving me a sense of the tempo of the language, this allows me to feel the material. Call it Method Writing. I need it. And I'm not alone. Gabriel García Márquez told me during our 1982 *Playboy* interview that when he was writing *The Autumn of the Patriarch*, he returned to his native Colombia because he required "the smell of the guavas" to create his novel.

If you've prepared for and conducted the interview properly, the actual writing of it should sing.

Of course, I scan my raw material for a story line, a theme. With Myrlie Evers Williams, for example, the theme was her thirty-year campaign to avenge the assassination of her husband, Medgar Evers. In between the narrative, I laced in contemporary news items, to give the story a nineties peg. But the spine was always her search for justice.

Once the theme is clear, I hang the assembled material on the skeleton of the piece, bit by bit, till it is shaped. My first drafts are broad, long. With each draft, I whittle the material down further. At the end of the process, I read the story out loud, to see if the voices sound conversational, to check that it all sounds plausible.

Beyond these obvious pointers, the rest of what happens in a session is art, magic, and chemistry. I'd be an "id-jet" if I tried to quantify it.

CD
New York, March 1997

SAINTS

The Dalai Lama of Tibet

In the summer of 1993, I went to *The New York Times Magazine* looking for an editing job. The magazine had been relaunched and redesigned under the leadership of Jack Rosenthal, editor, and Adam Moss, executive editor. Their idea was to open the magazine up, make it more visual, more experimental, younger.

"Why edit? Why not do the thing you're best known for—interviews?" Rosenthal suggested gently.

"I've never seen a Q and A in *The New York Times Magazine*," I returned, quite astonished.

"We can try it. Now, who do you want to talk with?"

"The Dalai Lama," was my immediate answer.

And so—after a few weeks of crash-reading on Buddhism—I was on my way to Tucson, Arizona, where the Dalai Lama was giving a five-day teaching on the fine and useful subject of patience. As a way of getting a pre-interview sense of him, I sat in on many of the teaching sessions and found that I, one of the most impatient humans extant, learned bookloads about patience and tolerance.

What was particular fun was watching him give a kind of "Dear Dalai" Q and A at the end of each lecture. Basically, he answered everyday questions that people came to him with. It was a little like the Pope doing Ann Landers. "Your Holiness," one questioner began, "My husband left me and our children so that he could be with a younger woman. He has destroyed our finances and our lives. How do I keep myself from the sin of hatred?"

"The hatred will hurt you more than anyone," he answered with great practicality and simplicity.

From observing these moments, I constructed my interview. I kept my questions as literal and concrete as possible—nothing airy, nothing too mystical. There seemed to be a charming earthiness to this monk. I hoped that I would be lucky enough to be able to show it.

His Holiness Tenzin Gyatso, the fourteenth Dalai Lama of Tibet, the exiled secular and religious leader of the Tibetan people, the winner of the 1989 Nobel Peace Prize, the world's leading exponent of nonviolent political change, was somewhat out of place at the glitzy Tucson, Arizona golfing resort called the Sheraton El Conquistador. Yet there he was, dressed in his traditional maroon robes, surrounded by Buddhist monks and non-Buddhist bodyguards, astonishing tourists as he rushed past the snack bar.

The Dalai Lama had come to this unlikely corner of the world to give a series of interpretive readings from "A Guide to the Bodhisattva's Way of Life" by Shantideva, an eighth-century Buddhist saint. For five full days, 1,500 attendees risked bad backs and cramped hands to sit for hours taking notes on the nature of patience. For them, participants in the expanding Buddhist movement in the Western world, this was a rare opportunity to study with the head of the faith. Moreover, many of the aspirants were more secular types, veterans of the 1960s who'd come to regard the Dalai Lama as the Rev. Dr. Martin Luther King Jr., the Mahatma Gandhi of this political moment. It is a forum the Dalai Lama clearly enjoys, a needed break from his routine as head of the Tibetan government-in-exile in India. "I am a simple Buddhist monk—no more, no less," he often says of himself. At the teachings, he gets to be that.

Yet his life has been anything but simple. Born in 1935 to a peasant family in northeast Tibet, he was, at the age of two, identified after the death of the 13th Dalai Lama as the 14th reincarnation of the Buddha of Compassion. That recognition brought a new name; Lhamo Thondup now became Jetsun Jamphel Ngawang Lobsang Yeshe Tenzin Gyatso (Holy Lord, Gentle Glory, Eloquent, Compassionate, Learned Defender of the Faith, Ocean of Wisdom). Taken to Lhasa to be educated, he grew up in a 1,000-room palace, surrounded by doting monks who tutored him in subjects like philosophy, medicine, and metaphysics, and gave him a childhood of pure magic.

The magic ended in 1950 when the 15-year-old Dalai Lama was called upon to assume full powers as head of state—this at the very moment the People's Liberation Army of China was invading Tibet. For the next nine years, the young ruler attempted to negotiate with Mao Zedong and Chou En-lai, who were intent on absorbing Tibet into China. Then, in 1959, after China brutally "quelled" a Tibetan civilian uprising against Chinese rule, the Dalai Lama fled to India; some 100,000 Tibetans have since followed him across the Himalayas.

In India, he was permitted to set up a government-in-exile in a small village, Dharamsala, a long day's drive from New Delhi. "His Holiness reconstructed a viable Tibetan community in India, preserving the culture of Tibet," says his close friend Robert Thurman, professor of Indo-Tibetan studies at Columbia University. "He held the Tibetan people together in exile and gave them hope during the very severe, even genocidal oppression in their homeland. He's also the first leader of Tibet to become a world leader, even without a political base —just on his moral force."

In Tucson, on September 16, 1993, a day after his teachings were completed, the Dalai Lama met with me in his suite. As would be expected from someone who has been worshiped as a demigod since age 2, he greets strangers with a mask of pleasant formality, which soon melts as he becomes engaged in ideas and conversation. An hour and a half becomes three; formality turns to laughter. One senses he's a little bored by the adulation that is his daily fare. The most striking thing about the Dalai Lama is his capacity for joy—how widely he smiles, how amused he is by his own contradictions, his own human foibles. The journalist William Shirer once said of his interviews with Gandhi in the 1930s, "You felt you were the only person in the room, that he had all the time in the world for you." This is true of Tenzin Gyatso also.

The interview was conducted in mid-September 1993, and ran in the *Times Magazine* on November 28.

Your Holiness, you seem such a happy person. Have there been moments in your life when your faith in human goodness was tested?

No.

You've never felt in danger of becoming cynical?

No. Of course, when I say that human nature is gentleness, it is not 100 percent so. Every human being has that nature, but there are many people acting against their nature, being false. Certainly there have been sad moments for me. The Chinese suppressions in Lhasa in 1987, 1988, now that was sad. A great many people were killed. I am sometimes sad when I hear the personal stories of Tibetan refugees who have been tortured or beaten. Some irritation, some anger comes. But it never lasts

long. I always try to think at a deeper level, to find ways to console.

I understand that you were very angry during the 1991 Gulf War, as angry as you've ever been.

Angry? No. But one thing, when people started blaming Saddam Hussein, then my heart went out to him.

To Saddam Hussein?

Yes. Because this blaming everything on him—it's unfair. He may be a bad man, but without his army, he cannot act as aggressively as he does. And his army, without weapons, cannot do anything. And these weapons were not produced in Iraq itself. Who supplied them? Western nations! So one day something happened and they blamed everything on him—without acknowledging their own contributions. That's wrong. The gulf crisis also clearly demonstrated the serious implications of the arms trade. War—without an army, killing as few people as possible—is acceptable. But the suffering of large numbers of people due to a military mission, that is sad.

Did you say that killing sometimes is acceptable?

Comparatively. In human society, some people do get killed, for a variety of reasons. However, when you have an established army, and countries with those armies go to war, the casualties are immense. It's not one or two casualties, it's thousands. And with nuclear weapons, it's millions, really millions. For that reason, the arms trade is really irresponsible. Irresponsible! Global demilitarization is essential.

In Tibet, from the late 1950s until the early 1970s, one of your brothers was involved in leading a guerrilla movement against the Chinese. In fact, the guerrillas were supported by the CIA. How did you feel about that?

I'm always against violence. But the Tibetan guerrillas were very dedicated people. They were willing to sacrifice their own lives for the Tibetan nation and they found a way to receive help from the CIA. Now, the CIA's motivation for helping was entirely political. They did not help out of genuine sympathy, not out of support for a just cause. That was not very healthy.

Today, the help and support we receive from the United States is truly out of sympathy and human compassion. In spite of their desire for good relations with China, the Congress of the United States at least supports Tibetan human rights. So this is something really precious, genuine.

To change the subject, you have spoken, as few religious leaders have, of the dangers of global overpopulation.

Well, the population problem is a serious reality. In India, some people were reluctant to accept birth control because of religious traditions. So I thought, from the Buddhist viewpoint, there is a possibility of flexibility on this problem. I thought it might be good to speak out and eventually create more open space for leaders in other religious traditions to discuss the issue.

How do you feel, then, about Pope John Paul II's continued opposition to birth control?

That's his religious principle. He is acting from a certain principle— especially when he speaks about the need to respect the rights of fetuses. Actually, I feel very touched that the Pope has taken a stand on that.

Can you also understand the needs of a woman who might not be able to raise a child?

When I was in Lithuania a few years ago, I visited a nursery and I was told, "All these children are unwanted." So I think it is better that that situation be stopped right from the beginning—birth control. Of course, abortion, from a Buddhist viewpoint, is an act of killing and is negative, generally speaking. But it depends on the circumstances. If the unborn child will be retarded or if the birth will create serious problems for the parent, these are cases where there can be an exception. I think abortion should be approved or disapproved according to each circumstance.

I understand you've experienced a major change in thinking about the role of women in the world.

It's not so much a change. I've gained an awareness of the sensitivity of women's issues; even in the 1960s and 1970s, I didn't have much knowledge of this problem. The basic Buddhist stand on the question of equality between the genders is age-old. At the highest tantric levels, at the highest esoteric level, you must respect women—every woman. In Tibetan society, there has been some careless discrimination. Yet there have been exceptional women, high lamas, who are respected throughout Tibet.

In a recent issue of the Buddhist magazine Tricycle, the actor Spalding Gray asked you about your dreams, and you said you sometimes dreamt of women fighting.

Women fighting? No, no. . . . What I meant was that, in my dreams, sometimes women approach me and I immediately realize, "I'm bhikshu, I'm monk." So you see, this is sort of sexual. . .

In your dreams, you realize this and you "fight" the feeling?

Yes. Similarly, I have dreams where someone is beating me and I want to respond. Then, immediately I remember, "I am monk and I should not kill."

Do you ever experience rages? Even Jesus had rages.

Don't compare me with Jesus. He is a great master, a great master. . . But as to your question, when I was younger, I did get angry. In the past thirty years, no. One thing, the hatred, the ill-feeling, that's almost gone.

So what are your weaknesses and faults?

Laziness.

It is said that you get up at four in the morning. How can you be lazy?

It's not that kind of laziness. For instance, sometimes, when I visit some Western countries, I develop an enthusiasm to improve my English. But when I actually make the effort to study, after a few days, my enthusiasm is finished. [Laughs.] That is laziness. Other weaknesses are, I think, anger and attachments. I'm attached to my watch and my prayer beads. Then, of course, sometimes beautiful women. . . . But then, many monks have the same experience. Some of it is curiosity: If you use this, what is the feeling? [Points to his groin.] Then, of course, there is the feeling that something sexual must be something very happy, a marvelous experience. When this develops, I always see the negative side. There's an expression from Nagurajuna, one of the Indian masters: "If you itch, it's nice to scratch it. But it's better to have no itch at all." Similarly with the sexual desire. If it is possible to be without that feeling, there is much peace. [Smiles.] And without sex, there's no worry about abortion, condoms, things like that.

Sir, your laugh is world famous—what makes you laugh?

There is something in my family. . . a tendency to laugh a lot. One brother, Gyalo Thondup, doesn't laugh too much. Another, Lobsang Samten, was very fond of cracking dirty jokes. A third, Taktser Rinpoche, he also laughed a lot. And Tibetans generally are very good-natured. In my childhood, I had a religious assistant who always told me, "If you can really laugh with full abandonment, it's very good for your health."

What do you do for leisure, to relax?

I like to let my thoughts come to me each morning before I get up. I meditate for a few hours and that is like recharging. After that, my daily conduct is usually driven by the motivation to help, to create a positive atmosphere for others. I garden . . . gardening is one of my hobbies. Also, reading encyclopedias with pictures. [Laughs.] I am a man of peace, but

I am fond of looking at picture books of the Second World War. I own some, which I believe are produced by Time-Life. I've just ordered a new set. Thirty books.

Really? Why does the Reincarnation of Compassion have such a fascination with one of the most terrible events in human history?

Perhaps because the stories are so negative and gruesome, they strengthen my belief in nonviolence. [Smiles.] However, I find many of the machines of violence very attractive. Tanks, airplanes, warships, especially aircraft carriers. And the German U-boats, submarines. . . .

I once read that as a little boy in Lhasa, you liked war toys.

Yes, very much. I also had an air rifle in Lhasa. And I have one in India. I often feed small birds, but when they come together, hawks spot them and catch them—a very bad thing. So in order to protect these small birds, I keep the air rifle.

So it is a Buddhist rifle?

[Laughs.] A compassionate rifle!

Let me ask you a difficult question in that regard. You are indispensable to your movement. Are you ever afraid you might suffer the same fate as Mahatma Gandhi and Martin Luther King Jr.?

The thought sometimes crosses my mind. As far as being "indispensable," people can carry on without me.

Asian scholars say that the Tibetan nation wouldn't have survived after 1959 if you had not been such a skilled political leader. That being the case, aren't you concerned that the Chinese might try to finish off the Tibetan independence movement by killing you?

Some Chinese have frankly said to Tibetans: "You only have one person. If we take care of that, the problem is solved."

Have you prepared yourself for the possibility?

Not really, although in general, as a Buddhist, my daily meditation involves preparation for death. Death by natural causes, I'm fully prepared for. If sudden death comes, that is tragic—from the viewpoint of practitioners.

In September, the Palestinians accepted a compromise for regional autonomy. If the Chinese offered such a deal, would you accept?

Actually, for the past fourteen years, my basic position has been very similar. There is one difference: in the Palestinian case, virtually every government viewed the Territories as occupied and showed concern. In the Tibetan case only the U.S. Congress and some legal experts consider Tibet an occupied land with the right of self-determination.

What was your feeling when you watched the recent signing of the Middle East peace agreement?

It's a great achievement. This issue is just one year older than the Tibetan issue. Our problem started in 1949, theirs in 1948. In those years, a lot of hatred developed. Imagine: Palestinians were taught to hate from childhood. That was seen as good for the national interest. In fact, it was rather negative; a lot of violence took place. Now, both sides came to an agreement in the spirit of reconciliation, in the spirit of nonviolence. This is wonderful.

Are there any signs that the Chinese might accept a compromise?

[Quickly] No.

You once wrote that the Chinese want to rule the world. Do you still think so?

I didn't mean it that way. The remark was related more to the Marxist world intention, rather than Chinese national historical expansionism.

Do you think that still is the case?

It's changed, I think. That kind of spirit...perhaps in the 1960s, with the Cultural Revolution, it was there. On the Soviet side, Khrushchev realized around 1956 that that kind of goal was not realistic. By the end of the Cultural Revolution, in the 1970s, the Chinese realized that it was out of the question. Now I think the issue is Chinese nationalist historic chauvinism. To them, all other people are barbarians.

Including you?

Oh, certainly! Of course! They are a proud nation. With Marxism gone, the strategy is to reach the economic levels of Western countries. They consider themselves a champion of the Third World, particularly after the Soviet Union collapsed. They see Russia as having become a part of the West. So what you have is the most populous nation, the worst kind of totalitarian system, the rule of terror—with nuclear weapons and with an ideology that force is the ultimate source of power. Their economy was poor, but now it is improving—without changing those other things. *Time* magazine has called them "the super-power of the next century."

Does that scare you?

We already lost our country. But I'm concerned about the world! The world community has the moral responsibility to see democracy in China. Now, how to bring it about? The Chinese intellectuals and the students, they are already a strong political force, and very essential. The world community must give every encouragement to that force. We should not indulge any act which discourages them.

Did you think at the time of the Tiananmen Square uprising that the democracy movement would succeed?

Yes. Actually, the events of the fourth of June shocked me. I did not expect them to fire on their own people.

But if the Chinese Communists have been as ruthless against

Tibetans as you charge, why not against pro-democracy demonstrators?

Because it was their own people! How could they shoot them? During the Cultural Revolution, this was understandable. Tiananmen Square proved that a regime that would have no hesitation to shoot their own people, such a regime. . . . There should be no doubt about their attitude towards other nationalities.

Given that not-so-optimistic assessment, what possible scenarios for China and Tibet do you see?

Basically, the Chinese Communist regime, it's only a matter of time, it will change. Worldwide today, there is a growth of freedom and democracy. And the democratic movement, inside and outside China, is still very active. Once the Chinese are willing to listen to others' problems, the Tibetans will not be against the Chinese nation. My approach is in the spirit of reconciliation. Certainly we can have an agreement.

In the meantime, the international community must support Tibet and put pressure on China. Without that, our own approach, according to the last fourteen years of experience, has no hope of response.

In closing, I read somewhere that you are predicting that the twenty-first century, unlike the twentieth, is to be a century of peace and justice. Why?

Because I believe that in the twentieth century, humanity has learned from many, many experiences. Some positive, and many negative. What misery, what destruction! The greatest number of human beings were killed in the two world wars of this century. But human nature is such that when we face a tremendous critical situation, the human mind can wake up and find some other alternative. That is a human capacity.

•••

The Dalai Lama—II

To celebrate the one hundredth anniversary of *The New York Times Magazine*, the editors were spending the summer of 1996 assembling a special issue on what the next hundred years might look like. Experts from every corner of society were being asked to prophesy the future.

It was Gerald Marzorati, the magazine's articles editor, who proposed adding the Dalai Lama to the mix. Buddhists, after all, believe in reincarnation; for all we know, His Holiness might be around in a hundred years—at least in some form—to see how it all turns out.

For several weeks prior to my appointment, I did a combination of theologic and futuristic studies, talking to experts in both areas. And so on a brilliant summer morning I arrived in Bloomington, Indiana, where the Dalai Lama had ventured to lay the cornerstone for a new Buddhist temple. I brought a sackful of interesting questions, about the rise of religious fundamentalism, women in religion, ethics in the cyber-age, abortion, war, and Hollywood Buddhism. I thought they were very clever questions. But ha!, how could I *not* have known this: Buddhists aren't terribly interested in the future. It's the present, being "in the moment," that counts.

"I don't think about the future," he kept answering, flatly.

"I know, Your Holiness, I know," I responded, embarrassed, "but, I'd be so grateful if you could give it a shot anyway."

And so, for two hours, Tenzin Gyatso, the fourteenth Dalai Lama of Tibet stretched and pulled and tried to think about the future, but, I felt, didn't do too well at it. When the interview was over, I returned to my hotel room and cried. And then I went back to the Tibetan Buddhist Center of Bloomington, Indiana, took one of his assistants aside and put my cards on the table. "I don't think that first session is quite good enough to get printed," I told His Holiness's personal assistant, Tenzen G. Tethong. "Couldn't we find some more time?"

Somehow, another half hour was found the next day.

This, my second interview with the Dalai Lama, appeared as nine hundred words in *The New York Times Magazine's* Special Centennial Issue of

September 29, 1996. I've expanded it here from additional material from those two July 1996 sessions to approximately two thousand words.

In the next hundred years, thanks to organ transplants and genetic therapies, people may be able to live much, much longer lives. If you had the chance to do that, would you take it?

Mere living is not so important. The important thing is usefulness. So if I could get another hundred years more and be useful, then . . . good. Otherwise, you just create more problems for others. And then, from the Buddhist viewpoint, isn't it better [through reincarnation] to have another young body? There's a Buddhist story, about an old monk who was dying and everyone was very sad. He said, "Don't be sad. Right now, I have an old decaying body. But very soon, I get a fresh young body."

Three years ago, you predicted that the next hundred years would be a century of peace, hope and justice. Since then, there have been massacres in Rwanda and Burundi, the Northern Irish Peace discussions have been blown apart, and the Chinese have kidnapped the young boy you designated to be the Panchen Lama. Are you still optimistic about the future?

Oh yes. Of course. A handful of shortsighted people have always existed. But overall, their day is over, because the public's attitude towards war and violence has become much healthier than at any time in history. People used to be much more jingoistic and nationalistic compared with the way they are now.

Recently, I was talking with the English Queen Mother. She is 96 and I asked her, "What changes have you seen in your lifetime?" She answered, "When I was young, we had not much concern about the outside world. Now, people have a great concern about what is happening all over the world." This is a very positive change.

So I believe that due to [the information revolution], generally speaking, any leader, if he tried to mobilize the whole nation for war—would find it impossible. In previous times, it was quite possible. Well, small scale wars, perhaps they can still do it. But large scale wars, I think, are not likely. Now, I do believe that in the next century our efforts should be for no more nuclear, chemical or germ weapons. After that, we have to seriously think about putting a complete stop to the arms trade. Once you make a bullet, it's purpose is to kill. Some people use them as paperweights. But how many paperweights does the world need?

A hundred years in the future, what will be the role of women in religion?

I think, improved. Because women want it.

Can you see a situation where there might be a woman Pope, a woman Archbishop of Canterbury, a woman...Dalai Lama?

In the Buddhist world, there's not much problem. Some of the Lamas of high reincarnation are women. So I am always telling people, in the future if the Dalai Lama's position should remain, if the Tibetan people wish, than under certain circumstances a woman Dalai Lama could be more effective.

Could you envision a woman Pope?

That answer, I cannot give—and secondly, my speculations are inappropriate.

Buddhism has become quite popular in the West. Could you see a future American president who is a practicing Buddhist?

No, I think someone in the Judeo-Christian tradition would be better. I prefer for people in Western countries to follow their own traditions. I have no desire to propagate. I don't even like seeing missionary work among Tibetans and Hindus...it eventually creates unhealthy things, improper things.

Is it possible that you, the fourteenth Dalai Lama, might be the last?

It is possible.... Not as the result of external force, though. If the majority of the Tibetan people feel that the Dalai Lama institution is no longer relevant, then the institution automatically will cease. Now, if that happens while I'm alive or just after my death, then, I am obviously the last Dalai Lama. But if my death comes in the next one or two years, then most probably, the Tibetan people will want to have another incarnation... of that I'm quite certain. Of course, there is the possibility that Tibetans [will] become insignificant in our land and all decisions [will be] made by the Chinese. It is possible and very sad.

What if the Chinese interfered with the choosing of the next Dalai Lama as they have just done with the second highest Tibetan religious leader, the Panchen Lama—would that end the institution?

Well, should another reincarnation be what the Tibetan people want, then my reincarnation will certainly appear outside of Chinese control. The reason is that the very purpose of the reincarnation is to fulfill the work started in the previous life that has not been accomplished. I intentionally escaped from Tibet to do something for the Tibetan nation that is still not accomplished. So therefore, it is logical that my reincarnation will not become an obstacle for the work which I started.

How do you rate yourself compared to your previous incarnates?

Ask some other people. [Laughs.] I consider myself not the best, but not the worst. Compared to the first, second, third...the fourth Dalai Lama, I might be able to compete. Then, the fourth Dalai Lama, in terms of tantric power, there's no way I could compete with him. He was famous for it. With the fifth Dalai Lama, [there's] no hope of competition. [This seventeenth-century figure is revered as the greatest of all Dalai Lamas— he unified Tibet and also was the first Dalai Lama to serve as Chief of State.] [With] the sixth Dalai Lama, I have, in some aspects [similarities]; in others, no possibility of competition. He disrobed. I [have] not. [Legend has it that he was murdered at the order of the Chinese emperor.] With some Dalai Lamas, I am much lower. Compared to others I'm a little better. But then of fourteen Dalai Lamas, in terms of popularity with the outside world, there's no match. [Laughs.]

But it's not through my own good qualities and abilities. It is the time...the era. Though I have no doubt, that if the sixth Dalai Lama had come to the outside world, he'd be very popular. [Laughs.] Especially in America. [He gave up his monk's robes for a woman.]

The Chinese seem to be waiting for this Dalai Lama to die ...?

Oh, they've openly stated that. "The whole of your Tibetan freedom struggle is based on one person and that person is getting older and older. If that one person dies, so does your movement." Some Chinese officials in the early 1980s stated that.

But right from the beginning, we sought to defeat that, by educating our refugee children.... We also formed a democratically elected Tibetan parliament-in-exile. So we've made every effort to build a community outside of Tibet and to make sure it doesn't all depend on one person. Of course, if I die, while we remain outside, it will be a setback and there will be some shock, but as far as the freedom movement is concerned, there will be no problem.

I've heard that three Chinese agents were recently found snooping around your compound in India—and that this is something new?

It was a new thing. Previously, Tibetans trained by Chinese come to India, and once they arrive, they inform us of it. But this was three persons whom people got suspicious about and they did not inform us.

Let me ask you frankly, do you think the Chinese are trying to solve their political problem by assassination?

I don't think so. I think they sent these three to create local trouble and division among Tibetans in India.

One hundred years from now what would you like to be remembered for?

As a Buddhist practitioner, I have no interest in that. So long as I am alive, my time and my life must be utilized properly. Then, after my death, I don't care how people remember me. If I'm seeking for people to say nice things about me, then I'm seeking worldly fame.

But you have worldly fame.

It didn't come because I wanted it.

One could interpret your question as meaning, "What do I desire people to remember the fourteenth Dalai Lama for?" I don't care about that. But then, there's another side to your question and that is, "By thinking about him, they might get some benefit. What were the qualities that people might remember a hundred years from now that could be beneficial to them?"

And what are they?

I don't know.

Perhaps that you fought for your people?

People will know what I've done. Also, that I taught non-violence—as did others in this century, Gandhi, Nelson Mandela, Martin Luther King. That there was a series of people devoted to non-violence. I don't know. I don't know. Of course some people say, "Oh, the fourteenth Dalai Lama did many wrong things. During fourteenth Dalai Lama's time, the country was lost and there was a lot of destruction." There are others who say that I was too soft with the Chinese and the right of the Tibetans to be independent. I'm not looking to what I hope the legacy will be. People say many different things, and you can't tell.

Is it true that you like to go shopping when you travel?

I like it. I'm a human being. I think human beings have a lot of curiosity. I go in Los Angeles. Sometimes, I shop for myself. Shoes... small electronic equipment... cat food. I go to shopping malls just like they were museums.

Have you noticed how in America, shopping malls are something like temples, worldly temples?

Perhaps . . . perhaps.

The sixth Dalai Lama died a violent death. Are you concerned you might too?

It is possible, I don't know. Airplanes trouble me. Dying in the ocean—and ending up in the stomach of a shark.

Many people get a sense of God by observing nature. What will religions be like in a hundred years if there is little nature left on earth?

The world itself *is* nature. The sun, the moon, they are nature. Even if there were no more animals, nature would still be here.

For those religions that believe in a creator, they would have to find reasons to explain why our beautiful blue planet became a desert. The explanation will help practitioners improve their practices. Take the issue of death. The worst thing that can happen to a human being is dying. Yet, when people are dying, they don't doubt about their faith in God. Nobody who believes in a creator says, "I doubt the creator because someday we have to die." Even in such difficult times, the belief in God definitely helps them.

You're always the optimist, Your Holiness.

If you ask me whether it's good or bad, of course it's bad. [But] in the Buddhist tradition, something like that would not change our attitude. We believe the whole world will come and disappear, come and disappear—so eventually, the world becomes desert and even the ocean dries up. But then again, another new world is reborn. It's endless.

What will you miss most about the twentieth century?

My present feeling is, it's better to think something pleasant about the future and not think so much about the past. The past is the past.

•••

Andrew Young

*I*t was a scant few weeks after the 1996 Olympic Games had folded its tent, and Andrew Young, the outgoing co-chair of the Atlanta Committee for the Olympic Games, was putting the closing touches on the last of Olympic business. There were employees to say goodbye to, photographers to sit for, T-shirts to ship off to friends in South Africa.

"I've always had a sense of mission," he said when we met in August of 1996. "But, now, for the life of me, I don't have the slightest idea what to do next."

For Andrew Young to be at a loose end seems odd. This United Church of Christ minister has lived one of the most hectic careers in contemporary politics. In the 1960s, he was the right-hand man to Martin Luther King, Jr., assisting him in his most dangerous civil rights campaigns. After King's assassination—which Young witnessed—he turned to electoral politics, serving in Congress for two terms from the Fifth District of Georgia. He was elected for a third term but vacated the seat when Jimmy Carter called on him to be the U.S. ambassador to the United Nations. There followed two terms as Atlanta's second African-American mayor, culminating with last year's triumph of the Olympic Games. Young's memoir, *An Easy Burden: The Civil Rights Movement and the Transformation of America*, has just been published to excellent reviews.

For a man who has been so close to centers of power, there's an amazing openness to Andrew Young. He has a kind of transparency that's rare in a public figure. Perhaps it is all his years as a minister, and then as a lieutenant in the glory days of the civil–rights movement, that make him unusual. He's not packaged, he's emotional. The private side of his history-making experiences is as important to Young as his public achievements. As we began flashing back to the 1960s, there were tears in his eyes.

You're crying!

I have an eye condition called blepharitis that tears my eyes. As I get older, I can't seem to stop it. But if my only problem at my age is my eyes, then OK. [Laughs.] I cry a lot anyway. The least little thing can trigger so many rich memories. Most of the time, I'm crying for joy rather than sadness.

That stands to reason. Yours has been a life of contrasts—much good, many sorrows. Were you fated to live out great extremes?

Well, I don't really see the bad. Maybe that's a part of being religious. My wife, Jean, died. That was *bad*. But we had forty years, three months, and nine days of a wonderful marriage. I have since married another woman who shares many of my religious values. It's almost like, "What right have I to be so lucky twice?"

When Martin Luther King died, I thought that was the end for us in the civil–rights movement. Yet that terrible moment turned out to be a beginning. The last formal meeting I had with Martin before he went to Memphis was about how to take the movement into politics. After he got killed, I helped do that.

So while I mourned a good friend, I never lost Martin. When I think about it now, I realize that I can't make a speech without it sounding like him, without understanding how much he influenced my life. The same is true of my mother, father, uncle. You are the sum of the spiritual contributions made by others.

Considering the "I've been to the mountaintop" speech he gave the night before his murder, many people believe Dr. King foretold his own death. Did he?

The thing he talked about *most* was death. He was stabbed at twenty-nine. A demented woman stuck a letter opener in his chest and it pressed against his aorta; if he had sneezed he would have died. To remove the letter opener, they had to cut his chest. The scar was shaped like a cross. "Every morning when I shave and look in the mirror," he said, "I realize this day could be my last. It makes you realize, if you haven't found something you're willing to die for, you're not fit to live."

This was Martin's way of constantly challenging those of us working with him to live so we wouldn't mind dying for the things we were trying to do. So when his death came, we were prepared.

Were you really? The civil-rights movement went into a tailspin after his assassination.

We were prepared for Dr. King's death, but not the *others*. I mean, if Dr. King had died and Robert Kennedy or John Kennedy had lived, we would have a different America now. A lot of good people died in and around the period of his assassination. I'm talking about the mid to late sixties. Ralph Bunche was beginning to get very sick. Walter Reuther was killed in an airplane crash, so labor was denied his leadership. All those deaths signaled the passing of an era. What you had left was George Wallace and Richard Nixon.

You hint in your book that a lot of the deaths of 1960s public figures were political assassinations. Strong charges, especially since you don't substantiate them.

Everybody I knew in the 1960s who was in a key position to change the world for good died mysteriously. I mean, Stephen Currier [who helped fund the civil–rights movement] was lost in the Bermuda Triangle. His plane was never heard of again. Author Bernard Fall [authority on Vietnam] was as sophisticated as any writer about war. He stepped on a land mine. That's unbelievable to me.

Who do you suspect is responsible for these deaths?

I feel they were all linked and planned by a vicious, insecure, and irresponsible group of people in power. Because I saw the relationship between Martin Luther King and the FBI, I've always thought the FBI might have been involved in some way.

So you're saying the FBI—not James Earl Ray alone—killed Martin Luther King?

Him, maybe all of them. You have to remember this was a time when the politics of assassination was acceptable in our country. It was during the period just before Allende's murder. I think it's naive to assume these institutions were not capable of doing the same thing at home or to say each of these deaths was an isolated incident by "a single assassin." It was government policy. And it didn't stop being policy until I was in Congress and we started an intelligence-monitoring operation and changed all that.

A review of the book in The Washington Post *called you "dismayingly irresponsible" for making unsubstantiated charges about Dr. King's and the other 1960s assassinations.*

I said my *feelings* were unsubstantiated. I made no claims. I may be paranoid and I admitted that, but I never said there was an official conspiracy. It was not just *who* killed Dr. King, but *what.* It was a fear of human rights, of integration, of the brotherhood of man becoming a reality.

At Martin's funeral, Ralph Abernathy preached from the story of Joseph: "Here comes the dreamer. Let us slay him, and we will see then what will become of his dream." I always felt the important thing was that the dream live on. So when I was in Congress I chose not to be on the House Select Committee on Assassinations. Instead, I started working for Jimmy Carter—for the ideal of human rights going from a domestic–policy issue to an international one. To elect a President who was going to help make King's vision a reality was more important than finding out who killed him.

If Dr. King could be murdered so easily, did you ever think twice about trying to "make his vision a reality"?

Nah. Keeping the dream alive'll get ya killed, too. When I was at the U.N., almost every African leader I met urged me to be more cautious. "You don't have to take on all these battles," they said. "We need you." I said, "Everybody's got to die. My only concern is that I die doing something worthwhile as opposed to falling down the steps."

You know, the one certainty about life is death, and it's the thing we're least prepared for. Martin made us very comfortable with the idea of dying by making a joke out of it—by "preaching our funerals."

When Dr. King "preached your funeral," what was his eulogy for you?

I was the Uncle Tom. "Oh, the white people who killed him don't know what a mistake they've made!"
If we could laugh at death, we could overcome our fears.

Have there been any moments when you truly felt fear?

There was this sense all through the movement—any time we took on a new city—that any day could be your last. When we went to Birmingham, there were sixty-something unsolved bombings there. When we went to Selma, there were four people killed in that region.
A CBS reporter came to me and said, "Please forgive me, but I have to keep a camera on Dr. King at all times. If he gets killed and I don't have a picture of it, I'll lose my job." It was expected.
The only time I was *really* afraid was in South Africa. A hundred policemen surrounded me all of a sudden and moved my assistant out of the room. To me, that's a signal you're being set up. It seems they were covering themselves by showing how "well protected" I was.

Martin Luther King had a lot of protection around him in Memphis when he was shot, didn't he?

We had more security around Martin than ever. There is a picture of me pointing to the building where the shot came from while the security men are running toward Martin. I was trying to get them to go where the shot came from. They weren't there to protect him.

Did Jesse Jackson really wipe Dr. King's blood on his shirt?

Yeah, and it's irrelevant. In the middle of a crisis like that, people do crazy, emotional things. I mean, to identify with the blood of a friend is no problem.

What about wearing it on television the next day, as he is reported to have done?

No, I don't think that is a problem.

You don't say much about Jesse Jackson in your memoir. What is your opinion of him?

You know, I trusted Martin because he was reluctant in his leadership. I don't trust people who want to lead. That's because if they really want to take charge of the world, they don't know what the problems are.

You consider Jackson more of a prophet than a politician?

Prophets tend to move you, and that's how people respond to Jesse. But he has not, in any place, implemented his prophecies. I tried to get him to run for mayor of Chicago. I tried to get him to run for Congress in South Carolina. For mayor of Washington. But that's OK. My role was to do it; Jesse's may be just to philosophize.

Another "prophet" is Louis Farrakhan. Harry Belafonte said in a recent interview that Farrakhan is the only black leader out there doing battle with the system. Do you favor his approach?

Farrakhan tends to mimic the anger of the oppressed, but nothing is ever done to assuage or alleviate it. So he recognizes the anger. Fine. All right.
I'd rather light candles than curse the darkness.

What was your take on the Million Man March?

I thought it was wonderful. But that was *our* march. Those people were there not because they were angry but because they were successful. They came because of jobs generated by the civil-rights movement.

But the traditional civil-rights groups didn't organize that march. Farrakhan did.

Nah, he announced it and people came.

Then how come the civil-rights movement didn't make its own "announcement"?

We could have, but what was the point? See, what we're about in the 1990s is integrating the money. People in the private sector are now the civil-rights movement.

We have a group of men here in Atlanta called 100 Black Men and some went to the Million Man March. But what they're *doing* is more significant. They adopted an eighth grade class from a school with one of the highest drop-out rates in the state. Ninety-four percent of those kids graduated from high school and 90 percent of those went on to college because these guys started working with them ten years ago. It's much better to put your money into sending a kid to college than going to Washington and staying in a hotel. It's not that the civil-rights movement is not doing anything—it's just not doing what it was doing in the sixties.

Although the movement changed the political landscape of America, many sociologists say the condition of the urban black poor is worse today than at any time in history. Did you ever think the civil-rights victory would be this bittersweet?

Listen, the only thing we have not done that we tried to do is wipe out poverty. And that's the root of all urban crime, and welfare problems. We're not going to be a great nation until we find ways to do that.

The best thing you can do for poor people is create jobs. You cannot wipe out poverty without economic growth. You also can't get people to share their wealth when they're afraid of losing it. We created more than 85,000 jobs in Atlanta from the Olympics and had 40 percent affirmative action—and no white people complained. That's because everybody was working, everybody was making money.

On another subject, you've been in the public eye for more than 30 years. Is it difficult being a prominent public figure, not to mention a prominent black public figure?

The problem is not just related to blacks. Betty Ford wouldn't have been an alcoholic if her husband hadn't been president. The number of prominent people who've had children who committed suicide scares the hell out of me.

But to answer your question, I've had experiences. I'd be coming out of the Waldorf and a guy would come out, see the only black person around, and hand me his car keys. And I was the U.S. ambassador to the United Nations.

What did you do?

I took them over to the guy who parks the cars and said, "The man over there needs some help." Another time, I was in a London hotel and taking some of my laundry down to the bell captain and a guy put his head out the door and said, "Excuse me, can you take my laundry, too?" You get things like that all the time.

Does it ever bother you?

My parents raised me to treat racism as a sickness. And you don't get upset at sick people.

Do you get upset when you see so many African-American politicians get targeted by law-enforcement sting operations?

Every high-ranking black official has had problems with the police. I really don't want to believe in conspiracy theories, but everybody believes that all politicians steal. Most folk would say that all black people steal. So you get a black politician and the assumption is, "He's guilty—you just got to find out what he's doing." Actually, I can't think of any black mayor who's been convicted.

Marion Barry?

Um, yeah. But he wasn't convicted of any fraud or malfeasance. He was convicted of drug possession. In a deliberate entrapment.

The problem was, he was entrapable.

Yeah, but almost everybody is. J. Edgar Hoover was probably a transvestite and a homosexual, yet he used the FBI to go after Martin Luther King. When I was being harassed by an Atlanta newspaper, I knew about all the sexual-harassment suits being brought against the guy at the newspaper who was trying to get me.

The thing is, it's unrealistic to think of perfection in human beings. Or to require it. The Bible tells you that all men and women sin and fall short of the glory of God. In public life, all that ought to be required is that your weaknesses don't interfere with your responsibilities.

On a more personal subject, you remarried on March 28, 1996, just eighteen months after Jean died of liver cancer. Was it difficult to start over again so quickly?

I was 22 when I first married, and the only life I'd known was married life. I really needed a relationship of trust and permanence that allowed me to continue growing. Dating wasn't for me.

After my wife's death, I went on a trip from Los Angeles to Tokyo to London to South Africa to Germany, and everywhere I went, people set me up with women—some of the most beautiful and intelligent women in the world. They felt since I was recently widowed I needed female companionship. But I wasn't that interested because they didn't want to be friends.

They were looking for something else.

It was like I was a sexual challenge. [Laughs.] They had to bring me out of my misery. And that wasn't the way to do it. So I was very boring. I mean, I'd get up in the middle of an evening, go back to my hotel room, and read a book. I'm not cut out to be a playboy.

Then how did you find someone appropriate so quickly?

Well, I had known Carolyn [Watson] for a long time and we'd been pretty good friends. She was in the process of getting a divorce so we found ourselves talking all the time. I would call her, principally to check on her, but really to find someone to talk to who wasn't "after" me. It developed into a very comfortable friendship.

You take very strong exception to the revelations that have come out in recent years about Dr. King's personal life, particularly the reports of his extramarital affairs. Why?

Because they were irrelevant. Nothing Martin did, or didn't do, interfered with his effectiveness or detracted from his devotion to the cause. The pressure he was under was like a battlefield. People in war do things they wouldn't do in peace. My understanding of sin is that which separates you from God. Alcohol is not a sin unless it gets you so bloody drunk you can't do anything.

Look at the record: some of the great men in American history— Thomas Jefferson, Franklin Roosevelt, even Eisenhower—had an earthy streak. The press and the opposition were very hard on Jefferson, accusing him of having a black mistress, which was probably true. The fact that Roosevelt went on a U.S. cruiser to the West Indies and a woman, supposedly his girlfriend, was on the ship is irrelevant compared to the fact that he conceived of lend-lease on that trip. One of the only presidents I know who didn't have an earthy streak was Nixon, and he was dangerous.

Speaking of being earthy, did President Johnson really tell Dr. King, as you say in your book, that his criticism of the Vietnam War made him feel that Dr. King had raped his daughter?

Yeah, he said it. Now, Lyndon Johnson was a complicated man. When you grow up with Southerners, you're not shocked; it's par for the course.

What about another Southerner, Jimmy Carter?

I think the lack of earthiness in Jimmy Carter, whom I love much, was a weakness in him. He is a very good man who lives under a similar kind of thing Martin lived under— the constant sense of the nearness of death. Everybody in his immediate family died of pancreatic cancer. *Everybody.* His father, brother, sisters. So he orders his life in a very structured and disciplined way—so many minutes for phone calls, so many for reading, so many for woodworking. I think this is one of the things that kept him from being a great president.

Why is that?

One of the things you get from the literature of the saints is the dark night of the soul, the raging of passions. I think men are driven to greatness by these raging passions. If you're too much in control, you're not available, not free to take on the toughest challenges in life.

One of the challenges you took on for President Carter was serving as U.S. ambassador to the U.N. Why is there so much antipathy in this country toward the United Nations?

Because there's always been an isolationist trend in the United States. Ronald Reagan, for example, found it was easier to whip up Americans with isolationist rhetoric than to deal with complex international problems.

Some claim President Reagan's get-tough policies with the Soviet Union eventually resulted in the end of the Cold War; that's hardly isolationist.

I don't think he stopped the Cold War. When the Berlin Wall came down, they sang "We Shall Overcome." That's hardly a Republican fight song. What stopped the Cold War was an increase of human-rights pressures within the Soviet Union and Eastern Europe—that policy is more President Carter's than it is Reagan's!

The Soviet intelligence community, I think, began to see that Russia's military might was exaggerated and couldn't keep up with the U.S. That made Gorbachev realize he had to find another way to compete. He saw himself as a Communist Franklin D. Roosevelt and thought he could save Communism by moderating it—but the human-rights pressures swept him away.

What other problems plague the U.N.?

No leadership. Ever since Dag Hammarskjöld, the one who got elected has been the weakest choice—we put in Kurt Waldheim knowing he was a Nazi! Both the Russians and the Americans have had a sinister conspiracy to keep the U.N. impotent ever since Hammarskjöld, who some of them had killed—we don't know which side.

You're saying someone had Dag Hammarskjöld killed? Can you substantiate that statement?

Again, this is part of my sixties paranoia. [Laughs.] And there's no way to substantiate it. Nor would I try. It may be my sickness, but I think mine is a far more realistic view of the world than just saying all these important "accidents" happened around this time and nobody has to think about them—to just forget them and wipe them away.

Why was there so much antipathy in the Clinton administration for U.N. Secretary-General Boutros Boutros-Ghali?

I don't understand it. The U.N. is a pretty big and cumbersome bureaucracy, and the U.S. was trying to pressure him to cut it back. He was doing so but not at the pace the administration wanted. Then Boutros-Ghali got angry and started talking about people "who owe billions in dues."

The other side of the story is the political one. In the middle of the campaign, there was a feeling the Republicans were going to make a big issue out of the U.N., so not doing something would have raised an issue. I'm guessing.

Since you mentioned politics, how do you feel about the last Congress ending "welfare as we know it"?

I think these people are mad. I mean, they are trying to destroy the America I know and love. It's sinful. Unless Jesus is lying, a lot of these people are going to hell.

How can the so-called religious Right be so callous about poor people's opportunities and cater to the basest instincts of humanity—rather than the generosity of spirit that I've always associated with religion? Now that the bridge has gotten them over, they want to blow up the bridge.

If Dr. King had seen the activities of this last Congress, he would see these as very dark days for the country. There are no jobs for these women, no day care for these women's children. You're going to put women and children on the streets. They are going to either beg or be prostitutes.

The mood now is that the government has no obligation for a safety net and that it should make poor people—and the elderly and the infirm—responsible for their own poverty.

Speaking of a safety net for older people, you'll be sixty-five on March 12. What's your opinion of all the measures floating around to "reform" Social Security?

Like most Americans, I don't intend to ever get old or sick. I'll probably work till my dying day. So I haven't worried much about retirement or long-term investments. That's why I'm grateful to Social Security because it's probably all I'll have—I can't afford to get sick! Like the old Negro spiritual goes: "I ain't got time to die."

•••

Aung San Suu Kyi

T hinking back on it now in January 1997, I realize that there was only one window in the last seven years when it was possible to go to Rangoon and to do an extensive interview with the Burmese democracy leader, Daw Aung San Suu Kyi. The time was late fall of 1995. I was very lucky. I caught the moment.

Aung San Suu Kyi, freed from six years of house arrest since July of that year, was beginning to test the limits of civil possibilities in her country. She was pushing the population of Burma—or Myanmar as the ruling junta, the SLORC, insist on calling the country—to act as though they were a free people. Though the military regime banned opposition rallies, Suu Kyi was holding free speech meetings in front of her house on University Avenue each weekend. Thousands were attending. Just like any normal political leader in a normal country, she was giving weekly press conferences. In a sense, she and her party, the National League for Democracy (NLD), were telling the SLORC generals: "Let's find a way to normalize civic life here. And if we can't do it together, we'll just do it ourselves."

Peaceful change seemed possible. Burma/Myanmar was seeking to enter various Asian and world councils. The United States was blocking Myanmarese loan applications at the World Bank and the International Monetary Fund. In fact, Southeast Asian scholars believed that Aung San Suu Kyi had been released from her six years of internment partly in response to international pressure. What's more, the SLORC, which had long closed off the country to most Western visitors, had declared 1996 "Visit Myanmar Year," another sign of possible liberalization.

Through a source, I managed to smuggle a letter to Aung San Suu Kyi telling her about my wish to interview her and asking for her cooperation. Then I made tentative inquiries about a visa.

"Visit Myanmar Year," might well be on the horizon, but the Myanmarese embassy did not permit people to come by and make visa applications. To apply, one had to send a letter explaining chapter and verse of one's intentions, and *then*, they'd consider faxing out application forms.

Should one pass muster, the documents would be subsequently shipped off to Rangoon where SLORC officials might or might not make a determination to grant entry to the potential visitor.

I rang up Congressman Bill Richardson, a New Mexico Democrat who is now U.S. Ambassador to the United Nations and who was then rumored to be dialoging with the SLORC Generals about opening up the system. Might he be able to help?

Amazingly, Richardson managed to coax a visa out of the Myanmarese.

Thus, on an icy New York November 1995 morning, I was off to Rangoon, all the while thinking about Kipling, and George Orwell, who, ironically, had been a policeman in colonial Burma.

Rangoon seemed a place of dreamy incongruities. Buddhist monks in maroon robes toting huge umbrellas walked the streets, while soldiers, seemingly thousands of them, patrolled in heavily armored trucks. There were vast and ancient golden pagodas everywhere—and a huge military museum where the SLORC celebrated itself. And there was a munitions factory right outside my hotel's front door. I had this feeling that if one mixed North Korea with Shangri-la, it would look something like Rangoon.

After settling uncomfortably into a Soviet-built marble nightmare called the Inya Lake Hotel, I phoned up Aung San Suu Kyi's house, spoke to one of her associates, and was shocked to hear him say something like, "Very well now, she can see you for a half-hour on Tuesday."

My breath stopped. This was an interview that her people had agreed to. Did this mean that I had scored that almost-impossible-to-get visa for nothing? I mean, goodness, even Arizona Senator John McCain had recently been denied a visa. Functioning on equal parts of fear and adrenalin, I flew downstairs, negotiated a taxi and directed the driver to Suu Kyi's home, where I demanded a quick visit with the gentleman on the telephone.

For the next forty minutes, I stood on Daw Aung San Suu Kyi's front lawn, begging, explaining, cajoling, bargaining, but never shutting up: "You don't understand what an opportunity this could be for you—an opportunity to tell the world your story."

"But she doesn't have any time," one of her aides kept answering. "She doesn't even have time to eat a proper supper anymore. We never give anyone any more than a half-hour."

"But this is so important and you promised . . . I came all this way."

"There are all these other reporters coming from *Le Monde* and from the *Far East Economic Review* and *The Guardian.* She must give them time too."

"We are more important," I responded, a little embarrassed, though not too much.

The jet lag hit. I began crying. "Oh, this is terrible," I sobbed, and then from nowhere added, "I do think my heart will burst."

Suu Kyi's staff found that funny. They began laughing at me, though sweetly. I laughed too. I knew what they, as Buddhists, were thinking: how can anyone want *anything* so badly?

Finally, after a huddle with "The Lady" there came a decision. I'd be given two hours on Tuesday. And yes, there'd be additional time for the photographer, Magnum's Steve McCurry, who was expected from the battlefields of Sri Lanka any day. And also, they'd see about further interview time, depending on scheduling.

Ah, normal breathing returned. I had my foot in the door.

In the days afterwards, I would find countless excuses to be at Aung San Suu Kyi's house. Being there almost daily put me in an excellent position to ask for and get more interview time; moreover, it relaxed Suu Kyi to my presence, which was important, because the Nobel Peace Prize winner could be spiky and cold with reporters. My strategy was to just get her used to me, and I did that to such an extent that Military Intelligence guys outside her gate soon came to smile at me and say, "Oh yes, Miss Claudia from *The New York Times.*"

I also remember the coolly cynical voice of a certain Burmese gentleman who was said to be the SLORC's official mouthpiece to the West when I asked him why they couldn't find a way to open the system up. "Between you and me and the doorpost, they are not going to talk to her," he snorted. "They will not recognize her because they will say, 'Why?' Your American companies are already here and they feel that Congress won't stop them. They will come. We have plenty of gas. American companies have already done the preliminary work. The Thais want electricity from our rivers."

On weekend afternoons, a time when we didn't do interview sessions, Daw Aung San Suu Kyi, then fifty, would climb up on a fence in front of her crumbling lake-side villa, take a microphone in hand and speak of democracy. Thousands of Burmese came from all over the countryside to hear her. They carried tape recorders and video cameras. And though Suu Kyi would explain such concepts as freedom of the press and the right to assembly in the most elegant Burmese, I'd hear certain English phrases seep through: "social contract," "Martin Luther King," "it's not fair."

From what I could see, very little was fair in Burma/Myanmar, Southeast Asia's second-largest nation. Indeed, for the six years in which Suu Kyi, the daughter of General Aung San, the founder of modern Burma, languished under house arrest, she could not leave the premises or make phone calls. She could rarely receive visitors. She was separated from her husband of twenty-three years, the Tibetan scholar and British professor Michael Aris, and from their children Alexander, now twenty-two, and Kim, now eighteen. Aris was only allowed to visit her five times during her incarceration; Alexander, who delivered Suu Kyi's Nobel acceptance speech for her, was only granted a visa into Burma once. And just what was Suu Kyi's crime? Advocacy of democracy, of an open political system.

This interview ran in the *Times Magazine* at a length of 4,600 words. This version contains an additional 1,100 words.

It seems I have come to Burma at a strange political moment. After six years of house arrest, you are free to move around, receive visitors—yet the SLORC is as entrenched as ever. Am I correct?

No, I wouldn't think of it as strange. I do think Burma is at a crossroads. This next year is when it will be decided how quickly we get to our goals. It could go faster depending on how everybody involved reacts to the situation. Everybody includes the international community as well as groups within Burma.

But nothing seems to have changed in Burma since your release last summer.

Well, the authorities have not changed in their official policies. But our National League for Democracy is certainly a lot more active. Before I was released there was nobody who could talk to a foreign journalist like yourself. Nobody could say, "These are the problems. This is what our people are suffering from." But now I can say it, and I do—which means that others also say it.

So there has been practical change, more of that than policy change. There are changes that we've decided to bring about, rather than what the authorities have arranged.

During the 1980s in Eastern Europe, people decided that they would act as though they were free—even though they weren't. Is that your tactic?

Well, I am acting as though I'm free. I do what I think I should. But to be free, what does that mean? If you want to look at it from the point of view of our inhibitions, our family responsibilities, our duties, no one is ever really free.

I think to be free is to be able to do what you think is right, and in that sense, I felt very free—even under house arrest. Because it was my choice. I knew that I could leave any time. I just had to say, "I'm not going to do politics anymore." But it was my choice to be involved in the democracy movement. So I felt perfectly free. Also, I didn't hanker after the great wide world. I didn't feel I wanted to go out. I didn't want to go out visiting.

Did your Buddhism help you with that?

I suppose so. It's so much a part of me that it's difficult to say whether it was my Buddhism or part of my character. But I suppose my Buddhist upbringing is part of my character now. As I said, I felt very free. It was my duty. I suppose that I am by nature a rather disciplined person. I quite like a disciplined life. Some people are very much bothered by having a strict regime, but that doesn't bother me. And of course, I always took Saturdays and Sundays off.

During the week, I read things on the economic situation in Southeast Asia and on politics or political philosophy. That was work. The things I read for pleasure were a lot of biographies of political dissidents. That I found very interesting. It was like comparing notes. What happened to them and how did they cope? I liked Nehru's autobiography very much, and Sakharov and Sharansky's *Fear No Evil.* That was fascinating: the way he had to stand up to all those interrogations.

Were you ever interrogated?

No, no. The first time they came to interrogate me, I said I could not answer their questions until they had first answered mine.

And they asked if I would answer their questions if they answered mine. I said [that] if they answered them to my satisfaction, I would consider it. They went away.

They came a second time. And I told them, "Until you answer the questions I put to you, I cannot consider answering yours."

They came a third time, in 1989, to tell me that my political party had put me forward as a candidate for the elections in 1990. They had come to examine me as a proposed candidate. So I said, "Is this what you do with all the candidates?" They said, "Yes." And then they started putting to me the same questions that they had asked before.

Is it true that during your house arrest, there were times when there wasn't money for food?

Yes. So I ate less—and I sold furniture from the house when I needed money to buy food. The SLORC offered to give me money, but of course I would not take it from them. So we discussed the matter and I thought, "Well, I could sell some of the furniture." They agreed to give me the proceeds. I later found out that they had not sold the furniture. They had simply warehoused it and given me money.

Did you try to get these items back once you were freed? They had belonged to your parents.

No, I didn't. But since the SLORC wanted to give them back, I paid them for it.

So you now have your parents' furnishings?

No, I sold them off again. I am not attached to things like that. In any case, I need this room for meetings, so it is better that it is bare. My father is dead. My mother is dead. Why should I cling to their furniture?

After you were released in July, you said that President Clinton should be more consistent in his policy toward Burma. Officially, the United States has supported the democracy movement. So, what did you mean exactly?

At the time I said that, it was because the United States didn't have a firm policy. They were always trying to decide what their policy should be and we could do with a lot more consistent help. At the moment, I do not think the government is inconsistent.

So where was the inconsistency? Was it in the desire of many corporate leaders who wanted to set up shop in Burma?

Yes. But that's not just the United States—it's every country where businessmen would like to come in. If they think there's a chance to make money, they are not very concerned about the political situation—unless, of course, it affects their business.

The SLORC has named 1996 "Visit Myanmar Year" in the hope of developing tourism. Will it help human rights if tourists come?

How could it? A large part of the tourist infrastructure—roads, bridges, railways—has been built with forced labor. [In the rural areas] each household has to provide a certain amount of labor. If you can't do that, you've got to pay money.

In Mandalay [Burma's second-largest city], the people are made to replace their ancient wooden-and-bamboo fences with brick walls. I think this is meant to impress foreign visitors. They also have to put up brick facades to their wooden houses. And those who can't afford it have had to leave the homes their families lived in for generations. Everyone knows how a lot of villagers around Pagan were forced to move because they wanted to make the place look clean and proper for the tourists. A whole lot of settlers have been removed from the banks of the Irrawaddy [River] to make the docks look very neat.

You know, at the Shwedagon [Pagoda] they've started tearing down the stairways that are hundreds of years old. They are going to make it all very new. The roof above the staircase, bits of it were donated by people. From a Buddhist point of view, it is very wrong to tear these things down because these are the good works of others. You don't tear down the good works of people just to impress tourists. They should have restored them. But I don't think the SLORC knows much about restoration.

I spoke the other night to a man with strong connections to the SLORC, and asked him, "Why don't the generals just sit down and talk with her?" His answer was, "There's no need. The SLORC can do business with others."

Well, this is always their attitude. They will only do business with those who exactly agree with them. We don't. But that's why we need to talk.

My SLORC source said that they'd never let you govern. They thought you should do some kind of humanitarian work.

But why? Why would they want me to just do humanitarian work? If they think I'm inefficient, then they should not encourage me to do any work at all. What they are saying is that they do not want me involved in politics. And you have to ask, "Why?" And they never quite give an answer. Of course, they can bring up my foreign husband, but that's not a reason.

I think they just don't want to talk to me because I have too much support. In 1988, we started calling for dialogue and their response then was, "There are over 200 political parties—we can't talk to one and not the others. So since we don't have time for everyone, we can't talk to the NLD." The next year, over a hundred of the political parties said they were prepared to have me as their spokesperson. And then the chairman of the SLORC said something like, "Well, she will be representing more than 100 political parties and I'm just one. So that's not fair." They always find reasons for not talking. That's the way they deal with the country.... I think somebody once referred to it as "a fascist Disneyland."

Do you ever speculate about what makes the SLORC generals tick?

All of Burma does. I suppose it is a desire to hang on to power. And it is also that many of them have done very well in the last five or six years and they do not want to give up their privileged positions.

When one talks to people near the government, they insist on describing you as a creature of the West—not of Burma.

Oh, well, if that makes them happy.... How do they explain all the Burmese that support my party? We won 82 percent of the seats in the 1990 elections. I didn't even run. I was under house arrest.

What do you think of the notion that some of the SLORC supporters believe that democracy is an alien Western idea, unsuitable to Asia?

If we are going to make an analogy, a country which has not invented television doesn't say, "Well, we've got to invent television from scratch before we have it here." They just go and buy the televisions from the United States and Japan, and they would consider any country silly that refused to have television until they produced their own. It's the same thing with democracy. Why should we have to wait? Democracy has been tried out in other countries and we are able to judge its weaknesses and strengths and decide how to adapt it to our own circumstances.

You have said that when you were first put under house arrest, you thought a great deal about your husband and children who were living in England. Eventually, you realized this was doing you no good, so you stopped. How is it possible to do that?

Most political prisoners do that. Anybody who is sensible knows that it does no good to go on and on agonizing about things you can do nothing about. Political prisoners from everywhere in the world will tell you the same thing.

Because thinking about them hurts too much?

Because it doesn't do any good. You don't help your family in that way. It's just plain common sense.

How did you change during your internment?

People keep asking me that and I don't know. Actually, when I reflect on it, I realize that I'm much more patient now. I don't have such a short temper. That's because I had a lot of time to meditate. And I think meditating does develop a sense of awareness and that means better control over your emotions.

Did you, after a while, get used to imprisonment?

I got used to it immediately. I decided, well, I've been placed under house arrest and [laughs] I need to enjoy it as much as I can. It had better be as useful as possible. I managed to do a lot of things I thought useful—meditating, reading, exercising, sewing curtains for the house.

During one of his visits here from England, my husband brought me a Nordic Track. He had bought the thing for himself, but never got around to using it. When he heard I was having back trouble, he thought it would help. He also brought me the *Encyclopaedia Brittanica.* So there was enough there for me to read, even if they'd kept me under house arrest for years more.

I wonder if you didn't use your time here alone to reflect on the legacy of your father, Aung San. You were only two years old when he was assassinated by a political rival.

42

No, I didn't do that! Occasionally, of course, I thought about him. But that would have been very unhealthy. You do not live in the past. And my father is no longer alive and I'm very much aware of it. Now, I did draw on his spirit for strength and what he had done to help me decide what should be done in the future. But the idea of using my time in detention to commune with my father who had died so many years ago sounds perfectly unhealthy.

You once told a reporter that you used to look at your father's picture and think, "It's just you and me alone here."

Oh, I'd sometimes look at his photograph and think, "Well yes, it's just you and me." But I do it in a rather humorous way. You see, my father was very young when he died. So it's difficult for me to think of him as an old person. I tend to look upon him as a friend as well as a father. I feel as if he is somebody who would have stood by me when I was in trouble. I think, "I may be alone, but I know I have your backing."

Your mother was a remarkable woman, too.

She was. And my father was very much influenced by my mother. And one of the reasons why I think my father must have been a wonderful person is because my mother was very strong. She was, by choice, a career-woman, and was not the domesticated type. Until she married my father. And I think she was completely won over by his principles and by the fact that he was a very lovable person, of which most people are not very aware. People think of him as a tough soldier and an astute politician, but he was very warm-hearted and loving.

As for my mother, she was very strong and very strict—she brought us up as she thought my father would have. Her strength was above normal. Sometimes, I think that by nature she was braver than my father. I think my father, like me, had to learn to be brave. My mother was afraid of nothing.

I don't remember my father. He died when I was two. And my mother was the head of the household, and a capable one, and so without going out of her way to do that, she showed me that a woman can be as capable and as efficient as any man. But she did not spell it out for me. She was not of the generation that talked of women's rights. My mother, for instance, was Ambassador to India, but she did not think of it as something she'd achieved as a woman.

In your speeches, you often talk about how people need to develop a "freedom from fear." What do you mean?

That you should not let your fears prevent you from doing what you know is right. Not that you shouldn't be afraid. Fear is normal. But to be inhibited from doing what you know is right, that is what is dangerous. You should be able to lead your life in the right way—despite your fears.

Anyone facing a dictatorship has to ask himself, "What are you afraid of?" Are you afraid of prison—and what are you afraid of in prison? Are you afraid of the bad food, beatings? Whatever it is, you have to face it and decide how you shall cope. As one of our young [NLD] students said, "Well, if they beat me, I shall yell!"

Surely there have been moments during this ordeal when you have had fear?

Yes, of course. One does fear doing the wrong thing...decisions that you make as a politician could hurt others, not just yourself. But I believe that a real revolution is a revolution of the spirit. Just going out in the street and waving your fist will not do. It has to come from inside. People have to decide that they will change a system that is harming a country so much and they have to be determined to do this in any way they can. As I have. As others have. Think of [NLD associate] U Win Tein. He has five children. And for him to put the lives of six people including his wife in jeopardy for the sake of his beliefs, that's a lot more than I am doing.

I know that my children are safe. They are in a country (Britain) where their rights are guaranteed. They have a caring father. So I have no worries on that score.

I wonder: to what extent have you been influenced by the tactics the Dalai Lama has used in his situation? Faced with overwhelming power, he has simply refused to capitulate.

And I don't give in either. Is that a "tactic?" Or is that a state of mind?

Tell us the difference between politics and meditation.

Well, if you're meditating and a mosquito comes and bites you, you have to think, "Biting...biting...biting." And you are aware that the mosquito is biting and you just keep sitting there. You don't stop the mosquito and you don't try to shake it off.

But politics is not like that. We try everything we can not to hurt others and not to create feelings of antipathy. But if people are doing things that are unacceptable to us as the party that represents the democratic movement, we can't just sit there and say, "They are doing it.... They are doing it.... They are doing it." And not do anything. For instance, they have been sentencing our people unjustly to prison. We're not going to meditate and say, "They've been unjust...they've been unjust...they've been unjust." We're going to do something. We've appealed those cases, and let's see how it goes.

Many Westerners have wondered why it is that nations with such large Buddhist populations have so often had such terribly violent rulers— Cambodia, Burma, Tibet?

Sometimes I wonder if the countries that embraced Buddhism did so because they needed it, because there was something violent in their societies that needed to be controlled by Buddhism.

But of course, violence is not limited to Buddhist countries. It is true: it is very difficult for us to explain why we should have violent governments in Buddhist countries because the governments themselves claim to be Buddhist! If you stay here long enough and you watch television, you will see the generals...donating things to monasteries, praying at pagodas and behaving very much like good Buddhists. So one wonders why such violence exists. And I think the conclusion one would have to come to is that perhaps they are not practicing Buddhism anything like enough.

Do you think the military dismisses you, in part, because you are a woman?

I don't think they dismiss me. I think they pretend to dismiss me. But I don't think it's because I'm a woman. It's just because I represent a strong opposition to what they want to do...I think they do not like anyone who stands up to them.

The generals of the SLORC seem to be firmly committed to the idea that you and your party will never rule...

Well, it seems to me that they spend an awful lot of time thinking about me.

Over and over again, you've said to the generals of the SLORC, "We want to help you out of your dilemma...we want to help you make the transition to democracy." Yet they keep resisting.

Perhaps they do not really want democracy—this is something that one can't help thinking.

But you keep on putting out feelers, calling for negotiations, and hoping that the generals will respond?

They'll have to respond at one time or another because that is the way all these situations end up—at the table. They keep saying, "We'll never talk," and then they end up talking. I mean, look at Liberia or Angola, where they just insisted that they would find a solution by weapons. In the end, they all had to sit down and talk. The wiser people are, the quicker they get to the dialogue table so that the people don't suffer so much.

You know, when I was under house arrest, I spent a lot of time listening to the BBC and I followed very closely the events in South Africa and in the former Yugoslavia. In South Africa, they chose the path of dialogue; the white government finally came to the conclusion that they'd have to talk over their problems. They thought in Yugoslavia that they'd solve their problems by fighting. In the end, they'll have to talk it out, but look at all the suffering that they unleashed on the country because they were not sensible enough to talk in the beginning.

Yugoslavia is something like Burma in that there was a unity that was imposed on the country by an authoritarian government. It was not a true unity that came from the conviction of people that they could live and work together. Such a situation is at some time bound to be shattered.

It ended terribly. It was like a pressure cooker exploding, all the resentments and hatreds, all the injustices that people felt they had to put up with that they could not discuss. 1988 here [when there were massive street demonstrations against the military] was that kind of explosion. Not quite as bad as Yugoslavia. And if the people of Burma continue to be oppressed, if they are forced into a superficial form of unity, another explosion will come in time. And that may be far worse than what we had in 1988.

After all these years of dictatorship, have the Burmese lost their sense of trust in each other?

Yes, I'm afraid so. Not completely.... One of the ways the government tries to stop people from being involved in the democracy movement is to encourage them to take an interest in business and not in politics. That is, if you are concentrated on just making money in this country you have to indulge in a lot of things that are ... not quite strict. There is a lot of bribery and corruption going on. You do lose the morality if you are told to concentrate only on making money and if you are made to feel as long as you are making money, you won't get into trouble. So people think that it's much more dangerous to support the democracy movement than to bribe somebody.

I'm told that there have been all these whisper campaigns in Rangoon against you. The big charge is that you have a foreign husband. You've responded by saying, "What's wrong with loving someone of another culture?"

The Burmese people in general don't think there's anything wrong. Of course, they would prefer that I had married a Burmese. On the other hand, if I had, he probably would have been put into jail as well. During my detention, I was lucky not having to worry about my family the way my NLD colleagues did. They had to worry constantly about their families being at the mercy of the authorities outside. This was an extra burden for them. Whereas I was freed of that burden because my husband and children were abroad and safe.

Your husband seems to be one of the major saints of the 20th century. He raised the children alone in England. He organized support for you. He doesn't seem to mind your political commitment.

He's not a saint. But he is a very good husband.

Are there very many husbands on the face of this planet who'd say, "I understand you have to do this"?

Well, I was only recently talking to a young woman from upcountry, who was jailed for five years and had three children. She said her husband was simply wonderful. He brought the baby regularly to see her in prison. He kept everything going. And there are other husbands like that.

You've said that your marriage cannot be a normal marriage anymore. What did you mean?

That we live apart. That's not a normal marriage. I simply mean that we will have to be married across the water, as it were.

Someone was telling me that there were leaflets circulating in Rangoon saying "Not only does she have a foreign husband, but he's Jewish."

Did they say he was Jewish? Sometimes they say I have a Muslim husband. Well, I think sometimes they say I have several husbands! Sometimes, they say I have, I think, four husbands. They just say anything they feel like saying.

There was a very lovely old lady in one of the Burmese villages, who didn't believe all that. And when she heard that I was supposed to have four husbands, she said, "Well, if I had all her advantages, I'd have four husbands, too." [Laughs.]

Do your sons hate politics because it took their mother from them?

I don't think my children feel as strongly about the Burmese situation as I do. It's absolutely normal that they should not. They have not grown up in Burma and even now live abroad. So obviously, they would not feel about Burma the way I do.

My younger son plays the electric guitar. He can't bear to be parted with it. Last time he was here, he casually mentioned "my girlfriend." So he let me know that he had one. He didn't keep me out of the picture.

In one of your speeches, you exhorted the crowd not to hit their children if they wanted to become democratic people. Why did you do that?

It was because of the climate of fear in Burma. In a lot of countries—not just Burma—people teach their children by frightening them, smacking them, instead of reasoning with them.

And quite recently, I went to a house where a little child was picking at the snacks on the table and one of the older people asked her to stop, and she didn't. And the father said, "Why don't you listen to me— aren't you afraid of me?" I was quite shocked.

This is what I meant in that speech: that you shouldn't feel that obedience comes out of fear—that the good child is one who does whatever he is told to do because of fear. I do not like this way of instilling fear into the people of Burma. And it begins in the family.

Since I've been here, I've heard a lot of Burmese say, "Aung San Suu Kyi is our only hope." Given that, do you ever fear assassination?

No, I don't. It's something that I have to recognize as a possibility. I always say to my colleagues, "If they ever assassinate me, make sure you really make capital out of it." There's not much point in worrying about it. I know I'm going to die one day.

A lot of Burma watchers say that there's a strong possibility that the junta will re-arrest you.

49

Yes, though it doesn't affect what I am doing. But I always consider that this is a possibility.

Should that happen, what will you do—set up a disciplined regimen again?

It depends on whether or not I'm put under house arrest or into prison. Prison would be a new experience. It might be interesting.

Do you ever admit to anyone that they have hurt you?

But they haven't done that much to me. The things that they thought they were doing to me did not really hurt me. The terrible personal attacks that they made only made the people turn against them. Before the 1990 elections, we used to say, "Every time one of them opens their mouths, the votes come pouring down on our side."

What do you want people in the United States to know about you?

That we are not near democracy yet and that there are, so far, no signs that we are progressing towards democratization. The National Convention [that the SLORC was holding to draft a constitution], as it stands, is not a step towards democratization at all. I think a lot of Americans very much take their rights for granted. And I think many of them do not know what life is like for those of us whose security is not guaranteed by a democratic constitution. So I would like to ask them to try to put themselves in our shoes and ask how they would feel if they were deprived of all rights. I would like them to see us not as a country rather far away whose sufferings do not matter, but as fellow human beings in need of human rights and who could do so much for the world, if we were allowed.

Do you think your father would have been proud of what you're doing?

It's too early to say. I think he'd say, "Well, you haven't got there yet." I think, after we've gotten democracy, he would say he's proud of me.

POSTSCRIPT:

Aung San Suu Kyi spoke those words to me on November 22, 1995. Several days later, the SLORC held a session of a constitutional assembly that had been meeting since 1993 to draw up a document to legitimize military rule over the country. The National League for Democracy leaders asked for modifications in convention procedures to make them more democratic; when the SLORC refused to make even the smallest of concessions, the NLD members opted to boycott the event.

With that, the repression started again. Burma ceased being at the "crossroads" that Daw Suu Kyi had spoken about in our interview.

According to the international human rights monitoring organization Human Rights Watch/Asia, "The NLD's boycott of the convention marked the beginning of a year-long confrontation between the SLORC and the NLD which led to the detention of over 1,000 NLD supporters, between November 1995 and October 1996."

Among those detained were her assistant, U Win Tein, who was sentenced to fourteen years in prison, and an old friend of Suu Kyi's who'd served as a kind of surrogate uncle to her, James Leander Nichols. Two months after Nichols's arrest, he died of a heart attack while being pressured into making false statements about his relationship to the Nobel Peace Prize winner. In May of 1996, Aung Sang Suu Kyi's cousin, an apolitical businessman named U Aye Win, who was sometimes at her compound to give her moral support, was arrested. According to Human Rights Watch/Asia, "Nothing has been heard from him since."

By the fall of 1996, leaders in the government had grown impatient with the size of the crowds coming at weekends to hear Aung San Suu Kyi speak—and they ordered active harassment of those attending. Human Rights Watch/Asia reports that: "On September 27, barricades were erected across the main street leading to Daw Suu Kyi's house, and hundreds of supporters were arrested as they waited near the barricades to hear her. The barricades were taken up and then put back several times during October and then the weekend gatherings were effectively banned. As a counter measure, the SLORC forced thousands of people to attend mass political rallies during June and July [1996] where the crowds pledged their loyalty to the government. All civil servants were threatened with dismissal if they did not attend rallies, and school children, farmers and day laborers were ordered onto buses and taken to rally sites."

As 1996 drew to a close, Suu Kyi was confined to a kind of house arrest again. She now needed the military's permission to leave her compound, something she refused to ask for. In December, when student demonstrations for university reform broke out in the neighborhood near her home, the SLORC blamed Aung San Suu Kyi for inciting them—though the students insisted that they found the NLD and its leaders to be old-timers of another generation. Later in the month, when a bomb went off at the Kaba Aye pagoda, a religious shrine frequented by high government officials, the SLORC tried to tie Suu Kyi to the violence. The Secretary of the junta, General Khin Nyunt, held a rare press conference where he declared, "Taking advantage of the student unrest... both the NLD and the BCP (Burmese Communist Party) underground launched their activities to destabilize the country."

Just after New Year's 1997, the junta declared Aung San Suu Kyi's house "off limits" to journalists and diplomats, further isolating her. "Journalists can meet her at other places," Colonel Than Shwe told the Associated Press. Except, of course, that she needs the military's permission to go anywhere.

•••

PHILOSOPHERS

Arthur Caplan

I'm firmly convinced that every interview has its own innate length, and that it is the interviewer's job to find it from the raw transcript he/she has amassed. In that sense, the interviewer is like a sculptor; you must locate the hidden form in the rock, or the raw copy.

Most successful print Q's and A's run in the neighborhood of three to four thousand words. Any less than that tends to be too skimpy for a serious interplay between two voices. *Playboy, Penthouse* and sometimes, *Rolling Stone*, give more room, and that's one reason for the fierce loyalty interviewers from those publications have for their magazines; it's just too much fun to have eight thousand words to fool with.

At *The New York Times Magazine* the interviews are, typically, about 3300 words. Smart, dense editing makes these pieces come to life. But sometimes beautiful little bits of exchange are excised. And it just can't be helped. The story must fit the space.

With this interview, I submitted a first draft of about 3500 words. Editor James Atlas saw an unusual quality in it and asked me to expand to an unheard of 8,000 words. Oh, God, this was the interviewer's idea of being locked in the bakery overnight.

I went back to Arthur Caplan, interviewed him yet again, and handed in a fat and happy 8,000 words. But the revised story proved too long for the requirements of the magazine; it dragged. What ultimately ran was 4,000. I'm splitting the difference here: restoring some very much liked material that was cut from the magazine version, for a length of slightly under 6,000 words.

When I met him, on a warmish afternoon in November 1996, Dr. Arthur Caplan, forty-six, professor of bioethics at the University of Pennsylvania, and the director of that institution's Center for Bioethics, sat in his Philadelphia office, frantically plowing through some sixty-eight, yes, *sixty-eight*, telephone messages littering his desk.

Among the messages was a call from a Chicago reporter seeking a comment on Joseph Cardinal Bernardin's death from liver cancer. CNN was sending over a camera crew over for footage on Gulf War Syndrome—Dr. Caplan is a member of the Presidential Advisory Committee on Gulf War Illnesses, which had just concluded hearings. A journalist from Southern California wanted Caplan's views on the big local story: the indictment of famed fertility expert Dr. Ricardo Asch for alleged improprieties at his Orange County clinic. And oh, yes, *Nightline* wanted to book an appearance.

"Gosh, people are in the grips of bioethics fever today," said Caplan. A burley, unprepossessing figure in rumpled nothing-special clothes, he talks at breakneck speed. "It used to be that I'd have to fight to get any coverage for these kinds of issues. Nowadays, there's so much bioethics in the news that there are times when I can't keep tabs on it all."

This is a problem that Art—as everyone calls him—Caplan, Ph.D. has made for himself. And one that wins him little sympathy from his academic peers. In the booming specialty of bioethics—an interdisciplinary splice of philosophy, law and health-policy planning—Dr. Art Caplan, philosopher, is both a serious scholar and a popularizer.

Caplan's particular skill is an ability to identify, analyze and explain the extremely complex moral questions that grow out of changes in health care, science, and medicine. As Director of the Center for Bioethics, he runs a combination think-tank and ethics fire-station for that institution's vast system of hospitals and research laboratories.

He does what he calls "hands-on philosophy," which means that he advises the university hospitals on the everyday bioethics problems on the wards, teaches medical students about moral ambiguities in their work, helps researchers design ethically-consistent projects. He has been a health policy advisor to the Clinton administration, writes a syndicated newspaper column, "A Question of Ethics," and produces a blizzard of professional publications with hybrid titles like, "Why The Problem of Reductionism in Biology Won't Go Away" and "What Are the Morals of our Treatment of Renal Failure?"

"He's a very complicated figure in philosophy," says Dr. Jane Caplan, a psychologist, and his wife of twenty-five years. They have a twelve-year-old son, Zach. "When he was a student, he never really fit in with the rest of the Columbia philosophy department. He was a guy who admitted it when he was wrong, who loved to argue and thought it was fun. To this day, he loves showing how complicated an argument is, and he believes the public is educable. A lot of people in his field don't. To them, applied philosophy is second rate."

Actually, Caplan is a classically trained philosopher with all the right credentials. He did his masters and his Ph.D. at Columbia University in the early 1970s, where his mentors were Ernest Nagel and Sidney Morgenbesser, two giants in the philosophy of science. In 1976, while still a graduate student, he took a part-time job teaching ethics to medical students at Columbia College of Physicians and Surgeons and found himself hooked on the moral dilemmas of the medical setting. That post lead to Caplan attending a national bioethics conference, where he was spotted by the founder of the field, Daniel Callahan, who asked him to work at the Hastings Institute, which was then and to some extent still is, the cutting-edge bioethics think-tank. Caplan would eventually become Associate Director at Hastings.

After seven years at Hastings, Caplan was offered a bioethics program by the University of Minnesota. Three years later, he got an unrefusable offer from the University of Pennsylvania: an annual budget of nearly a million dollars, hands-on involvement with some of the cutting-edge research in genetics at the school, and an income of about $200,000.

Caplan's Center is located on a bleak Philadelphia avenue—near the University of Pennsylvania's Medical School, but not within it. "I wanted to say, 'We're new!'" he explains. "I also didn't want to be located on the medical school campus. I wanted to be partners. Not beholden."

Give us the job description of a bioethicist.

I spend a lot of time trying to identify ethical issues in health care and science and then thinking through ways of arguing about them to change behavior. Or policy. Or both. Sometimes, I will come into a medical setting and suggest changes in practices, simple things like, "Will you please stop interviewing hospital patients while they are going to the bathroom." It can be as crude as that. Or as elegant as, "Have we thought through how sperm cell transplants could be misused?" I've been laboring in the bioethics vineyards for more than twenty years, but my mother still has a hard time figuring out what I do for a living.

How do you know what is moral?

Ask patients—they'll tell you. Also, know what the law says and what the customs of the tribe [of the medical profession] are. The good bioethicist will get some help from looking at traditions, the norms of right and wrong, and also, from what the law says. If you're operating on someone without a signed informed consent, there may be a good reason—but you're probably doing something wrong. If the law says that people are dead after their brains have stopped functioning and you are still treating somebody after that, you may be doing something wrong.

Are you seen as a charlatan by your peers?

They wouldn't go that far. But I have my critics. Mostly, they think I shouldn't spend time yakking to the masses.

My answer to them is that philosophy as it's often done is too removed, too disengaged, and renders many of its practitioners unemployable. To me, the whole point of doing ethics is to change people, to change behavior. Why else do it?

What we do at my Center is a kind of applied philosophy. For instance, right now, the Center staff is looking at a gene therapy trial that is being conducted at the medical school here. There's a gene therapy being developed to kill off tumor cells in a fatal brain cancer called "glioma." In order to test this stuff, you have to try it out in low doses on people with the disease.

The first people who get it are never going to get cured.

In fact, the goal of the first trials is to see whether you kill the subjects by giving them the gene therapy as opposed to letting the brain cancer kill them. Among things we want to know, when they sign up for these experiments, is whether the patients really understand that no cure is being offered them. Do they nevertheless come in with hope? And if they do, is it right to tell them, "There's no hope?" Should we be telling them the truth? Can they even hear the truth? It's not so easy to say to a dying person, "All we've got is the ability to experiment on you." No one wants to say it and, certainly, no one wants to hear it.

So on one hand, we're looking at the way informed consent is given in this particular experiment. But we are also in the trenches, doing real-world, real-life ethics here. And that's what philosophy ought to be—about real people, speaking to human concerns—not armchair fantasies about right and wrong.

What are the roots of your bioethics obsession?

When I was six, I had polio. Not a bad case, but I missed a good chunk of first grade and went to rehab for many years after. That definitely got me interested in ethics. You don't have to get Freudian, it's right there. I thought about things like why didn't the hospital let your parents stay over. I wondered about why such a bad thing had happened to me since I was such a good kid. Truthfulness bothered me a lot. The doctors and nurses at Mass. General Children's Hospital would never tell you when a kid was going to die. And on my floor, a lot of kids died. You couldn't get a straight answer. Johnny would be in the next bed, looking terrible and they were saying, "Johnny is going home now." And then, suddenly, there'd be this empty bed.

It has never ever left me, that not being truthful is a tricky thing in medicine. That experience reminded me that people in health care get a lot of information from other patients. So it's better for them to have good information.

Why didn't you become a doctor?

I loved *thinking* about medicine, but I didn't like doing it. I could never adjust to the idea that you had to cause people pain in order to help them.

Do you think science will be able to give people the ability to achieve a kind of immortality in the near future?

Yeah, well, sort of. I can envision a situation where by transplanting your heart, liver, spleen, lungs and bone marrow, you can be transformed into an immortal-like thing.

It will be done by excising diseased human body parts and by grafting on human and animal parts. I don't see a problem with it. Now, a lot of people might say, "It sounds intrinsically yukky to have ten animal organs keeping me alive." But we can adapt to that, much as we have to other kinds of bio-engineering. No one complains much nowadays about the unnaturalness of heart-transplants.

I do think it has a social cost, though. The dollar price of pursuing an extended life is big. We can wind up distorting the health care budget to add five, ten, twenty years of life to those who can afford it. But to do that, we might be pulling social resources away from people who can't get fifty years because they were born in India or West Philadelphia.

Do you fret about the ethics of using animals as an organ source for humans?

If you believe in an animal's right to life, then you should begin at the breakfast table, not the surgery table. The number of animals killed for bacon is incredible.

Well, pigs are not endangered. Chimpanzees are.

In the long run, nobody is going to use primates for transplantation. You can't use a sixty pound chimp's heart to support a two hundred pound man.

Oh, of course, it's sad to have to kill an animal, but it's something I would consider doing, even to the point of killing thousands of pigs to get parts for people. I think these pigs will lead very happy lives so that they will be healthy when their organs are put into you. It is just a mistake to think that the only way you can give moral worth to something is to equate it with us. There are degrees of moral worth.

How do the popular television doctor-dramas, ER, *and* Chicago Hope, *cover bioethics?*

C-plus, at best. They do a pretty good job at laying out clinical issues.

Should a drunken man get a liver transplant? Should we allow a baby who's been through a lot to die? But there's never any attention to the economics of modern medicine: "How do people pay for this?"

Every doctor on *ER* fights hard for their patients, without ever having an administrator say, "Enough! This guy doesn't have any insurance." In fact, there's very little of the nitty-gritty of money and bureaucracy that dominates a lot of what the American health care system is about. I certainly don't see enough challenge to the system.

Sometimes, the producers of these shows phone me for story ideas. I told one a while ago about a case I'd worked on where I'd gotten a call from the operating room and the doc was saying, "We've got a guy open on the table, on a heart-lung machine, and we dropped the heart we were going to put into him on the floor. There's no choice—we've got to use this heart. When he wakes, do we have to tell him about what happened?"

"You've got to *offer* to tell him," I said. "Because people have a right to know if you're putting them at risk of infection and death." That became one of those TV episodes.

OK, let me ask you the **ER** *question. Should a drunk be able to get a liver transplant?*

Yes. Sin does not belong in bedside rationing decisions.

But the fact is that someone who's been drinking a lot—Mickey Mantle, for instance—is not going to give that liver the mileage it deserves.

Effectiveness certainly counts. If someone can't survive with a new liver, there's no point in giving them one. And that was true of Mickey Mantle. But the real question is, "Will it work?" Not, "Is the person good enough?"

What's your take on that eugenic sperm bank that opened up in Southern California a few years ago?

You mean the Nobel Sperm Bank? The Repository for Germinal Choice? It still runs. The guy who is executive director is Robert Graham, as in Graham crackers. He'd actually go to scientific meetings, eyeball people and kind of say, "You're good enough." Then, he'd send them a canister and a note asking for a donation. Hardly anyone was doing it. So the Nobel Sperm Bank started out with Nobel laureates. Then it became smart scientists, but they couldn't get enough people to do that. So now, it's business leaders, celebrity types, "people of achievement," athletes, this quintessentially American notion of fame. O.J. Simpson is a great athlete. He could be in the bank, for all I know.

The whole thing is bonkers. Even if parents could select for eugenic possibilities, you might be able to increase the odds of having a kid with certain traits maybe just a little bit. If you look at families, there's enough variation between the slug sibling and the genius sibling to show that having the ace parents doesn't guarantee a championship outcome.

But let's say you could do it. To what extent should parents be allowed to put their tastes and values onto the biological design of their kids? There's something weird about saying, "I had my kids because I want them to be little exemplars of traits I value." You can almost see the parents complaining, "I had you to be a violinist, and what's this, you're tone-deaf!"

So the Nobel Sperm Bank may not be the best way of generating Alpha babies. But surely, some of the new developments in genetics and reproduction technologies could get us there?

Oh yeah, definitely. I think that the eugenic dreams and biological perfectionist aspirations of the Nazis and others were hindered, in part, by their not having the science. Well, look out, world: THE SCIENCE IS COMING.

In genetic testing, for instance, huge leaps are being made—and they bring with them, big, big questions. Let me give you just a few: What will happen when we can, with precision, tease apart the genetic contribution to violence, aggression, mathematical ability? Will that mean that we will start to have a lot of public debate about social programs, arguments linked to the wisdom of the genetic identification of the violent, the nasty, and the mentally ill? People are sure to be asking, "Should we step in early and do something about that?" That will quickly lead to new arguments about "What is man?"

I'm really interested in how the sale of genetic information and the sale of genetic perfectionism is going to shape us. The early signs are not good. I think that there will be an attempt to generate markets for people to feel bad if they don't get genetic report cards for their embryos and reproductive mates. Soon it will be, "How dare you create a child with a known mental disorder." In a market society, notions of perfection will sell. You can almost see the shops at the mall: "Genes R Us."

There's an experiment being done here at Penn by a man named Ralph Brinster. He can transplant sperm-making cells of rats to a mouse, and have them continue to make rat sperm cells! This opens the door to a rather different type of sperm bank where instead of taking little samples and freezing them, what you may have down the road is [the ability to] take a piece of your testes and put it into a carrier and have an unending supply of sperm because now you've got the sperm-making cells. This also opens the door to the manipulation of those sperm cells to try and alter them for eugenic purposes. No one has really known how to do that, but if you can get the sperm-making cells out of the body, and keep them working, and manipulate them, then "designing our descendants" moves from science-fiction to reality.

Can you see a time when we are not just designing our offspring, but ourselves too?

Oh yeah, it's coming—cosmetic enhancement of our mental engineering. Prozac and Ritalin are early versions of that. In twenty-five years, perhaps less, we may be faced with a whole set of moral questions about the desirability of changing mental functioning through drugs and implants. In the near future, we'll be asking, "Should everybody have an implant that diminishes aggressive impulses?" Or, "Should we swallow a 'niceness' pill?"

We'll also be wondering what to do with virtual technology and pleasure enhancement. Should everybody be allowed to go in a box and have all their sexual fantasies acted out in their mind with what's called prioperceptive or feedback loops?

Instead of getting genital stimuli, it will all be going on in your brain. Now, my question is, "Is there anything wrong with spending a lot of your time doing that?"

Anyway, these issues are going to be real. Not for our generation, but for the next one.

No, our boomer cohort has to contemplate Dr. Kevorkian. Tell us: Why do you loathe him?

How much tape do you have? I think he's a zealot and fanatic. You don't want an advocate for the right to die to be the same person making the judgment [on who should die]. If you watch some of his video tapes with people, there's no psychiatry, no psychology and he's not exactly the most warm and giving guy that's ever been around.

Part of the reason he troubles me so much is that he's so into his movement, which means he is the least likely person to be able to achieve a true informed consent and to weed out the depressed, the despondent, and the dingy from those who truly do want to die. Some of the folks he's seen seem to me to be just depressed, not necessarily in need of his services. I also don't trust him because I think he's obsessed with death. I think he's obsessed with trying to control death.

So you're saying he wants to be God?

Yes, he wants to make sure that death doesn't sneak up on him. Or anyone else. But it's both arrogant and hopeless to think that you can control it.

Is medically-assisted suicide a form of cowardice?

There's almost no one who can't find a way to kill themselves, if they really want to.

What Kevorkian is asking for is different; assistance by doctors. And that's troubling. People come to docs and say, "I can't do this myself." But what they mean is: "I can't do it because I might be cursed in the afterlife." They have all sorts of religious baggage they bring to the subject of suicide. It's just that no one likes to admit it.

I think this is one place where a person ought to take personal responsibility. It should not be easy. Or made easy. Besides, medicine's job is to make the case for why you should stay here. How will people be able to trust doctors if they know that under some circumstances, the doctor can kill you. I can see nursing home patients wondering, "When the doctor offered me assisted suicide, was it time for me to go? Or was it my bill?"

The bigger reason his movement disturbs me [is that we] still don't have a national system of health care. To have the right to die before you have the right to treatment, seems a little bit backwards. I worry about abuse. We may end up saying, "We've got assisted suicide—we don't have to worry about fixing up the pathetic nursing home system for the frail, old, and disabled. They can kill themselves if they don't like it."

Wait a second, isn't the opposite happening? I have the impression that the over-medicalization of the terminally ill is a much more persistent problem.

That's fair. It's a very real problem. But it comes from an era that's ending as we speak, an era when medicine was paid for by procedure. The more you did, the more you made. Now, it's the less you do, the more you make.

Have you wondered at all about what all the changes in birth and reproductive technologies do to traditional concepts of parenthood?

Oh yeah, and a number of very serious things have already happened to motherhood. With advances now available, the pregnant person might have no genetic relationship to the baby. Right now, you can take sperm from one man, put it in a dish with an egg from another woman and put that embryo into a third woman. In a situation like this, it's not at all clear who is the mother and why.

I think this leads to situations where you can make babies for money simply by using technology. We've seen some recent cases that should warn us about where we're going.

For instance, it's alleged that Michael Jackson, a man who is unlikely to pass social work-muster in terms of adoption, supposedly hired a woman, whom he subsequently married, to be impregnated artificially and carry his baby.

Here's an example that shows how much we need some controls. James Alan Austin of Bethlehem, Pennsylvania, a fertile single man in his late twenties, hired a surrogate to be artificially inseminated with his sperm. Upon payment of the fee, the child was delivered to him. A few weeks later, he murdered the baby. He never really explained why. I think he said something like the baby wouldn't stop crying. The standard excuse. Why a fertile man should be allowed to buy a baby with no screening or check on his character or motives is not at all clear to me.

What's the difference between pimping and surrogate-brokering?

Nothing. I think that buying babies is a practice that society should not accept anymore than it does paid exploitative middle-men dealing in sex.

I've talked with lawyers who broker surrogacy arrangements, and I've felt that the distance between them and a kind of brothel arrangement was not all that far. They sit there, sort of saying, "What type of surrogate do you want and these are the women we have in our book and who would you select and here's the fee."

You were an adviser to the Clinton administration during the failed health care reform effort of the first term. Any advice for the President this time around?

He should go back to the plate, but he needs a more modest agenda. I would say stress four things: managed care reform and children . . . children . . . children. The American people know that taking care of our kids is morally the right thing to do.

This time, though, he must be sure to frame the debate in moral terms. The big mistake in 1993 was to launch the health reform discussion with a lot of technical plans, bureaucratic maps and indecipherable language. The reform effort failed because the administration spoke an economics-jargon familiar only to policy wonks and not the values-talk most Americans relate to. None of it should have happened that way. The American people were ready to wrestle with health care. Clinton missed his appointment with history.

During the battle over health reform, Harry and Louise—the Insurance Institute's Every Couple—scored points when they complained in television ads about the loss of choice if the Clinton plan went through. Three years later, consumers appear to have everything they didn't want—less choice, less accountability and generally, more insecurity. How did we get here?

When the Clinton reform effort went down in flames, all that was left standing was the marketplace, and the decision to let business contain costs. Cost-containment became the only goal of American health care. And interestingly, costs are down. But complaints are up, too.

Name the four biggest secrets of the American health care system.

First, money is omnipresent in everything that happens.

Two: privacy is a myth. Medical information is not protected and confidential. In fact, medical information is bandied about, whipped back and forth with very few qualms, with lots of people peering at it, finding it, using it. An everyday reality of managed care is that dozens of people have every right to see the most intimate details of your medical records. A precondition to get care is to waive your privacy.

Three: that we have a wonderful acute care system, but a scandalously rotten chronic care system. I think that's because we Americans don't like to think about old age. Or decrepitude. In an autonomy-crazed culture, old age and infirmity is a filthy little secret to be hidden.

Four: that we ration health care. Americans hate this idea because it violates the national belief that when it comes to matters of life and death all lives should be treated equally. We cannot, as a society, admit that anybody is worth more than anybody else. So we ration, but we don't ever confess that we do.

In Oregon, they admit it. In the Medicaid insurance system, the procedures the state will pay for are clearly prioritized. Will we all be following Oregon?

It was incredibly courageous what they did there. They took on the issue in a public way that was unprecedented and hasn't been duplicated since. I admired it, *but*... it also had a fatal flaw: the effort to think about rationing was confined to the poor. It focused on Medicaid, a population politically unable to look out for itself and who were not represented at all in the state-wide dialogue.

Oregon shows both what can be done—put the public on notice that they must grapple with hard choices, and what should not be done—confine discussions of rationing to the weakest, most vulnerable amongst us.

You've been doing some bioethics work around Gulf War Syndrome as part of a Presidential Advisory Committee on Gulf War illnesses. What are the bioethics issues that the veterans' complaints bring forward?

Most concretely, which values drive decisions about calling something "a disease." It's not enough to have illness, you need a cause, and in the context of the military, it's better that the cause be physical than psychological.

People who are sick as a result of service in the Persian Gulf do not want to be seen as malingerers or cowards or chronic complainers. Moral values are therefore a key element of what looks like, on the surface, a simple medical question: is there Gulf War Disease?

It almost sounds like you're saying here, "They are somatizing."

I know. But I don't mean to. Your question shows the problem. If people have psychological and mental complaints, they may well be in their head, but it certainly can also be in their bodies.

Wait just a minute. We know that some of our troops were indeed exposed to chemical weapons. And even if that hadn't been proved true, they were breathing oil fires, dust, fuel oil, taking various prophyoplatic drugs. Our troops were exposed to all kinds of hazards that could easily create sickness.

Absolutely true. But it doesn't mean that these things did not produce psychological as well as physical problems. Nor does it mean that we really understand anything at all about single or multiple causes that might have lead to their complaints.

But nerve gas is toxic. That's the point of it.

But not everyone who is sick was exposed to nerve gas. And the available data on exposure to chemical weapons does not link them to the kinds of symptoms that veterans report.

To really know why soldiers get sick in modern technological warfare, the military is going to have to rethink its approach to monitoring the health of soldiers. What we need is a recognition that wars fought in strange environments where toxic substances can be used as weapons, or are a by-product of battle, do not fit the old mind-set of how to count casualties.

What was the biggest moral crisis you've faced?

Going for a draft induction physical in 1971, the middle of the Vietnam War. Many people were going to Canada or not showing up. My wife Jane didn't want me to go to the physical. She thought Canada looked better at the time, but I re-read Socrates's discussion in Plato's Dialogues about why he was going to take the hemlock. He argued that since he'd accepted society's benefits, it was wrong for him to reject society. This led me to decide, "I don't support this war, I'm going to argue against it, but I'm going to go."

As it happens the doctor who gave me the induction exam was one of the guys who was exempting anyone he could. When he heard that I had had childhood polio, he said, "You should not be going to Vietnam." But I never did anything to get out. It wasn't patriotism. It was just a feeling that you shouldn't rip off the system.

Have there been moments when you've not lived up to your own standards?

Sure, and I felt like a dodo afterwards. The strongest example I can think of was when I was at medical school at Columbia and there were some doctors in the neonatology department who told me that they thought a little girl should be permitted to die because her brain was all bashed up. They wanted me to help convince the parents to let this baby die. And I did that.

But the parents made it clear that they weren't going to let this baby die and they could love a baby even with severe intellectual impairments.

69

And later they came to me and said, "Why did you push us around by throwing your moral weight on the side of the doctors—you didn't even know much about us." They were right.

Do you believe in the small lie?

Oh yes, absolutely. One of the lubricants of social comity is the small lie. It's like learning to use any small sharp object—you have to use it carefully. I certainly don't have a problem with a small lie, if I'm trying to save a life.

For instance, early in my career, I realized that by paying attention to the ethics of what good informed consent is, I was missing something. Whenever I'd been involved in a case of a Jehovah's Witness who was refusing a life-saving blood transfusion, their family and clergy were present. It occurred to me that maybe they were pressuring the patient to say, "No, we don't want blood." So the next time I had a Jehovah's Witness case, I got everyone out of the room and talked to the patient alone: "Do you really want to refuse the blood? Because if you don't, I am willing to make sure you get a blood transfusion and lie about it."

The first time I did this to a car-accident victim with internal bleeding, the guy didn't want it, and he died.

Some months later, I had another Jehovah's Witness case, a guy with a small aneurysm, and this man said, "I want the blood, if you won't tell anyone." This was true informed consent. A life or death decision like this had to be made in a pressure-free environment. We did go out and say to his relatives, "Gosh, it was a lucky recovery. We thought he needed blood, but we see he can make it through without it." The dominant value there was to let a person make his choices free of coercion.

With kidney donations, I began having questions on the way we were counseling family members who'd been called upon to donate live organs. I realized family ties could be coercive. So I went in and talked to our transplant team and said, "Before we accept any more live kidney donations, we'd better be prepared to give people a medical excuse, lie for them—so that they feel that they don't have to withstand the wrath of their family if they say 'no' to having someone cut them up and take one of their kidneys." And I got a guy right away who, when offered the chance, said no to donating to his brother.

Was that the right thing to do—somebody probably died there?

Well, it was, if you believe that to take organs from someone, they have to have a truly free choice about it. The way bioethics works is that all the questions of right and wrong aren't always all up for grabs at the same time.

•••

Kareem Abdul-Jabbar

*T*his was the unexpected interview. I was in Chicago, attending the convention of the American Bookseller's Association, and for reasons not altogether clear to me, found myself at a reception for basketball player Kareem Abdul-Jabbar.

Now, I know next to nothing about athletics. And I arrived at this party at a restaurant called "Grappa" not knowing a soul, and only having a vague sense of who the guest of honor was. Dimly, I understood; he's to basketball what Babe Ruth was to baseball. So, I drank champagne and ate interesting little Italian appetizers, and when I tired of making small talk with strangers, I retreated to a bench in a corner. Not long afterwards, this seven foot giant of a man sat down beside me, and receded, it seemed, into his own thoughts.

The giant was Abdul-Jabbar, suffering an attack of shyness.

It was fascinating watching him obliterate his public self at his own party. This huge physical presence just went deeper and deeper into a shell, till he was, frankly, gone. Out of nervousness and because I can't stand silences, I mentioned the book Abdul-Jabbar had just written on African-American history, *Black Profiles in Courage*.

"Your book is going to be very useful," I quickly said. "You know, I teach non-fiction writing at City College in New York and many of my students are teachers in the public schools and they always talk about how they could use such a book."

Abdul-Jabbar glanced down at me. "You teach at City College?," he half-sneered. "Well, how can *that place* consider itself a real university as long as it has Leonard Jeffries there?"

Dr. Leonard Jeffries, Ph.D., who had headed and was removed from leadership at the CCNY Black Studies Program, made international headlines with his insinuations that a lot of African-Americans' sufferings were the fault of the Jews. At City College, Jeffries was a much worshiped and much loathed figure, depending mostly on where one stood. On one side were those who said he was destroying the university; on the other were those who claimed him to be just a persecuted truth-teller. Abdul-Jabbar thought him a lousy scholar. "I'm an amateur historian. I love history. And that guy doesn't know what he's talking about," he said.

Now, when I pick an interview subject, I am always looking for someone who will astonish me and more importantly, surprise the reader; the famous subject talking in a new way. I'm always scanning television talk-fests and radio programs to get a sense of how people talk—are they verbal? Do they have a good story? Is something there?

Now, this *was* a new look at a sports hero. The little I knew about Abdul-Jabbar included the fact that he had been famous since he was a teen, as a young man he'd converted to Islam, changed his name from Lewis Alcindor to Kareem Abdul-Jabbar, and was a strong advocate of black pride. Given all that, his vehemence about Jeffries intrigued me. Here was a black hero who hated what Jeffries, a black nationalist, stood for.

When I returned to New York several days later, I approached my editor with the Kareem suggestion. The news peg here: Abdul-Jabbar in retirement; his second career as an author; a black role model's dissent on the tactics of some black leaders. The substance of his differences with Jeffries interested me less than the strength of his anger against him; I just sensed that unexpected spark I always search for in my stories.

I was also struck by something I'd seen at the Chicago party—the shyness of the public man. Spend even five minutes with Kareem Abdul-Jabbar and you see a person whose nature is very, very private. I wondered how he'd endured public life. And more importantly, what it had cost him.

Some weeks later, on a Los Angeles day so hot that the freeways seemed to be melting, Jabbar's associate, Lorin Pullman, drove me to the secret corner of Beverly Hills where the basketball star lives. I knew that Kareem rarely let reporters anywhere near his home. I knew he had a reputation for remoteness with the press. And all of that worried me. What if, despite a carefully negotiated appointment, he saw my visit as an intrusion? What if he closed down? The thing a reporter always dreads is coming home without the story.

I needn't have worried. Kareem Abdul-Jabbar, then forty-nine, easily the greatest basketball player to ever shoot a sky hook, stood in the hallway of his glass and wood Japanese-style Beverly Hills mansion while I took off my shoes—as is custom in Islamic homes—and asked to see his famed collection of African-American artifacts from the nineteenth-century American West. Quickly, the ice melted into the burning California morning as Kareem proudly showed off the collection. In one corner were armaments, helmets and uniforms of the U.S. Army's Tenth Cavalry, the black Buffalo soldiers, who fought the Indian Wars and made white settlement possible. On the walls were original photographs: Sitting Bull, Ulysses S. Grant, Colonel Charles Young, one of three nineteenth-century blacks to graduate West Point, and Abner Doubleday—the hero of Gettysburg, who went on to command a "colored" army unit in the Indian Wars in the years before he invented baseball. "A great hero," Abdul-Jabbar smiled shyly. "A great American *hero*."

Kareem Abdul-Jabbar loves history, adores it with the kind of wholehearted passion that he could never quite give to his fame or his unearthly athletic talent.

"If I had led anything like a normal life, I would have been a historian," he later admitted over a lobster lunch in his dining room. Abdul-Jabbar-in-person gives off an odd mixture of shyness and confidence. He doesn't usually let reporters into his gorgeous perch high over Los Angeles, and there was a slight tension to him that read, "Should I Really Be Doing This?"

The reason for this sweetly reluctant hospitality had been, of course, the publication of *Black Profiles In Courage*, a book he'd written to tell young people about heroes minimally mentioned in standard texts—black history-makers like Crispus Attucks, Joseph Cinque, and Harriet Tubman.

"My son was doing a black studies project for school and there was no really good sourcebook for him," Abdul-Jabbar recalled. "So I wrote one. In this book, I'm kind of trying to say to black youth, 'Hey, this is your story, too.' They don't feel that the American story relates to them. Black kids feel that their ancestors were brought here, more or less, like cattle, and that the story ends there. They shouldn't be allowed to turn their backs on all our ancestors invested in this country."

This interview was conducted in late August 1996 and ran in *The New York Times Magazine* that winter at about 900 words. Here I've expanded it to 2,500 words with unused material.

Of all the figures in your book, which one has the most resonance for you?

Bass Reeves. He was a lawman [in the old American West] and so was my dad [in post-War New York]. As a kid, I always wanted to be a cowboy anyway, but then, I never saw a black lawman on television—so I found Reeves's story very moving. He was among many blacks who were lawmen, who upheld the constitution, fought crime and got no credit for it. That's a tribute to my dad.

You were in grade school during the civil-rights movement. How did that affect you?

When those girls got blown up in Birmingham, I wanted to hurt somebody. At first, it was indiscriminate. Any white person would have been all right. Eventually, I got through it and realized that justice is supposed to have some meaning to it.

When we met some months ago, I mentioned that I teach at the City College of New York and you snapped "that place can't consider itself a real university as long it has Dr. Leonard Jeffries [the now deposed head of the African-American studies program] on the faculty." Why such vehemence?

Well, I didn't mean to put it in such radical terms. Of course, CCNY is a university. Didn't Colin Powell go there? I was referring to the black studies department, not the university itself. I think Jeffries is a joke, man. He wants to argue things irrationally. I mean: use facts—it's as simple as that. He's just a guy with a great chip on his shoulder, posing as an academic. Actually, he reminds me of the guys when I was in high school who were the professional black nationalists. They all had the hair and the garb and it was an act! They needed attention, they needed approval, but they weren't trying to solve any problems.

You seem troubled by the way some black studies is taught?

Yes, because it often continues the separation of the black experience from the American experience. The book I've just published, *Black Profiles In Courage*, is an *American* history book. It's black, but it's more American than anything.

You're not a big fan of Nation of Islam leader, Minister Louis Farrakhan?

He's part of the problem and not part of the solution. He uses racist demagoguery instead of trying to deal with real problems that need real solutions. And I don't respect his constant attempts to make people angry at each other.

Besides, what they're talking is not Islam. I mean, it uses some Islamic trappings. And then somebody taught them this weird stuff about Yacoob. This man wants us to believe that there are black scientists driving around the universe in a spaceship called "the mother ship." I don't take them seriously.

You are a devout believer in Islam, yet you were educated in Catholic schools in New York. How did you come to convert?

In high school, I started reading things that made me question Catholicism very seriously, especially when I read of the Papal involvement in the slave trade—that really disturbed me. Finding out how much money the Catholic Church made off the slave trade totally turned me off the Catholic Church. For life! I couldn't continue to be Christian. I couldn't have done that, no matter what.

But Christians weren't the only group involved in the slave trade. Weren't the slavers of Zanzibar Moslem?

Yes, but Christianity was the religion mainly involved in the slave trade to the western hemisphere. And reading the accounts of the Christian slave traders talking about how good the name of Jesus sounded while they were ferrying people from Africa to America, that completely turned me against that whole thing.

Are you still as religious as you were when you first converted?

I've become pragmatic. I understand that I can't be a saint. I have to forgive myself and others for excesses that my humanity forced me to do... but I still believe in Allah, and the Day of Judgment, and I'm going to try to save my soul.

You were quite devoted to Malcolm X's teachings when you were younger. Define his appeal, please.

I liked Malcolm's approach to things. He was defiant, but he wasn't trying to get anybody killed. And he articulated the depth of arrogance of the dominating society. I was angry. I thought that Dr. Martin Luther King was too accommodating. I was about 35 years old before I could view Dr. King with appreciation. Funny, what opened up Dr. King's teachings for me was seeing a movie on Gandhi, the one by Richard Attenborough. Dr. King often quoted Gandhi. And then I saw what it meant to Gandhi to be non-violent, and the strength it took, and I saw how Dr. King was emulating that, and how it was the wisest way.

Speaking of movies, did you see **Hoop Dreams***?*

No, but I read reviews of it. I hope that when people saw it, they got to understand how totally exploited college athletes are. But that's started to happen anyway because of all the kids going from high school to the pros. Now, all of a sudden the NCAA is saying, "Gee, maybe we ought to pay these athletes while they are in college." Which would have solved the whole problem in the first place, but they are too interested in getting off scott-free. See, the NCAA is like an unpaid minor league for professional sports. And it's interesting that in amateur athletics the only people who are amateurs are the athletes. The universities, they all make money off of it. The only people who can't make money are the talent.

Did you feel exploited by UCLA?

Of course—I *was* exploited! I don't know exactly how much money

UCLA made winning the NCAA three times in a row, but it was millions. I didn't get a penny.

White kids have been going into professional baseball and tennis right out of high school all along. They are making large amounts of money early and nobody says anything about that. But black people are perceived as needing education more than whites, so there is more said about it for that reason.

Could you have excelled at any sport other than basketball?

Maybe, I could have been a pitcher. I also could have probably done a few things in track and field.

So then you understand Michael Jordan's brief excursion into baseball?

No, because Michael, he's very competitive. He's got to be beating someone at something all the time. So when he went into baseball, that couldn't work for him; going from being a basketball great to being a mediocre baseball player. Besides, it wasn't like he needed more money.

During your years on the court, were there moments when you said to yourself, "Wheee!!!, I'm the best in the world?"

No, because you get into that, and then being "the best in the world" will become your focus and pretty soon you won't be.

When you quit pro ball in 1989 at the age of forty-two, you were the oldest player to ever retire from the NBA. What made you finally leave the game?

It was time. I had saved money. I would still be able to send my kids to school. I could still do all the things I had to for my family. So when I thought about it, I realized I had experienced all the best moments of the game a *number* of times. Charles Barkley would like to experience some of the things I experienced, just once. He's playing now and making these gazillion dollars a year, but the professional reward I enjoyed was really unique. I tried to get into that and appreciate that.

But actually retiring was strange, disorienting. At first, nothing made sense. You can't really get into a new structure till you leave the old one and so you have no idea what it's going to be like. The notion that I'd been living a really crazy life came home to me after I attended the first training camp after retirement. I had gone there to work a little bit with the guy they'd gotten to replace me.

Were you there to teach him sky hooks?

No, he had no ability to learn anything like that. Anyway, when that was over, I went home and then I paid attention to where the team was and it was about four or five cities a week. It was ridiculous. I couldn't keep up with it. And I thought, "I used to live like that?"

So how did you get used to being "a civilian"?

I did a book about my last year on the road, *Kareem*. In the spring I had a book tour and that helped. But after that, it was, "what do I do now?" Fortunately, my kids needed to spend time with me. So my boys came to live with me for large periods of time and I was able to play catch-up as a parent. Now, that really helped because that's something you can get into with your heart.

And then I did have work to do. After I retired, I did marketing. Basically, I do the same kind of marketing deals that Michael Jordan does. I did these books, I got into movie production. I did some projects that related to history. I produced a television movie, *The Vernon Johns Story*, about the Birmingham minister who preceded Martin Luther King to the pulpit of the Dexter Avenue Baptist Church. If it wasn't for him, the civil-rights movement would never have happened. If that's the only thing I ever do in films, I'll be proud.

Weren't you going to produce a feature film about the 761st Tank Battalion, the African-American World War II army unit that supposedly liberated the Buchenwald concentration camp?

That got sandbagged. The people who did the original documentary [on that same subject, for PBS] made claims that were a bit farfetched [and the controversy killed prospects for a feature film]. In truth, the 761st was the first unit through the door in Buchenwald, but they were not the only ones. [In the documentary] it was made to seem like the 761 Tank Battalion alone and by itself freed Buchenwald when they were the first through the door. There were others involved in the effort, and eventually they came around—infantry people, and people from headquarters.

Is there a lesson from that, and from much of what we have been discussing, about the uses of history?

Yes—when people use history to prove their worth, it's wrong. To distort history means that you're lying about something and by connection, it means you are lying about your worth.

I don't know who it was—someone was speculating that black people, black Egyptians were the first people to discuss the principals of aerodynamics because of some Egyptian drawings he saw. He was claiming that blacks discovered aerodynamics. There's nothing to support this. That type of thing is counterproductive. It's a lie. There are valid contributions of blacks to history and science and we can talk about them, you don't have to make up things.

There's a theory in sports that the intellectuals go into basketball and the boobs head for football. Any truth to it?

Well, that's been my experience with a lot football players. Football is about speed and strength. Basketball requires more skills. You have to be clever and everything to use those skills, but in basketball you have to develop a lot more. Speed and strength is just where you start. So it requires a different type of personality. You can't just run over people.

At home, retired, do you ever miss being the greatest basketball player of all time?

Not really, because I always thought that basketball was my job, but that I was more than that. Since I've been home, I've come to think of the pace of my new life as good. What they say about taking the time "to smell the roses" is true.

•••

Alvin Toffler and Heidi Toffler

Seventeen years ago, when I first interviewed a futurist named Alvin Toffler for *Newsday*'s Sunday magazine, two remarkable things about him never made it into print. The first was that Alvin worked in a room filled with all kinds of electronic boxes and ticker-tape looking equipment. In those days, writers who worked on an IBM Selectric were the definition of high-tech. But Toffler had this whole room full of Frankensteinian gadgets all on a huge U-shaped desk. At the end of the interview, he pointed to all these mysterious objects and declared that in the future, "all writers will work on a system like this."

"Gimmick-meister" was my reaction then.

Now that I've owned six generations of computers, my tone is considerably humbler. I've come to think of Al Toffler as the man who saw the future first and saw it could mean liberation from retyping.

The second thing that was so interesting about him was that he introduced his wife, Heidi, to me as "the editor of my books." Now in those dark retro days of not too long ago, lots of male writers had muse-wives who edited their copy, typed the manuscript, and proofread the galleys. Typically, they might be thanked with a note inside the published work. But they weren't given the full credit of having this as a job. Up to that point, I hadn't seen anyone but Alvin Toffler credit his wife in such an egalitarian way.

Sixteen years later, Adam Moss and Jack Rosenthal asked me to do an interview with both Tofflers for *The New York Times Magazine*—Heidi now had a by-line right alongside Alvin's. The couple had just been declared Newt Gingrich's favorite thinkers, and Gingrich, at that 1995 moment, was riding high on electoral victories that swept in a Republican Congress. The first thing Al said when I pitched him was, "Yes, we'll do it, but you have to promise to include Heidi in the piece. We do lots of joint interviews and then the reporter edits her out of the story. It's almost like people won't accept that we are really partners."

"I won't do that," I promised.

This was an exciting time for Al and Heidi. Then newly elected

House Speaker Newt Gingrich's required reading list for his fellow Representatives included the Federalist Papers, the Declaration of Independence and *Creating a New Civilization* by Alvin and Heidi Toffler, then available only in hardcover. Not long afterward, Turner Publishing announced the mass-market paperback release of that book—the Tofflers' eleventh—with a foreword by Gingrich.

For the Tofflers, futurist authors who for three decades have been forecasting the ways computer technology would change society, Gingrich's endorsement was something of a career-reviver. Though they had published bestsellers in 1970 (*Future Shock*) and 1980 (*The Third Wave*) and though their ideas were regularly solicited by prime ministers and industrialists from Singapore to Stuttgart, Alvin and Heidi had become marginal figures in American intellectual circles.

"If you're not writing gobbledygook that ordinary readers choke on, you're not regarded as 'serious,'" complained Alvin, then sixty-six, sitting in the couple's spartan Los Angeles office. Heidi, then sixty-five, added that with Gingrich's help, "a public discussion on the future has been launched. Our publishers are reissuing a lot of our books, and people are buying and reading them."

Interviewing this couple was tough. Talk to one Toffler privately and the other will phone—to make additional points for the interview, to make lunch plans, dinner plans, updates on the lunch and dinner plans, and so forth. The First Couple of the Future were never long out of touch. Interview one Toffler separately and tales of the other will fill the conversation. The Tofflers have been married nearly fifty years and like many long-married couples, they've spent decades working out the knots of togetherness. Heidi, outspoken in private, often stepped back when Alvin was around. Alvin, in turn, accepted Heidi's smoking and her strong opinions. They often fought and argued, but did so without any real anger. It was more an exercise they found challenging, and perhaps even fun.

I met with the Tofflers in February, March, and April of 1995. *The New York Times Magazine* ran the interview in June.

One of your critics, former Secretary of Education, William Bennett, recently said, "If the Tofflers are so smart about the future, why

don't they play the stock market instead of write their books." O.K., Al and Heidi, why don't you?

Alvin: Two points. One, his statement reveals an inordinate focus on money that says something about his values. Secondly, this is an uninformed commonplace attack on futurism, on the assumption that futurists claim to know the future. Actually, we always say that...

Heidi: ... Nobody knows the future. Including Bill Bennett! Listen, we don't even know the man. He seems to be saying that to write books just to expound ideas is a waste of time—the only valid reason is to make money. I mean, compared to his enormous best seller, which earned millions, he must feel we shouldn't waste our time!

Alvin: I don't think the issue is Bennett. I think it's a sneering attitude, held widely, about people who think about the future. It's a total misunderstanding of the functions of futurism.

Explain what futurists do.

Alvin: What Heidi and I do is look for connections between events, connections that make patterns. We are pattern detectors. We think of change not in terms of Right and Left, but in terms of a multiplicity of forces interacting. Thus, technology has a major effect. So do changes in family structure and education. What you have is a whole series of forces impacting on our lives, forces that have different time frames.

Now, all of us are futurists. We all make assumptions about what is going to happen after this moment. The difference between us and others is that most people make these suppositions unconsciously. We do it deliberately—and build models. Our batting average has been better than most. In *Future Shock* we talked about how cloning and new birth technologies were creating new moral dilemmas, about the coming of cable television, about the workplace moving into the home. We also talked in that book about something, which was in those days called EVR, and which you now know as the VCR.

So, to take your example, in the late 1960s you saw a prototype for the VCR and you asked, "How will this change our lives?"

Alvin: Right. I had seen it. And we asked, "What will it do? What are the social effects?" Our guess was that it would help desynchronize society. The VCR meant you don't have to watch the same thing at the same hour that ABC, CBS or NBC chooses to transmit it. You can watch the six o'clock news at midnight.

What are some changes you see on the horizon now?

Alvin: Genetically altered agriculture. What that will mean is the customization of agricultural products, and the ability to grow food in parts of the world now considered non-arable. The ability to tailor crops to local climatic and soil conditions may make the difference between hunger and survival. I also think we will face a crisis in eugenics. Give a totalitarian government the advanced tools made possible by the biological revolution, and we can see a world of competing eugenic strategies as arrogant regimes play God with future generations.

Virtual reality points to a boundless capacity for deception. Not simply by governments or corporations, but by hostile individuals acting on each other. We can do this today, but we are increasing the sophistication of deception faster than the technology of verification.

The consequence of that is the end of truth. The dark side of the information technology explosion is that it will breed a population that believes nothing and, perhaps even more dangerous, a population ready to believe only one "truth" fanatically and willing to kill for it.

Have you ever been screamingly wrong in any of your forecasts?

Alvin: Sure. In forecasting a throwaway society, we said people would wear paper clothes. We were right about the throwaway society, but paper clothing never caught on.

Before going further, would you explain the keystone to your books, your Third Wave theory of history?

Alvin: We believe that the most basic of all changes in human social organization have been the result of three processes. Starting 8,000 to 10,000 years ago, agriculture was invented in the Middle East—probably by a woman. That's the First Wave. Roughly 250 years ago, the Industrial Revolution triggered a Second Wave of change. Brute-force technologies amplified human and animal muscle power and gave rise to an urban, factory-centered way of life. Sometime after World War II, a gigantic Third Wave began transforming the planet, based on tools that amplify mind rather than muscle. The Third Wave is bigger, deeper and faster than the other two. This is the civilization of the computer, the satellite, and the Internet.

But this change is not just a matter of technology. It's also of family styles, culture, politics, and the structure of social organizations. If the Industrial Revolution gave us mass production, mass consumption, mass media, mass education—the Third Wave reverses the direction: customized production, micro markets, infinite channels of communications, heterogeneous family styles, and instead of mass political movements, we see thousands of single-issue grouplets.

What makes you so unafraid of the future?

Heidi: Who says we're unafraid? There are a lot of things that can happen out of the blue. The amount of damage that can be done by a small group, or by an accident, or by a lack of communication is tremendous.

Alvin: Also, there will be massive dislocations. Just like at the time of the Industrial Revolution. And this current change is even bigger, moving faster and covering more of the planet. So there will be a lot of social upheaval. There are terrifying pieces to the future. Race-specific weaponry. You can zero in on ethnically linked genetic characteristics and target those who carry them. This is genetic warfare, a modern version of giving the Indians infected blankets. Terrifying. Absolutely.

People who think we are blindly optimistic have us confused with John Naisbitt—who *is.* If you read our work, you will see an underlying melody which is bittersweet. Life is a mix of events and forces and processes that have diverse consequences. Some will look good to us, but our grandchildren will hate them. Others will look bad, but they will have a side effect that produces wonderful things.

Was the bombing of the Federal building in Oklahoma City in any way related to dislocations you've been forecasting?

Alvin: It didn't surprise us. In 1975, in a book called *The Eco-Spasm Report*, we actually talked about private armies and paramilitary groups. In *War and Anti-War*, we looked to the danger of electronic terrorism. The kind of terrorism we've seen until now is no different from that described by Joseph Conrad in his novel *The Secret Agent*, published in 1907. Today's terrorists are technological klutzes compared to what's coming. New methods will soon be available. Intelligence experts know that there are probably ten crucial electronic nodes in our society, which if struck could literally shut America down. A terrorist could shut down the Federal Reserve computers if he attacked those computers with an appropriate virus, and spread financial chaos.

The fact that there are now paramilitary groups around the country reflects intense alienation, linked to paranoid theories of history—and intensified by millennialism. My hunch is that we'll see a proliferation of political and religious sects, some of them armed with weapons of mass destruction that go far beyond fertilizer bombs.

When did you first meet your pal Newt Gingrich?

Alvin: I always thought it was in 1975. But recently he reminded me that we had met earlier, in 1971 or 1972. I had given a speech in Chicago after *Future Shock* came out. And he had flown up from Georgia, where he was a young professor, to hear me. He was obviously bright and anyone who took the trouble to fly all the way from Georgia for my speech was obviously... [laughs] a man of impeccable judgment.

Then in 1975, at the initiative of some Democrats, we organized a seminar in the Senate, the Conference on Anticipatory Democracy. This is where we argued that Congress was a particularly anti-future place. Newt came to this. Later, he organized the Conservative Opportunity Society and he invited us on occasion to speak to them. There were times when he and his wife, Marianne, would come to New York and stay at our place.

There were times when I would go to Washington and stay at his.

It's a great fascination to people that we're friends with Newt Gingrich. But it is totally neglected that we talk to the Democrats, too. Some of Newt's ideas we disagree with strongly—prayer in the school, family values, the Christian Right. We are *not* Newt Gingrich. Newt Gingrich is *not* Toffler. Can we put that in caps? NEWT GINGRICH IS NOT TOFFLER! We are friends who think together and very often disagree. However, he does want to move in directions we think vitally important. We do think that de-bureaucratization and de-centralization and a weakening of Washington and a dispersal of power downward is where we must go.

Have your lives changed much since Gingrich put your works on the required reading list for members of Congress?

Alvin: The phone hasn't stopped ringing. The dominant reaction has not been to our work, but to Gingrich. In today's society, Gingrich is a lightning rod. We are perceived to be standing next to the lightning rod.

Heidi: And we've struggled for thirty years to get our ideas recognized. And they are, everywhere else in the world. They aren't here. It's too big a country. I think also we don't have a tradition in this country of revering the intellectual. This is why Hemingway and the others were expatriates.

In Washington, a lot of important Republicans are upset that you are so close to their man.

Alvin: I'm sure that's true. And the further right you go, the more true it is. We're not Republicans—so they're not keen on our having any intellectual influence on their leader.

Heidi: One of the things Newt said when we first became friendly was, "Look, you're going to agree on 80 percent of anything I say, and detest the other 20 percent." But you know what? I can't think of a single friend that isn't true of!

Alvin: Besides, we cannot agree with 100 percent of anybody's view. We have friends whose ideas we detest absolutely. It may shock some of your readers, but we once spent three hours with Nicolai Ceaucescu. We have spent lots of time with world leaders whose ideas were thoroughly detestable. You can learn from ideas you detest.

Heidi, people who've interviewed you say that you're more interesting when Al isn't around. Is that true?

Heidi: Oh, it's hard when we are together because Al wants to be liked more than I do. Al doesn't feel as strongly about things as I do. And maybe that's one of the reasons why Al and I have such a good partnership. Somebody once said that when I'm talking, Al is listening very raptly—as if he's hearing it for the first time. That's because Al never knows what I'm going to say. I pretty much know what Al is going to say. Newt and I are more similar in temperament, in strength of conviction. Al is a Libra, he's more balanced and less of a social animal. I'm a Leo, an individual.

How did this Libra and this Leo get together?

Alvin: At NYU. This was the late 1940s. I had a very close friend, now a world-famous scientist, who was dating a young woman. And she had a friend who was Heidi. I had come back from the South where I had gone to register voters for the Progressive Party. I went to the campus and there was Heidi, and that was it.

What attracted you?

Alvin: She was smart, beautiful and she paid attention to me. From the beginning, we argued about everything. It's part of the creative tension between us. She will say something, I will attack it almost instantly. I will say something, she will give me hell. We'll do that till we sort out our views.

Heidi, what was your first impression of Al?

Heidi: An air person—somebody who was up there. After we met, Al worked at a bookstore. The day after he got paid, the money was gone—he bought books with it. I had to supply him with lunch and carfare. I was supporting Al from the day I met him!

Does being married make for greater efficiency in futurizing?

Alvin: Oh, I don't know if it's incredibly efficient. We work hard. We're a one-family think tank, an "electronic cottage," a term we invented in *The Third Wave.* There is no line that I write that we haven't discussed. I do the writing. Heidi can write. But she doesn't enjoy it. The thinking, the organizing, the structuring and the outlining we've always done together.

Heidi: We talk to each other in shorthand. After all these years together we're like those comics who give punch lines and everybody laughs because they already know the joke.

But what happens to your writing when you fight?

Heidi: If it's about something intellectual, we keep arguing, trying to convince each other...

Alvin: No, it's simple. Heidi says, "You're a moron." Now, if the argument is about the kinds of things most couples fight over—one person is neat and the other one is a slob—those are the things that can really make you angry.

Heidi, how do you feel when people dismiss your contribution to the books you two have written because you're merely "The Wife"?

Heidi: "Wife" is the worst word in the English language. I remember once we were at a meeting in New Orleans and Al introduced me by saying "This is my wife and my collaborator." And people looked around for "The Collaborator." "The Wife" couldn't be that. There had to be another person. It bothers me when men come up to me and say, "We just want to tell you how wonderful we think your husband is, giving you all this credit." What they're really saying is, "I wish I could be as generous with my wife—you obviously don't merit it."

Your feminism must give you some problems in conservative circles. For instance, last January while both of you were speaking at a Washington conference, Arianna Huffington accused Heidi of "Second Wave" thinking because of her advocacy of women in politics.

Heidi: Oh, I don't think she even knows what Second Wave means! To her, it's just an epithet. She was talking about the Republican Party and volunteerism. I said the Republican Party doesn't have much of a future unless it has more candidates who are black, minority and women. And she said this was a Second Wave idea—it wasn't important to hold office. So I said, "Women have volunteered for hundreds of years and they got nothing for it." I didn't say, "Why did her husband dump $28 million down the drain, if it wasn't important to be in the Senate?"

Huffington's said to be quite brilliant.

Heidi: To me, she is not brilliant. But I haven't heard a single woman say she's brilliant, so maybe that says something. I think, also, we have tendencies to believe that if somebody was a Rhodes scholar or went to Cambridge she has to be brilliant.

Alvin: Well, look at Clinton. He attended Oxford. I don't think he's brilliant. He's intelligent, quick, articulate. But I have not heard a single original or profound idea out of Clinton. Not that I expect a lot from politicians during political discourse. Maybe if I sat down in a room with Clinton, and we spent a few hours talking, my image of him could change entirely.

Are there any Democrats you like?

Alvin: Tom Daschle and Al Gore. I think Gore is probably the best thing that the Democrats have, but his hands are tied. On reinventing government, he's all right, but tepid. The changes he'd like to make, he cannot. The Democrats need the Civil Service unions and their votes— and that effectively blocks the Democrats who wish to reinvent government. The idea of privatizing shakes those unions.

Heidi: We try to talk to Democrats about our ideas. I remember, some years ago, Al spoke at a Democratic midyear policy convention. On the platform was the then-head of the U.A.W., Leonard Woodcock. I sat with Woodcock's lawyer. When Al finished, I said to the lawyer, "Would it be possible to get together with you and Woodcock to talk?" And he turned to me and said: "Why would we want to do that? I didn't understand a word your husband said."

What defines a Third Wave person?

Heidi: A Third Waver understands that there's a profound shift in this country and that knowledge is the key factor in production. A Third Wave person says: "Teach people how to think. There are no facts. Everything is open to interpretation."

Let's play a game: Who's Third Wave and who's not. What about Bill Gates, Ross Perot, Lee Iacocca, to name three industrial leaders?

Heidi: Gates? No. I don't think so. I think he's a technician, a programmer. Obviously very shrewd, but I wouldn't characterize him as Third Wave. As for Ross Perot, he doesn't understand that we're moving to a world that's pluralistic. The idea of running this country like a business, it's insanity. Finally, Iacocca. Oh, God, no. His claim to fame was that he got the government to lend Chrysler all that money. But his view of the world is Second Wave. He's one of the people who're responsible for the American automobile industry being overtaken by the Japanese and the Germans.

As a young person, were you influenced by science fiction writing?

Alvin: More by movies about scientists. I've been a movie buff since I was a kid and it really troubles me that the stuff coming out of Hollywood now is absolutely... sick-making. *Dumb and Dumber?* At the time when society needs to move from a brute force to a brain force economy, we put out this shit that teaches kids that being stupid is OK. Now, *Forrest Gump* was different. I don't think it popularizes stupidity. What it's doing is answering *The Bell Curve*. It says that life is not just IQ. That there are other virtues and sometimes there is a kind of wisdom that comes up in the strangest places.

Heidi: I think one of the reasons we see all of these movies about dumbness and nothingness is that people feel overloaded by information. Their knee-jerk reaction is, "I can't keep up, so let's glorify stupidity."

What was your take on Jurassic Park?

Alvin: *Jurassic Park* was spectacular in its effects, deleterious in its philosophy. It was essentially science-phobic, depicting science as evil, with only occasional modifying remarks. I think it comes from their hating their math and science courses in college.

Is Newt Gingrich really a Third Wave man?

Alvin: Well, I believe that Newt picks up on the core of Third Wave ideas. Newt wants to make it easier for people to work at home. He is in favor of continuing to explore space. He has an image of an American society transformed by information and knowledge. And I believe that Newt is not racist and not uncompassionate. For instance, Newt and the Republicans were regarded as heartless when they made fun of the Democrats' "midnight basketball" provision in the crime bill. Newt made fun of that all over the place. But what I heard Newt say was, "If they had said, 'Let's not have midnight basketball, let's have midnight computers in the black communities,' I would have supported that."

So you didn't find his "Let 'em eat laptops" proposal absurd?

Heidi: Oh, he caught himself on it the next day. I think Newt was saying that since information is the critical factor today, he doesn't want poor children deprived of access. We were with him and he said: "I think I made a mistake. Because who is going to give them to the kids?" I think this was a wish of his. And so he came up with a centralized solution.

What I find puzzling is that your books forecast a new era of personal freedom, diversity in life-styles and tolerance of minorities. Yet, your friend Gingrich rails against gays in the military, single mothers, "countercultural" McGovernites.

Heidi: I think if you sat down with him, you'd find . . . the Speaker was divorced himself and he understands perfectly well. I think when Newt says, "Family Values," he means that we have responsibility. Newt is a tolerant person. If he were against diversity, he would disown his sister, who is gay. When a friend of his, a member of Congress, came out of the closet, a lot of people shunned him. Newt didn't.

You've said in other interviews that people try to get at Newt by getting at you?

Heidi: That's the downside. The upside is that with Newt's help a public discussion of the Third Wave has been launched.

Alvin: So our ideas are beginning to be part of public discourse as they were not in the past. We're pleased—not just as Mr. William Bennett might say, "because it means royalties." The important thing is that the ideas are going to be discussed.

Heidi: The thing we want people to know is that we're not conservatives. We're not Republicans. We're not Democrats. We are authors!

Alvin: Sometimes I wonder if we're Tofflerites.

•••

CITIZENS

Barney Frank

In February 1995, an editor with *Mother Jones*, the West Coast political magazine, phoned asking if I might, in the wake of what was then the Gingrich sweep of Congress, interview Democratic liberal legislator Barney Frank.

The interview proved fascinating. Most political figures are so reticent about their personal lives that one would think they didn't have any, and maybe they don't, but Frank, an openly gay Congressman in a committed relationship with gay rights activist Herb Moses, was unusually... well, frank. The stories he told—of going to White House dinners and never dancing because he had to pretend straightness; of all the lies he had to live before he came out, were remarkable in their humanity. You just didn't hear any politician, gay or straight, talking about their private struggles with such openness.

Well, you could have knocked me down when I saw the published story. Almost no personal material was included. Most of the piece was Frank's witty attacks on Newt Gingrich and his prognostications on the coming political year. The story was nice enough, but awfully conventional. The story was fine. But I ached for another shot.

So I took the *MJ* piece and the transcript to Alan Burdick, at the time my regular editor at *The New York Times Magazine*, and made the case that here was an interview that still waited to be printed—the private life of an openly gay Congressman. If the personal is political, then let's learn first-hand what the personal means.

The editors of the *Times Magazine* agreed. Some months later, I was back on the Barney trail. We met again in September and October 1995, on Capitol Hill, in taxis around Washington, D.C., and at the Frank-Moses home near Dupont Circle. The *Times Magazine* ran the interview on February 4, 1996.

"He's left me out!" Representative Barney Frank said with a frown one Washington morning when we met for a second interview. "Can you believe this? Oliver North writes up a list of the twenty-five most dangerous liberals in Washington and he leaves me out!"

It did seem an oversight. In Washington, Frank, then fifty-five, was considered among the last of the old-time liberals, a man who still believed that government is good, that public service is honorable. He was Newt Gingrich's nemesis, a pit bull of oratory, the point man of the House Democratic leadership for floor debates and a star of C-SPAN. He was also an unofficial adviser to President Clinton and was a force behind the administration's recently proposed gay rights bill.

Growing up in Bayonne, New Jersey, Frank watched the Kefauver hearings on television and dreamed of someday fighting the good fight in Washington. His first political job was as an executive assistant to Mayor Kevin White of Boston in the late 1960s. In 1972, he won a seat in the Massachusetts State Legislature. Eight years later he was elected to Congress, where he quickly made his mark with his parliamentary skill and his sharp tongue.

The Congressman's rising star, however, was shadowed. He was a closeted homosexual. For years he considered coming out, but advisers feared that would imperil his career. He came out anyway, in 1987, in an interview with *The Boston Globe*. Some months later, he met and fell in love with Herb Moses, who works for the Federal National Mortgage Association and is a gay activist. They soon set up house and have been together ever since.

In 1989, the roof fell in. Steve Gobie, a male prostitute with whom Frank had a brief relationship in 1985, appeared in the news with lurid accusations.

"When the scandal first broke, I decided I would not run for re-election," Frank says, surrounded by a sea of papers in his House office. "I was afraid that because I had been dumb and indiscreet that I might damage other Democrats. I was grateful that the House Ethics Committee was fair and let me disprove most of what he said."

Frank retained his seat, and now relishes his outspokenness, political and personal. He is "very lucky," he says. "It was unimaginable that I could live as a gay man with someone like Herb and have an emotionally satisfying private life that was not an interference with public life. In my own life, things have moved forward."

Eight Democratic Senators have announced that they will not seek re-election. What do you make of this exodus?

Actually, I was delighted when Sam Nunn said he wasn't going to run again. Nunn's been an outstanding bigot. This man has shown very little zeal in his career, but he was astonishingly active when he was leading the charge against gays and lesbians in the military. Nunn has acknowledged that he, early in his career, fired two men who were gay because he said they could be security risks. There are right-wing Senators who could keep closeted gay people on their staffs, but Sam Nunn fired two men because they were gay! Also, I think the *sine qua non* for rational public policy is a very substantial cut in the national security budget. Sam Nunn was the major obstacle to a rational defense budget.

New Jersey's Bill Bradley is also stepping down. At a news conference, he said he could do little good in the Senate because "neither political party speaks to people where they live their lives."

Shame on him if that's true! Why didn't he? My least favorite politician is the kind who says, "I am the only honest person here and a pox on all the rest of you." I don't understand how Bradley can claim to believe in what he does and then find everybody equally morally wanting. I mean, Bradley's been a Democrat all these years. Where was he, like, on Mars or on Venus? What was he doing to change this?

You appear to be thriving in the current Congress. In fact, you're one of the few Democrats who seems to be having fun. Why is that?

I'm a counterpuncher, happiest fighting on the defensive. Besides, I really dislike what the Republicans are doing. I think they are bad for the country and for vulnerable people. I feel, "Boy, this is a moral opportunity—you've got to fight this." Also, I'm used to being in a minority. Hey, I'm a left-handed gay Jew. I've never felt, automatically, a member of any majority. So I started swinging from the opening bell of this Congress. It got to the point where Newt Gingrich was saying, "Barney Frank hates me."

Do you hate Newt Gingrich?

Oh, yeah. I despise Gingrich because of the negative effect he has on American politics.

What's different about politics now as opposed to twenty years ago?

New rules. It used to be that a politician was never supposed to answer an attack. Now you'd better. Not answering attacks made sense when people had a good opinion of politicians. But in the atmosphere we've been in for the past fifteen years, in which the public is generally angry at government and politicians, you'd better answer the attacks because the public is predisposed to believe the negative.

There's one other big change that I think is actually good: that the wall behind which you can be hypocritical has eroded. For instance, if someone is a closeted gay member of Congress, and is generally supportive of anti-discrimination measures, I regret the closeting, though I understand it. On the other hand, if someone is privately gay and publicly a gay-basher, that's a hypocrisy and should be exposed.

Whom are you thinking of?

I don't want to name them. But from time to time I want to threaten to. I've used the threat twice. In 1989, when Tom Foley was about to become Speaker, several Republicans spread the rumor that he was not only gay but that he had sex with underage children. So I made a public statement: "Republicans are trying to use an accusation of being gay as if it were a bad thing. If they continue to do this, I'm going to out some people." And they backed off.

I did it again last year, when President Clinton issued an executive order abolishing anti-gay "security clearance" rules. And Bob Dornan and others said something like: "The president made a mistake. These people, particularly when they are in the closet, are a security risk because they can be blackmailed." So I said: "I do not believe that gay people, in or out of the closet, are a security risk. But if the Republican Party gets through Congress a law that says that closeted gay people are a security risk, I will send a list to the Ethics Committee of all the closeted gay Republicans." And they did back off. Bob Dornan accused me of being a bully.

There are three openly gay members of Congress: you, your Democratic colleague from Massachusetts, Gerry Studds, and the Wisconsin Republican Steve Gunderson. With Studds and Gunderson retiring, will you be feeling isolated here?

If this were an Agatha Christie novel, it could be called, "And Then There Was One." I think having openly gay and lesbian people here helps dispel prejudice. So going from three to one is not good.

Yet there are several other gay members of Congress and the Senate.

But they are not out. The fact that the other gay and lesbian members are still in the closet shows that prejudice is still strong.

Why do you think Gunderson is retiring?

I think it's because it is impossible for him to live as both an openly gay man and as an elected Republican. Why else would a very able guy at forty-five, who enjoys it, walk away? Steve shouldn't have had a tough primary in his eighth term. But he did.

And despite that, you still advise gay politicians of all parties to declare their sexuality publicly?

I do. I think public service is wonderful, but it's not worth your mental health. You read about people from time to time who say, "Oh, he or she is so wrapped up in his or her work that they don't need a private life." Yeah, right, and Elvis is still alive. I don't know any human being

103

who doesn't have a combination of physical and emotional needs that allows them, without cost, to exist without a personal life.

When I first ran for office, I made a decision that I would sacrifice a private life for politics. After a while, I became increasingly jealous of the people who were "out." I thought, "Why am I leading this unhealthy life where I have to be dishonest?" People said to me: "Well, you don't have to be dishonest. Just don't mention it." I defy any human being to get through a week in which you honestly answer every question put to you and not give away your sexuality. "What'd you do last night?" "Are you married?" "Are you seeing anybody?" Unless you're a total hermit, you're going to give away your sexual orientation.

Did you take women to fund-raising dinners and balls so that you could appear heterosexual?

I stopped doing that in the early 70s. For a long time, I just went alone. And then by '84, I started taking men. By then, I was living kind of half in and half out. People knew. They didn't say anything. I came out in 1987. I had wanted to much earlier.

The event that pushed me was the death of Stewart McKinney. He was a bisexual member of Congress, a Republican, and he died of AIDS. There was at first a lot of denial, including about how he'd contracted AIDS. I went to the funeral and I was saddened by his death. And there was this unfortunate fight in the press: was he gay, was he not? I thought: "Boy, this is crazy. I've got to make sure this never happens to me."

You asked that we run a photograph of you and Herb Moses, the man you share your life with, to illustrate this interview. Why?

Because I think the fact of gay couples is important. There are so few stories in print of gay people that aren't tragedies, scandals or disasters.

The Clintons have entertained you and Herb at the White House. Is this different from the political events of the past?

Oh, sure. And it's very touching. Herb and I have gone to White House events together since 1987. But we went only at times when any member of Congress and their spouses could go. The Clintons and the Gores have invited us when there were only about ten Congressional couples. That meant a great deal to us. It seemed one more step toward prejudice being over.

You've been critical of gay groups for not being pragmatic enough in their battle to achieve civil rights. What do you mean?

Well, because we've been a minority that has had to hide, cultural self-expression is often seen as a political statement. The truth is, it is and it isn't. It doesn't influence public policy. During the gays-in-the-military debate in the spring of 1993, the gay community on the whole didn't want to be political, and therefore the best we could do was some kind of compromise. I didn't like Nunn's compromise ["Don't ask, don't tell"] and I tried to get a better one, and some gays and lesbians said, "Oh, no, we're not going to compromise at all." It was hard to get many parts of the gay community involved in lobbying for a better measure. People were much more interested in demonstrations and marches.

The problem is, the Left is a victim, to some extent, of its own ideology. People on the Right are more likely to believe that America works in the textbook sense: "This is my government, this is my Congressman. How dare he not listen to me." People on the Left are more likely to say: "Well, wait a minute, writing letters is nothing. We need a demonstration." That is absolutely backward.

The NRA doesn't have demonstrations. They write letters. In fact, direct action, as a political tactic, is second-choice. The first choice is to exercise political power, to scare them into voting the right way. Direct action is what you do when you have no power. Blacks in the South had to use direct action until they got a voting rights act. Another problem is, we listen to the critics who say, "Oh, these politicians don't want to listen to the voters, all they do is listen to campaign contributions." In fact, votes will beat money any day. Any politician forced to choose between his campaign contributors and strong public sentiment is going to vote public sentiment. Campaign contributions are fungible, you can get new ones. You can't get new voters.

You see this now with the Human Rights Campaign Fund. Their political tactic is just dumb and, I think, undignified. Last year they gave money to help Newt Gingrich stay Speaker and Dick Armey stay majority leader. It's one thing to give money to the individual Republicans who are supportive. But to give money to help Newt Gingrich and Dick Armey—that's stupid.

Last summer, Bob Dole returned a campaign contribution to the Log Cabin Republicans, a gay political club. Basically his message seemed to be, "Take back your perverted money; I don't approve of you."

Dole was stupid. He should have kept the money. He would have been better off. And the Log Cabin Republicans were stupid to offer the money; Bob Dole has a very anti-gay record.

After he got criticized, Dole blamed the incident on some staff error. That's contemptible. One of the least attractive characteristics of people in my profession is blaming the staff. But he still wasn't going to take their money. And then you had the Log Cabin Republicans saying, "Oh, please take our money anyway."

Steve Gunderson wrote to Dole—and this shows the dilemma of being a gay Republican—and said, "You shouldn't have treated the Log Cabin Republicans that way." He says Dole told him it was a misunderstanding. So Gunderson is still supporting him. Does this mean Dole is going to accept the money? No, he regrets that it happened. Well, I'm sure Mussolini, if we could ask him, would regret World War II. I mean, people often regret fiascos. But that doesn't mean that they have any change of heart, morally.

Your older sister, Ann Lewis, is deputy director of Clinton's re-election campaign. Do you have an inside track on how the election campaign is going to look?

It's this way. I think the Republicans won in '94 because they weren't us. And we're going to do very well in '96—winning the Presidency and probably the House—because we're not them. I think what the Republicans are doing is very unpopular. The Republicans never told people that they were going to reduce what Medicare would otherwise provide. They didn't tell them that they were going to endanger student loans or cut out low-income heating assistance. They basically gave people the impression that they could balance the budget fairly painlessly and now they are doing it in a very painful manner.

Gingrich took advantage of public anger with us to win in 1994. But he did himself a disservice because he made it seem too easy. I mean, he would have been better off being more honest. He did all the easy stuff first. He said, "We're going to balance the budget, we're going to do this, we're going to do that." And now he is in this incredibly difficult period of trying to make that real. And he's whining and complaining, "The president's being political!" Horrors! The president's actually being political!

The polls look good for Democrats at the moment. But the election is many months away, and the Republicans will play hardball.

Well, we're going to play tough, too. I think you can play tough without playing dirty, and I think Newt Gingrich's vulnerabilities will not go away and Bob Dole is a weak candidate.

Part of their problem is systemic. The Republicans' most extreme wing is both very strong within the party and very unpopular within the country. That was our problem in the early 1970s. George McGovern was able to defeat Ed Muskie for the nomination in 1972 by going so far to the Left that he made himself unelectable. Bob Dole is doing similar things. I think they've already locked themselves into some very unpopular positions. They were on the wrong side of the environmental issue, the student-loan issue.

Is it true that one of the few freshman Republicans you respect is Sonny Bono?

Yeah. Sonny Bono has a better understanding of the dynamics of Congress than almost anybody else. He is not a great student of the substance of the issues, but he understands the craft of politics. He is an analyst. What I've seen of Sonny is that instinctive understanding of how audiences will receive certain things.

On a more personal subject, your mother entered politics at the age of seventy. How did that come about?

That's a fascinating story. She's eighty-three, a very bright woman, never went to college, had four children and was widowed at forty-eight. In 1982, I ran for Congress against Margaret Heckler, who attacked me because I was an unmarried forty-two- year-old who had supported gay rights. I was an unbeliever in "family values." So my brother David said, "How about a campaign with Mother?" She made a very funny commercial that said, more or less: "I'm for Barney Frank and he's going to help the elderly. And how do I know? Well, I'm his mother!"

My mother started getting invited to speak; an elderly activist named Frank Manning asked her to join his organization. Today she is president of the Massachusetts Association of Older Americans.

You've often said that you knew you were homosexual from the time you were thirteen. As a teenager, did you try to see if the other life might be possible for you?

I wished it was. But it wasn't. I can't imagine that anybody believes that a thirteen-year-old in 1953 thinks, "Boy, it would be really great to be a part of this minority that everybody hates and to have a really restricted life." I think I always wanted a political career, but I didn't think it would be possible as a young person. Actually, as much because I was Jewish as because I was gay. In those days, there were very few Jews in elected office.

In 1989, when the Steve Gobie scandal broke, many observers speculated that you were through in politics. Today, you're a top Democratic strategist. Do you take pleasure in the phoenix-like quality of your career?

Oh, I don't think in those terms. I had one crisis in '89. I do not take pleasure in having had that terrible experience. Look, I was depressed. I think it did damage to the values I care about. As for being gay, I never felt I had much choice about anything. Maybe my weight a little bit. So just go out and be the best you can be. You can't make yourself a different person. I am who I am. I have no idea why. Maybe I'm more Popeye than phoenix: I am who I am.

•••

Benazir Bhutto

I'd long wanted to interview Benazir Bhutto. This was a woman who'd *twice* been elected as Prime Minister of the Islamic Republic of Pakistan, the first woman in modern times to ever head the government of a Moslem state. She was a fellow baby boomer, who appeared to be fulfilling not only the destiny of her family, but that of her generation in transforming her world.

After having been removed from office in 1990 on charges of corruption and mismanagement of the country, she had, three years later, forced a new election, won it, and was now back in power.

A confirmed appointment to see her in early March, 1994, in Islamabad was arranged through the Pakistani embassy in Washington. I quickly began talking with Asia experts for background. As I poked around Washington policy circles, I was shocked by the kind of intense personal loathing that her name generated. "Unscrupulous", "power mad", "empty", "corrupt", were the words one heard.

It was said that she ran the country like a feudal fiefdom, that she remained in power by giving the country's military whatever it wanted, that she lied to the West about the country's nuclear program, that she'd done little to improve the miserable lives of the Pakistani poor—particularly the women.

"Benazir Bhutto is the most corrupt and unscrupulous politician on the face of the globe," a foreign correspondent who'd long covered Asia for a major newspaper told me.

I flew to Pakistan suspecting that perhaps Ms. Bhutto was being held to a higher standard than a male leader might be. "Who says she has to be an angel?" I kept whispering to myself after I'd landed in Islamabad. This sisterly attitude was with me until I arrived at her press office and discovered that my appointment to see the PM had evaporated. I had traveled twelve thousand miles—for nothing.

I left a handwritten note and some books with her press attaché—including an illustrated copy of *The Little Prince* I had brought from New York for the prime minister's three young children.

I was scarcely back in my room at the Islamabad Marriott, when a call came asking if I'd like to join Ms. Bhutto on a week-end trip she was making to Karachi. We'd have time to talk during the flight.

In all the world there could not have been another plane quite like the official jet of the Prime Minister of Pakistan, Benazir Bhutto. The front section was a kind of office-cum-nursery, jammed with toys, briefcases, newspapers, nannies and Bhutto's children, Bilawal, then five; Bakhtawar, then four; and Asifa, then one. In the main cabin, political advisors, security commandos and generals were keeping an eye on the prime minister they cautiously supported.

"Hullo, gentlemen.... Hullo, babies," Bhutto called as she entered the plane.

It was both jarring and interesting to see soldiers saluting a woman with children on her lap. It was wildly surreal to be discussing nuclear weapons with a head of state while her four-year-old handed her candy hearts. But Benazir Bhutto—then forty years old and a woman supremely comfortable with power—has never lived an ordinary woman's life. She is a politician with the spellbinding looks of a 1940s movie star and a personal story played out on the Pakistani civic landscape.

"Sometimes I look at all the different stages of my life and think it reads like fiction," Bhutto muses, her accent hinting of Oxford and Radcliffe, her alma maters.

Benazir Bhutto is the oldest child of Zulfikar Ali Bhutto, the populist prime minister of Pakistan, deposed in a 1977 *coup d'etat* and hanged by the military regime of General Mohammad Zia ul-Haq. For much of her youth, Bhutto opposed the Zia dictatorship, spending six years in prison and under house arrest. Her martyr-like opposition might have gone on indefinitely had General Zia not died in 1988 in a mysterious airplane crash. In the election that followed, Bhutto became the first female prime minister of the Islamic Republic of Pakistan.

Winning votes, however, proved easier than running her chaotic, problem-ridden nation. Bhutto hadn't been in office two years when her longtime foe, President Ghulam Ishaq Khan, dissolved her government, on August 6, 1990, charging mismanagement and corruption. In subsequent balloting, Bhutto was replaced by the conservative Islamicist Nawaz Sharif. Undaunted, Bhutto assumed the role of parliamentary opposition leader, hectoring Sharif, fighting him at every turn.

In the late spring of 1993, she formed a coalition with her old adversary, President Khan, who was suddenly charging Sharif with mismanagement and corruption. With new elections called for October 1993, Bhutto stood on the threshold of a remarkable political comeback.

Then her brother showed up.

Mir Murtaza Bhutto, then thirty-nine, the only surviving son of Zulfikar Ali Bhutto, had been running an armed anti-Zia organization in exile and had been prevented from returning to Pakistan because of long-standing terrorism charges against him. Suddenly, with his sister near triumph, he decided to go home and run for twenty-four legislative seats. His sister opposed his political move, since it meant he was running against candidates of the Pakistan Peoples Party (PPP), an organization long identified with the Bhutto clan. Murtaza Bhutto, however, had the backing of the family matriarch, Begum Nusrat Bhutto, then sixty-five, who told everyone that her son was the true heir to the Bhutto legacy.

Benazir Bhutto won anyway.

When Ms. Bhutto and I finally got to talk on that airplane ride, we made a friendly connection. By the time we got to Karachi, we were on great terms. One sensed that Bhutto liked having a Western woman her own age around, someone to chat with about the whole changing world of women on the global political landscape—a subject that none of her male advisers seemed to have much interest in.

Pakistan is the most insular and conspiratorial society I've ever visited. One only had to read the local newspapers to see it. The Pakistani English-language daily I'd brought with me featured two subjects of great local interest—bad things happening to Pakistanis, and bad things happening to Moslems anywhere in the world. There was also a kind of gleeful tone about natural disasters and train wrecks in India.

Paranoia seemed to hang in the air like the humidity. My hotel phone at Islamabad's main hotel clicked as if it were wired to a flamenco troop. Almost every time I returned to my room some "porter" could be found rummaging through my things. Most importantly, I was ordered by Bhutto's people never to mention where I was going and when. In a country where so many knew the arts of the Stinger missile and where the dictator Zia ul Haq had died in a plane crash, the PM's flight departures were classified.

On the prime minister's flight was a flock of generals who seemed to be there to, well... keep an eye on Bhutto. There was one general, a doctor, who was introduced to me as her "military physician." I had the sense that he traveled everywhere with Bhutto to do the autopsy. She appeared to dislike him with unusual intensity.

Once during the flight, the prime minister mentioned she was suffering from a urinary tract infection. I mentioned that I had some medicine for that on hand—I always carried it for emergencies when I traveled. "Why don't you ask your physician if you can take it," I offered. She looked at me as if I were mad. "Oh yes, I'm really going to consult my *military physician!*"

I could see why she didn't trust him. In Karachi, he was always introducing me to this military man or that one, adding, "He is a great man. He will be prime minister."

Some days later, the prime minister invited me to join her while she visited her home-constituency of Larkana. I was under the impression I was to stay with the other women at her estate, which had a visitor's compound. But as soon as I'd put my things in the dorm room that had been assigned to the women visitors, Mr. Doctor-General and another general ordered me into a jeep. Next thing I knew, I was shut up at the military base in Larkana, in a room that was guarded by soldiers with machine guns—in a room that had scorpions crawling up and down the walls.

I took my interview tapes and notes and stuffed them into my purse and pockets and considered various strategies to protect them, if push came to shove.

Some time later, a soldier with a machine gun knocked on the door and announced that the generals were summoning me to supper in their quarters. I grabbed my purse and joined the gentlemen. The generals wanted to tell me how my article should read. "Pakistan is not a nuclear power. The military likes democracy. The Pressler Amendment is bad. Clinton should let us have jet fighter planes."

With the main points of my piece dictated, dinner was over. I went back to my room and slept surprisingly well, except that there were huge insects doing scary walk-ons in my dreams.

When I awoke the next morning, the armed guard was gone.

Instead, there was a car with a driver who asked, "Madame, where would you like to go?"

"The prime minister's house!" I said. "And quickly, please."

At the Bhutto estate, Benazir's cousin Jason greeted me. "Where have you been?"

The interviews were conducted in Karachi, Islamabad, and Larkana in early 1994, and published in *The New York Times Magazine* on May 15 of that year. This version is somewhat expanded from what was published originally.

What was your reaction last October when you were sworn in as Pakistan's prime minister for a second time?

There was this sense of *déjà vu*. The ceremony was at the Presidential House. The red carpet was the same. The men in the red, gold and white uniforms were the same. The bands playing. I was walking along. But none of my old nemeses were there. There would be a new president, a new military chief, a new intelligence chief. And as I went along the aisle, I thought, "My God, I am a survivor!"

Do you have a better chance to get something done this time around? Your first term was marked by gridlock.

It's a much better situation. I have the president with me, which is a great factor for stability and rules out the undemocratic act of dissolution, but I don't have an outright majority; I have a coalition.

When your first government was dismissed in August of 1990, did you envision a future comeback?

I was determined. I knew in our twenty months in office we had moved fast in a number of fields and the people of the country would stand by me...I was so confident that I didn't get a shock on August 6, 1990. I got a shock when elections were held on October 24, 1990. My worry was that the interim government would either disqualify me before the elections or they would not hold the elections. They rigged the elections. But before that, they did everything to get rid of me. I remember all our names were put on an exit control list where we couldn't leave the country. After a week, the list was lifted and my mother came to me and said: "I'm going to go and it's not safe for you. You should leave too." And I said: "Mother, you go. You've suffered so much. I must stay."

I begged my husband to go. And he said to me: "I cannot abandon my wife and children. I would rather die than abandon all of you." With that, I became hysterical. "It's just words," I told him. "People say they will 'die' for each other, but don't know what that means." Later, when he was in jail, Asif reminded me: "When I said those words to you, I didn't know what they meant. But I still made the right decision." So I think our bond grew much deeper as a consequence of his imprisonment, because he then shared what I had known and we became much closer emotionally.

It was a terrible time. Two officials came to tell me: "Leave the country. If you leave, nothing will happen. But if you stay, your husband will be hanged and you will be disqualified [from holding office]." And I said, "I won't go!" Later, some of them told me: "You don't have to go abroad now, but don't file [nomination petitions for the October 1990 elections]. Your husband doesn't file and your mother doesn't file. If you do, your husband will be hanged and you will be disqualified and imprisoned."

Forty-eight hours after I filed, my husband was arrested. It was a harrowing time. At one stage, a sympathetic police officer told me that the government would kill my husband and arrest me for the crime. So I addressed a press conference: "I have information that the government of [Pakistani province] Sind plans to bump off my husband and put the blame on me." And instead of denying it, the head of the government said, "Oh, yes, she wants to bump him off, but we're taking measures to keep him safe."

Is it true that Margaret Thatcher advised you on how to force an election?

Well, we were having dinner at the Dorchester [Hotel] before the change here. "Lady Thatcher, I'm so confused," I said. "The president wants to make a deal with me, but he just wants to use me against the prime minister. The prime minister wants to make a deal with me, but he just wants to use me against the president. I don't mind being used, but I'd like some concessions up front. Who do I go with?" And she said: "Neither. If they don't give you anything up front, don't give them anything. When my opponents do that, I just let them go at each other." I thought this was very good advice and I remained discreet. And they destroyed each other.

With your mother and brother opposing you during the elections, did that kill the joy of a comeback?

I used to dread going to bed not knowing what the next day's headlines would contain. But I also found that I had the emotional resources to meet it. Still, if somebody had told me six months earlier, "When the next elections come around, your mother's going to be campaigning against some of your candidates and your brother's going to be fighting in twenty-four seats," I would have perhaps fallen apart.

These elections, we fought very hard to get them. I did my best to relay a message: "Don't do this. Fight for just one seat. I'll leave a seat open for you. We won't contest it. And if you run uncontested, it won't put Mother in the position of having to campaign against her own party." But he was not prepared to listen. My brother's never listened to me on anything I told him.

Doesn't this split threaten your party?

There is no split in the PPP! But that's what my opponents thought they could engineer and that is why they used him. They used him at the time of the elections because they thought: "When the male son returns, aha, the party faithful will desert the daughter for the son." It didn't happen.

Will his behavior pave the way for General Zia's son to take over?

No. That's naive—as naive as my brother's belief that he can be successful just on his father's name.

In your autobiography you hint of great political differences between you and your brother during the years of exile. What were they?

Well, it was basically the course of struggle which he had adopted [alleged terrorism]. I did not think that it would lead to any gains, and the dispute was on that. In fact I thought that it would harm the Pakistan People's Party and it would harm the political movement that we were waging for democracy.

And it was used by the military dictator against us time and again. It was even used by Mr. Nawaz Sharif time and again, that I was mixed up with my brother in what he was doing, when I really never was.

Why is your mother backing your brother?

Listen, I love my mother dearly. I was always an obedient daughter and I always craved my mother's love.... But in our family it was always a joke that my mother had a soft spot for my brother. We all knew that he was her favorite, that she spoiled him.

She's saying such terrible things about you—even comparing you with General Zia. Why?

Because all my life I was such a dutiful daughter. And perhaps my mother found it difficult to accept that when the time came for a decision between political responsibility and obedience as a daughter, I chose political responsibility. She's basically angry with me because she was removed as chairperson of the party. She blames me for it. But that was a party decision endorsed by a party convention of several hundred people. Right now I'm trying to reconstruct my relationship with her.

As for my brother, I think he has to familiarize himself with Pakistan because at the moment he still thinks of me as "a sister." He doesn't think of me as a political leader who stayed behind and waged a political battle and triumphed.

Were you closer to your father than to your mother?

Well, I *do* think fathers have a special relationship with daughters. I was the eldest child whom he hoped would follow in his footsteps.

He often took me with him on trips abroad because he wanted me to have an exposure to international relations. He would take me with him on trips to the United States, to Moscow. He took me to Simla when we had an agreement with India because he wanted me to have an exposure to the climate of international relations and to world leaders.

Did you enjoy doing things that other girls couldn't do, didn't do?

To me, these weren't things girls "didn't do." I saw Indira Gandhi in India and Mrs. Bandaranaike in Sri Lanka and Mrs. Fatima Jenna in Pakistan.

In reading your autobiography, **Daughter of Destiny,** *one senses that your father wanted you to lead a public life and that your mother sought more traditional things for you?*

I think my father was a reformer. He liberated the women of Pakistan. He emancipated them. In my mother's family it was very, very different. I remember my mother telling me, "When you were born your grandparents were so disappointed they wept and wept and for three days nobody came to the hospital because they were so sad that a girl had been born."

But now I look back and see, well, maybe it was my mother who was disappointed. She had married into a feudal family, and perhaps, she felt that if she had a son it would secure her own position. When we were growing up she'd tell me how *her* mother wanted a son and she kept getting daughters.

So I think in her background, there was much more consciousness of the traditional hierarchical society. But my mother's a wonderful lady. I mean, she could be, excepting this. This is what I feel is a weakness or her blind spot where my brother is concerned. But otherwise, she's elegant, she dresses so well, she's so charming. I mean she could charm the birds off the trees. I've always envied her charm. I've always envied her ability to look so smart and to be, well, you know, something.

You said earlier that your father hoped you'd follow in his footsteps. Did you always seek a political vocation?

No, I feared politics. Because it took my father away from us for long periods. And it was dangerous. We had the '65 war when I was growing up. And in '66 when he left Ayub Khan's cabinet, I remember hearing that his shirt had blood on it and thinking, "My God, has he been hurt?" And then when he fought Ayub Khan's dictatorship, every time he left the house I was frightened—Would he come back? There were repeated assassination attempts on him. So for me, this was a fearful life. I knew he wanted me to go into politics. But I did not want it.

Even when I went to school, I opted to study psychology. But my father wrote to my dean and said, "Could you convince her to study politics or international affairs?" Then I took government.

Do you think of yourself as a particularly strong person?

Well, I think the most important thing is that if one does not know what is ahead, one can cope.

As you may know, I had a very carefree upbringing. I was a child who was pampered by my parents and sent to the best schools, had no responsibilities, never wanted for anything. And so I had no idea that I had the strength.... Now, I find that whenever there is a crisis, I'm very calm. When that moment of crisis comes, I'm thinking "this has to be done, this has to be done next."

For instance, I remember once [when I was out of power] we got a tip-off that there was going to be a raid on our house in two hours. A lot of people around me panicked, but I didn't. I started saying to different friends, "you must burn this, you must destroy this, if they're going to take us to prison, this is what we're going to need. Could you get some soap? Could you get some shampoo?" So I can be very clinical in a crisis.

Asia has produced more female political leaders than other parts of the world. Any theories on why?

Well, this part of the world lived under colonialism. When there were demonstrations against British rule, the women participated, too.

So the idea of women in politics was not so alien as in the traditional democracies where women had not played such a central role. Another thing, because we are not as literate a society, people look to symbols.

Thus, a female member of a family can become a symbol of a male's message. Indira was seen as the symbol of Nehru's concept of India and Mrs. Zia [of Bangladesh] was seen as continuing her husband's policies. But in Turkey now, there's Mrs. Tansu Çiller, elected on her own strength.

In 1990, President Bush cut off American aid to your country because he could not certify that "Pakistan does not possess a nuclear explosive device." An American law, the Pressler Amendment, required him to do that. Now the Clinton administration has requested a one-time exception to Pressler to release F-16 fighter jets to your country. Is this turnaround your doing?

It's not. But I hope to God it comes about. Pakistan is an old ally of the United States and it's very important to all the friends of the U.S. to know that the U.S. stands by its friends. So, I think this one-time lifting of Pressler will have a positive impact in Pakistan. It will send good signals to all other allies of the United States.

One question puzzles many outsiders. Why is the atom bomb so popular in Pakistan?

It's our history. A history of three wars with a larger neighbor. India is five times larger than we are. Their military strength is five times larger. In 1971, our country was disintegrated. So the security issue for Pakistan is an issue of survival. Even now, in 1994, the Indian president has said that "Benazir Bhutto believes in the myth of a two-nation theory." If an Indian president can say that Pakistan is a myth, implying that partition should never have taken place, well, it makes Pakistanis feel insecure. They wonder, "How can we protect our territorial integrity?"

So given that history, Pakistanis feel, "Well, we don't have to go all the way. But, God forbid, if there's a threat, at least we have the knowledge to go all the way, if nobody else comes to our rescue." Obviously, we hope somebody else will come to our rescue and that there will be a security solution. And it is why I have always said that this nuclear non-proliferation issue must be handled regionally.

Experts on the region say that if there is war between India and Pakistan, it will be over Kashmir. Since it is such a flash point, will Pakistan accept an independent Kashmir?

When people raise the question of an independent Kashmir, we feel this is a ploy to divide the Kashmiri vote. The Hindus are going to vote for accession to India because they are the minority. If you are talking about the Muslim majority deciding between accession to Pakistan or an independent Kashmir, the Muslim vote could get fractured and we could find ourselves with the status quo, where the Hindu minority accepts Indian rule and the Muslim majority does not accept it.

The people of Kashmir have always felt one with Pakistan. The British built the infrastructure in such a way that all the roads, the rails, run from Kashmir throughout Pakistan. So it's like Kashmir is the head of Pakistan. Kashmiris have a strong identification with Pakistan, not as a federated unit but as an autonomous unit within Pakistan.

Nobody had the right at the time of independence to choose to be independent. They had to accede to either India or Pakistan. If we now say that people have the right to decide for independence, then we are arguing against the *raison d'être* of India and Pakistan.

We are perhaps unleashing a process that could chain react into the Balkanization of the Indo-Pakistan continent. It could lead to greater instability and would be in no one's interest.

So your position isn't all that different from India's?

Kashmir was forcibly taken over by India, and India agreed to hold a plebiscite under U.N. auspices to determine whether Kashmir should accede to Pakistan or India. According to the U.N., it's very clear it's a disputed territory. It's not part of India.

But it's not part of Pakistan either?

Well, it is a disputed territory, in which the people have to determine whether they wish to accede to India or Pakistan.

What is your opinion on Steven Solarz's recent nomination by the White House as American Ambassador to India?

I've always respected Steve Solarz for his commitment to democracy... but I have always felt that he has a blind spot about India. He and I have argued about India in the past. But then, a good friend of Solarz's married a Pakistani girl. So... Solarz has some linkages to Pakistan, too.

You've often said that Islam is not as conservative towards women as it has been interpreted to be. Do you see yourself as a medium for showing the world this other side of Islam?

Yes, very much so. Because I was taught from a very young age that Islam is the religion of justice, compassion and tolerance. As I grew up, I found that many countries had deviated from these principles for their own narrow political reasons. And they were trying to reinterpret religion to suit their political needs. As a woman, I've always felt very proud that Islam is the first religion that says that marriage is a contract [in which] you can write anything you want; it's the first religion which gives the right to divorce; it's the first religion that says both parties have the right to negotiate custody. It's the first religion to give property rights to women.

Given that, many of your critics complain that you did little to help Pakistani women when you were in power for the first time. They say that you missed the historic moment to free the women of Pakistan from what General Zia did to them.

Well, I don't agree. I was only in power for twenty months. But despite that, many barriers were broken for women. Whether it was setting up a Women's Development Ministry, which had not existed before, or [releasing] the report of the Commission on Women's Rights that had been banned. No government had the guts to release it. It was *my* government that released a report that encouraged women's rights in a society which until that time had been hostile to receiving it. The government that I led lifted the ban on women taking part in international sports. We fixed a quota on jobs for women in government services so that working women would have opportunities. We set up a women's development bank.... Most importantly, while I was there, there were no more retrogressive laws against women.

So the time may have been too short to repeal all of the laws that had been passed [previously], but this did not mean that giant strides weren't made while I was there. I had five ministers and a Deputy Speaker of the National Assembly who were women.

The complaint I've most often heard is that you did little in your first term to eliminate the Zia-promulgated Islamic code that discriminates against women, the Haddood Laws.

Well, I never completed my first term. I was thrown out of power after twenty months.

Now, as far as the Haddood Laws are concerned, we have (since) sent them for examination to the Islamic Council of Ideology. In the light of their recommendation, we will be taking remedial steps. We certainly intend to reform the Haddood ordinances. We believe they are not in conjunction with the spirit of Islam, which is the spirit of justice. But we also need a constitutional majority to do so. So we will try to convince the opposition. I have a coalition government. I don't have a simple majority.

You know, I was just reading this terrible story in the paper today. I must show it to you. A cleric burned his wife internally with hot rods, tied her up.... Now, one of the things that I really feel helpless about is crimes against women. And as a woman, I feel very strongly about them. But it is up to the provincial governors, not the federal government, to resolve them. So I am writing a letter immediately to the chief minister on this and asking him to take action. This is such a brutal crime and it should not go unpunished.

On a personal note, your marriage to Asif Ali Zardari in 1987 was an arranged one. Why would someone as independent as you accept marriage to someone you hardly knew?

I *couldn't* have a love match. I was under so much scrutiny. If my name had been linked with a man, it would have destroyed my political career. Actually, I had reconciled myself to a life without marriage or children for the sake of my career. And then my brothers got married. I realized I didn't even have a home, that in the future I couldn't be in politics when I had to ask permission from their wives as to whether I could use the dining room or the telephone. I couldn't rent a home because a woman living on her own can be suspected of all kinds of scandalous associations. So keeping in mind that many people in Pakistan looked to me, I decided to make a personal sacrifice in what I thought would be a loveless marriage. The surprising part is that we are very close and that it's been a very good match.

At the time of your engagement, many women's rights advocates felt betrayed because they saw arranged marriages as part of the second-class status of women.

Well, I don't agree with that. People today do computer dating. Is that a betrayal? When it's difficult to find a man, for whatever reason, one has to look for mediation. I feel there is someone to spoil me, to take care of me, comfort me. It's so nice to have somebody who cares about you. I was so lonely after my father died. I felt I was taking care of everybody else. With Asif, for once, I had somebody with whom I'd lay my hair on the pillow and feel I was safe. I'd love to arrange my own children's marriages. I say that because I've been so happy.

Do you ever wonder what you would have done if this arrangement had gone badly?

That would have been really bad luck. And I would have found it terribly sad, personally. But I suppose it would have ended up a marriage of convenience. Because I did get married originally in an arranged marriage to have a political career...I didn't expect happiness. I was very, very happy to find a charming, humorous, intelligent person as my companion. He's very brave, very honorable. A little too stubborn at some times, but everyone has their failings.

Did Asif's arrest in 1990 evoke memories of your father's imprisonment and execution?

It was a replay, except when my father was taken I thought, "They couldn't do it." My father always said, "They wouldn't have imprisoned me unless they meant to execute me." With my husband, I knew they could do it. Because if they could have done it to someone like my father, they could do it to someone like my husband, who was nowhere near my father in stature. When Asif was released [two years later], I was crying not only with relief that he had returned home. I was crying because I was thinking of my father who never came home.

Do you sometimes look at old photographs of yourself and think, "Is that the same person?"

Well, I look at all the different stages of my life and think it reads like fiction. Because it's been through so many ups and downs. So now I understand the idiom, "Life is sometimes stranger than fiction."

Does it ever seem to you that your life has the elements of a classic Greek drama?

[Laughs.] Well, I hope not so tragic. Don't all Greek dramas end in tragedy?

POSTSCRIPT:
In August 1996, Ms. Bhutto elevated her husband Asif Ali Zardari to membership in her cabinet, eventually giving him the posts of Investment Minister, Chief of the Intelligence Bureau and Head of the Federal Investigation Agency. On September 20, Bhutto's brother, the man she feared could make a successful coalition with Islamicist forces against her, Mir Murtaza Bhutto, was killed in a gunfight with Karachi police outside his home. Mir Murtaza's widow, Ghinwa, immediately accused Zardari of having a role in the killing. Several days later, Bhutto had forty army officers detained in connection with a suspected Islamicist military coup against the prime minister.

More was to come. In early November of 1996, President Farooz Leghari dismissed Ms. Bhutto's government on charges of nepotism and corruption. She, in turn, accused Leghari of masterminding Mir Murtaza's assassination as a way of bringing down her government. Asif Zardari was then arrested, with hints that he was complicit in the Murtaza killing. By late December, a Karachi court ordered Zardari's release, citing a lack of actual charges against the First Husband.

In early February 1997, general elections were held in which Ms. Bhutto's party fared badly, placing her even further from power.

•••

Hanan Mikhail Ashrawi

*T*his interview started out in the winter of 1994 as an assignment to do a Q and A with Yasir Arafat for *The New York Times Magazine*. Several of the magazine's writers had previously tried to score an appointment with "The Chairman," but had been unsuccessful.

Small wonder. Getting Arafat to agree to an appointment was a study in frustration. Here's just a little of what I did to try to pry loose an hour or two of his time. I visited with his cousin, Nasar Al Kidwa, who was the PLO's U.N. Ambassador. Had a pleasant enough chat, but got nowhere. Two of the five American Jewish members of the Oslo Peace delegation, Menachem Rosensaft and Gail Pressberg, made inquiries for me. Pressberg phoned up Arafat's mother-in-law to see if she could enlist her help. I next called a good friend who is a parliamentarian in Germany, Karsten Voigt, and he soon had half the brass of the European Socialist International phoning on my behalf. I was sure that would work: the PLO was soliciting lots of development funds from Europe. But we got no response.

Hanan Ashrawi, the English professor from Ramallah, had been Chief Spokesperson of the Palestinian negotiating team in the period before the Oslo Accords. She was someone who'd lived on the West Bank throughout the Intifada, who—at the same time—was constantly involved in developing dialogues with Israeli counterparts, and who was a key player in creating the atmosphere that had made change possible. Because of her role as a member of the Palestinian negotiating team, she was known to readers. In fact, internationally, she was probably the second best-known face of Palestine—after that of Yasir Arafat. The citizen-politician aspects of her story interested me. As did the fact that she was a woman and a Christian functioning at high levels in Palestinian society. It was rumored that Arafat had asked her to a) head his office in Washington and b) serve as his Minister of Information, and that she had refused both jobs.

"Let's do the woman instead," I suggested to my editors once the

Arafat interview looked truly dead.

Thus it was on a brilliant May morning in 1994 that I arrived in Jerusalem and checked myself into the American Colony Hotel, a former pasha's palace located in East Jerusalem. Like the Europa in Belfast, the Camino Real in San Salvador, the Intercontinental in Managua, this was the place favored by the international press corps, a center of activity where I would find journalistic comradeship and—gossip.

At breakfast on my first day there, a group of Italian reporters invited me to go with them to Hebron where there was certain to be lots of action.

"No, thank you," I answered. "I'm off to Ramallah— doing a piece on Hanan Ashrawi."

"Why her?" one of them asked. "She is not important. She is not going to be a minister in the government."

"That's why I want to interview her."

The three-story villa of Hanan Mikhail-Ashrawi faced a prison. Built during the British Mandate, the gray cinder-block compound in Ramallah, on the Israeli-occupied West Bank, has housed political prisoners under successive British, Jordanian and Israeli administrations.

Because she found the jail so horrifying, Ashrawi would not cross the street if she could help it. "I'd like to think of myself as an antidote to that place," she explained over lunch in her dining room several days after the Cairo peace accords were signed. "Or at least, I hope I am."

If civic involvement and human rights activism are the antidote to steel and barbed wire, then Ashrawi was that. Ashrawi, then-forty-seven, had twice declined to be minister of information to the Palestinian National Authority that now governs the Gaza Strip and Jericho. Instead, she founded the Palestinian Independent Commission for Citizens' Rights, whose goal is to put civil liberties on the Palestinian agenda.

As a full-time activist without an official portfolio, Ashrawi spent twelve to fourteen hours a day working for her citizens' rights group, organizing Jerusalem Link—a feminist alliance she co-founded with Naomi Chazan, an Israeli member of Knesset—and writing a memoir. On most days, even when she was at home, Ashrawi rose at 6 A.M. to don makeup, heels and a tailored suit. With the press making constant calls, she said, "I can't hang around in old T-shirts."

Hanan Ashrawi understands the news media. She first came to international prominence as a fierce debater on the 1988 ABC *Nightline* Town Meeting on the Middle East; previously, she had been a community activist and an English professor at Bir Zeit University in Ramallah. For more than two years (1991-93), she was the spokeswoman for the West Bank and Gazan community leaders representing the Palestinian side at the peace negotiations. In that role, she gave a new face to Palestinian nationalism. If the old image was that of an unkempt terrorist, here was a well-groomed feminist with a sharp mind and well-developed ideas. Within a short period of time, Ashrawi—who is a Christian and a graduate of the American University in Beirut and the University of Virginia—established herself as the second-most-famous Palestinian, though one with a lot more CNN appeal than the unshaven enigma she calls Abu Amar—Yasir Arafat.

The Ashrawi household was pleasantly chaotic. (The house belonged to her father, a socially prominent Ramallah physician.) On a recent day, an assistant busily screened phone calls while a maid was preparing lunch in the kitchen. Ashrawi's husband, Emile, then forty-four, was repairing a fence in the backyard. An artist and a staff photographer for the United Nations who has a gentle, sixties-countercultural manner, he was the drummer in his own rock band when he met Hanan. The couple's daughters—Ama and Zeina, then sixteen and twelve—lounged about the living room watching *Ghost* on television. From time to time, Ashrawi broke off our interview session to run to the living room to hug Zeina, who had a cold. At other moments, the interview was interrupted by Emile, who offered me a special pistachio gelato made locally.

"If you're going to go out in the world and make peace," said Ashrawi, "you need peace within, peace at home. Except for what is in front of this house, I have that."

The *Times Magazine* ran this interview on June 26, 1994 at a length of around 3,000 words. Here I've added another 1,400 words from the original typescript.

In Israel and the West Bank, one meets few Palestinians with any enthusiasm for the Cairo peace accords. Why is that?

You mean the reluctant peace? The painful peace? It's true. It's hard to find a Palestinian who thinks, "This is it; this is a response to our dreams and aspirations." The most optimistic will tell you it is a first step—a difficult, painful and complicated first step. Palestinians have always talked about redeeming history, of finding a place for ourselves as a nation among nations. Now, through a process of shrinkage, political manipulations, the peace process has been transformed into a series of technical steps that led to fragmentation of our land, to placing Yasir Arafat on probation. The Israelis control every step.

Can you blame Israel for wanting certainty on security?

I can. This is short-sightedness: it's a functional, not a comprehensive peace. Even where the Israelis say they are withdrawing, they have created such an intricate and complex network that the whole thing has the risk of imploding. All we are doing is asking the Palestinian leadership to perform functions for the Israelis. The National Authority has no sovereignty over the land. It has no full authority over what are called "security issues." Even legislation is subject to the Israelis. Yet, this Palestinian governing authority is supposed to deliver. Well, they cannot maintain peace when they do not have the ability to really govern.

None of the members of the West Bank and Gazan negotiating team went to the Cairo peace signing. Why?

It was our choice. Faisal [al-Husseini, a prominent Palestinian leader based in Jerusalem] and I were in Jerusalem that day because we wanted to demonstrate to the world: "This is not it." Up to the last minute, we met, we called Tunis, we wrote. We asked for a postponement; we asked for changes. But there was a mad rush to have it signed on May 4. We said: "Since dates have never been sacred, how come this one is? Don't sign until it's an agreement that people can accept."

If the deal is that bad, why was it accepted?

Political imperatives. It's some kind of contemporary pragmatism that is reductive in nature, probably profane in nature, considering the real aspirations of people.

What will happen if the peace process doesn't widen—if Jericho and Gaza are all that Arafat can get?

Well, if you continue to maintain the seeds of discontent, I think you will see an eruption of violence that will have internal repercussions as well as external ones. After the ninth or tenth negotiating round, I remember thinking to myself, "I have premonitions of a big sorrow to come." Still, one has to ask, "Is this what we brought on ourselves? Could we have done things differently?"

Watching Arafat's performance at the Cairo ceremonies, I was struck by that old cliché of how much easier it is to be a guerrilla than a politician.

[Laughs.] Yeah. And then when you become a politician you become subject to all the manipulations, power politics and politics of self-interest of others. It's true. You are exempt in many ways from certain types of accountability. When you are making a national liberation movement, you operate by different laws, by different standards of etiquette.

Earlier you asked if you had brought this on yourselves. Well, did you? From the beginning, your negotiating team kept telling the Israelis: "We're not the game. The PLO in Tunis is."

We fought hard not to be fragmented and the PLO, to us, was a symbol of our national identity. The negotiators avoided the charge of being an alternative leadership. We felt that the recognition of the PLO was a recognition of our history. But the people who lived all those years in exile—they have to come home and be a part of the future here.

I've heard people here grumble: "Gaza-Jericho is a bad deal. We could have gotten better." True?

On the whole it is not the best deal we could have gotten. It's not just bad in terms of how it responds to Palestinian rights and aspirations, but in how it addresses the issues that have caused friction. If we had wanted the functional approach, we could have accepted the tasks of the civil administration, which were offered to us in '82, without negotiations, and we refused, because we weren't going to perform administrative tasks for the occupation. And if we had wanted Gaza we wouldn't have to negotiate because they were willing to withdraw from Gaza anyway, because it was a place they couldn't control or run.

Journalists covering the peace process say your team of West Bank and Gazan leaders had a tougher stance than the one Arafat settled for.

That's true. Our group was made up of people living under the occupation and so we had direct accountability. People came to our homes, questioned us about all these things. That's different from reading messages and faxes.

Were you surprised a year ago to learn that Arafat had gone behind the backs of your negotiating committee and made a deal with Israel?

No, I wasn't. First of all I had established the Oslo channel, which didn't start in Oslo but right here in this house. I had established many back channels because I was convinced that negotiations in the public eye were not going to lead anywhere.

At one point, I was told by PLO officials in Tunis, "The channel is succeeding," and I said, "Fine." Some time after that, we went to Tunis and we saw some of the documents of the Oslo accords. I was flabbergasted—not because Oslo had happened but because of the substance of the documents. It left out some major issues: the settlements, Jerusalem, human rights. And [the PLO] made commitments without getting commitments in return. I remember saying, "You postponed issues without getting guarantees. This could go either way: It could lead to disaster—or statehood, at some point."

Arafat has asked you to join his first government as minister of information. You've said, "No." Why?

Because I have another commitment: to founding the Palestinian Commission for Citizens' Rights. I believe this is a very badly needed part of nation-building. A nation is not just defined by its political leadership in government. One can serve by insuring that the process of nation-building is going in the right direction. This commission was organized because we wanted to make sure that the laws coming out are just and are applied uniformly. We want to safeguard basic rights, to work against the abuse of authority and misuse of public funds. So it's a tall order.

You've been under a lot of pressure to accept the ministerial post.

Some people said I was abrogating my responsibility, but I don't accept that. When Faisal and I started meeting with [then Secretary of State] James Baker, there was almost a consensus that we shouldn't. So I don't mind taking risks. It's not easy to establish a citizens' rights commission. Nobody wants a group of high-powered people with credibility telling them, "This is illegal and this is unjust." But somebody has to have the guts to do it.

I've heard that within PLO circles, you are resented as a woman?

By the men? Not at all. In fairness, Abu Amar has never discriminated on the basis of gender or religion. On the contrary, he always says, "Give me someone with abilities."

Well, how do you explain that as we go to press only one woman, Intisar al-Wazir, the widow of an assassinated PLO official, has been appointed to the governing authority?

I'm very unhappy about that. When I was in Tunis, I tried to talk to them about tokenism. I said, "Don't place one woman and say we have 'our woman' because by rights, by history, by ability, our women have the right to be there." Then Abu Amar said, "But you don't want to be on it."

133

I've been told that the PLO leadership doesn't particularly value you. A journalist I know who covered the White House peace accords signing in September of 1993, told me that the PLO people from Tunis treated you like some kind of secretarial-assistant, not a world-renowned diplomatic figure.

Oh, that person misunderstood the situation. In Washington in September, everything was a mess. Somebody had to take control and make some sense out of it. As usual, it's the women [who] tend to think of the work that needs to be done.

Nobody gave me orders [to do that]. To make Washington a success, there were practical things that had to be done. And very frankly, people didn't know how to do it. I had to establish contacts. Who's going to get Bush? Who's going to get Baker?

Do you think that your skills make you threatening to others?

Oh, yes, I'm sure. And I don't resent that on a personal level, no. Although sometimes I feel sad that we are quite willing to sacrifice substance and the cause for the sake of personal gratification. Instead of taking pride in the accomplishments of others, [it is] "I want to put them down because I cannot do the same." You know, I keep telling people, whenever any Palestinian does anything that makes me feel proud, it is a collective victory.

You're probably the second-best-known Palestinian in the world.

That's true. And that's because people need to identify with a face, with a human being, rather than abstractions and slogans. And because I consciously tried to convey the reality of a people in a human way— and that evoked a kind of honest response from people. And this I felt all along.

It is said that your great contribution to the Palestinian cause has been in the area of public relations: you transformed the image of a Palestinian from an anonymous terrorist to a person with a case to make.

That was true. I felt we had been excluded from the discourse and therefore, we have to intervene, we have to make ourselves heard and felt in ways that are recognizable—human, not defensive, to show who we are with all our flaws, with all our historic luggage.

It was in many cases our fault, the stereotyping. It wasn't entirely the fault of the West. We have to prove, first of all, that we exist and that we are more than the stereotypes that had been set up, that we are not who people think we are. We had been described as "the terrorists," "the demographic problem," "the two legged vermin," the "genetically violent people." We had to set a new semantic level. And it wasn't easy and it wasn't going to happen by itself.

You were one of the first Palestinians to engage in unofficial dialogue with Israeli citizens. To what extent did the dialogue make the peace process possible? Was it helpful in developing a common language and some kind of trust?

Yes, though [the effects were] probably not immediately visible. I started something here in late 1973 when I came back [to the West Bank]. The first two Israelis I met with were from the women's movement. They were people who early on grasped the need to a develop a common approach and a common language. It took quite a lot of doing. It wasn't easy. What was done was "a first" on both sides.

The Israelis didn't like it at all. Because to them the greatest threat was any kind of Israeli-Palestinian contact because that would dispel all the myths and distortions: "These are people who are inherently violent and who are going to kill us." And to find counterparts who'd say no, "This is not what we want." And [for people on either side] to demonstrate it, this was unusual.

Palestinians who did this too were killed?

Yes. We paid a very heavy price. There were some very courageous Palestinians who were perceived as traitors. . . . It was very painful. Many of them were my friends.

Were you surprised at the hunger of many Israelis for contacts?

135

Yes...yes. Some wanted to prove that under occupation, you can normalize. They were trying to find quislings and lackeys and create "village leagues." They were trying to find political equivalents who would normalize.... That didn't work. There was a second type [who were motivated by] guilt. Many Israelis didn't want to be occupiers.

There was a third type [whose actions were] much more immediate. We took risks together.

There were Israelis who came to demonstrate in Ramallah and they were given the Palestinian treatment. They were clubbed. They were beaten. Tear-gassed. I remember when this happened, there was an old Palestinian man who had onions with him and he gave them to the Israelis, who thought the onions were some kind of Palestinian hospitality ritual. No, it is something we use for tear gas—and he was trying to help them.

Gradually, this activism lead to political dialogue and it brought in people from the Israeli establishment. Gradually, this evolved into joint projects.

If you were organizing an ideal dinner party here in Ramallah, who would you invite?

First of all, it would be in the garden, which Emile has turned into a place of beauty and peace. I'd like García Márquez because of his imagination. Isabel Allende. I like the Latin American writers. Would I invite James Baker? Yes. I would invite Larry King. I liked him a lot. He has an immediacy and honesty. I'd invite Peter Jennings.

I've heard that you used to date him?

That was in another life. Another time and another life. Beirut. I dated many people when I was single.... Now, about that dinner party. I'd invite people I know—not necessarily famous people. I would invite the Swedish Foreign Minister, who I like. But I also like her predecessor. Certainly, Nelson Mandela. I like him personally.

Watching Mandela's inauguration on television these last few days, to me it was very emotional. For a long time, the ANC people used to tell us, "Don't forget us when you get your state." When he was being inaugurated, there was such a celebration. While, here after the Cairo signing there was all this wrangling about weapons and having the police come here from The (Allenby) Bridge. We need something to celebrate. Our history is one of tragedies. We're always involved in pain, and loss, and disasters, and so on.

For both Israelis and Palestinians.

Ah, yes, this competition for pain and victimization. It has to change. We've [both] been prisoners of the past. The past has to be acknowledged, but we cannot become captives of it. We've had to fight self-pity. Because a sense of victimization can be used to justify everything else that you do, and then this competition for pain is not helping either. I think the competition should be [to see] who can transcend it, who can see beyond it, and who can end the victimization, rather than who can use it as historical luggage and as a whip to flog others with. We don't need guilt. We need to change the situation.

Will the general elections for the legislative council be put off?

Probably a bit. We should have elections this year. If we allow for setting them aside, or forgetting them, or ignoring them, it means that we have already incorporated all the undemocratic seeds we were fighting against.

Could you see yourself running?

Yes, possibly. I haven't decided yet.

It's a different thing—elective office.

Yes, you have a popular base, a constituency and a sense of authority that comes from the people.

Your husband, Emile, is a believing pacifist. You're a nationalist who has been an ally of the PLO. Is there any intrafamily conflict over political stances?

He's a pacifist and I'm not for a military solution, so I don't know if there are that many differences. I oppose violence and believe there are responsible, civilized means for settling problems. I respect my husband's commitment very much. Except sometimes I challenge him: "Suppose somebody should come to hurt our daughters. What would you do?" And he finds it very difficult. He says: "If it's me that they want to hurt, I could still be a pacifist. But if they wanted to hurt them, I don't know."

How did you meet Emile?

I saw him at a pop concert in late '73 that his band had given in Jerusalem. It was called Bara'em, which means "blooms." It was the first rock concert I had ever attended that had national lyrics, Arabic lyrics, with contemporary music. Also, I liked the way he looked on stage. I thought, "This is one person who feels the music."

Not long after that, he came with his brother to my parents' house, where I was living, because I was being put on trial. The Israelis were charging me with anything you could think of because I had been in demonstrations: incitement, threatening the security of the state. So Emile and his brother came to my house. Everybody was giving advice about what to do in the trial and he was just very quiet and I was very impressed. Here was a man who listened.

People on the West Bank say that Emile is a most unusual man in this culture. But this man who introduced himself to me as a "full-time father and photographer" would be an unusual man in any culture.

Yes, he is. I met many people before Emile, and I was never convinced of the institution of marriage. In fact, I was determined not to get married because I said, "I do not want to be owned." And then we went out for a while. He was so confident of his masculinity. There have to be few men who don't define their manhood by subduing their women. He's very comfortable that my work goes out to the world. At the same time, Emile has created a sense of peace here in the house—[a sense] that the world is all right. In front of our house is a prison. But in the back he has created a beautiful garden so that the family can have a haven, a place of peace.

Your daughters, Amal and Zeina, grew up on the West Bank in the middle of the Intifada. What kind of a childhood did they have?

Tough. They have seen their neighbors and their best friends killed. They have been tear-gassed. They have seen endless meetings, day and night, and their mother's very unpredictable schedule. They have seen their schools closed too. They were robbed of their childhood.

Have there been times when things got to be so terrible you thought, "I just can't do this to my kids—I've got to get out."

Many times. But I didn't feel, "How do I get out?" I felt, "How do I rescue my kids from having to see these things?" Once, I took wounded students to the hospital and the car was filled with blood. We had to go through roadblocks and tear gas and shooting and then back for another load. When I got home, I was so pained and unhappy that I forgot to clean the car. So, the next day, when my two girls got into the car to go to school they screamed when they saw the blood. They were very young, four and eight. That was not the most shocking thing they ever saw, but it was especially terrible because this was bringing "it" home.

My children grew up too fast. We always talked about what I was doing during family meetings. They said, for instance, "We understand. You're out there, making peace for all of us and we want to support you." On the other hand, my oldest says on the phone when I'm far away, "Mama, I want to talk to you about being a teenager." Zeina, when she was six, said, "I've lent you to peace, but I also need my mother with me."

To change the subject, give us your personal take on former Secretary of State James Baker?

I liked him a lot. I found him to be a person of extreme intelligence, very sharp. He could engage—we could have a dialogue, a debate, a fight, an argument, but he was there. If you disagreed with him, he would fight back. [Laughs.] Last time I saw him, I invited him to Ramallah for dinner.

And Warren Christopher?

I never really knew him. I still don't. And I've met him many, many, many times. He has an invisible barrier there, a shield.

Would you invite him to your house?

No, because we haven't established the slightest personal rapport. I feel Christopher has his talking points, and he is a nice enough man. But when I invite people, I need to feel some engagement. Like Larry King— I invited him to my home and we had a very good discussion. I need to look somebody in the eye. Christopher never looks anybody in the eye, and it bothers me.

Might you invite Bill Clinton?

I would invite Hillary Clinton to my home. I'm a woman's woman, always fascinated with women who can make it, who can defy, who break the patterns.

In closing, your good friend Faisal Husseini characterized the Cairo agreement this way: "What happened in Cairo is like a birth after a long period of suffering. The infant is weak and his health is not what we hope. But he is still our baby." Do you agree?

That's Faisal's metaphor. The problem is to ascertain whether the infant is still growing, and whether it is still living. There are people who say it is still growing. And there are others who say it's very weak and it needs a lot of nourishment. I tend to think it's going to need a lot of nour-ishment. The odds are against it. Life is not going to be fair to it. And physically it is not equipped, really, to deal with the cruelty of the world it has been born into. So in some ways, it's going to need intensive, inten-sive care. But we're going to try our best.

POSTSCRIPT:

Later that summer, Michael Kelly, then a staff writer for the *Times Magazine* and now editor of *The New Republic*, eventually got to see "The

Chairman" in Gaza. In the November 27, 1994 *Times Magazine*, Kelly reported: "It is axiomatic that the less power a politician has the longer he will make you wait for an audience. I spent most of my last week in Gaza hanging around the Palestinian Broadcast Center, watching the guards fondle their guns, the sleekly suited West Bank bankers come and go and the delegations of well wishers and favor-curriers file in and out for their few minutes in the president's company. When at midnight on my fourth night of waiting, the call came, I was led into a small room in the back, where Yasir Arafat sat at the end of a long table. . . . He spoke for about half an hour, and I think intended to use the interview to register his strong protest at the treatment he was getting from an ungrateful, uncooperative world. . . . It was not so much an interview as a protracted whine."

As for Hanan Ashrawi, she ran in the general elections for membership in the Palestinian National Authority and won herself a spot. She is currently Minister of Education. Lately, as the peace process has stalled, she again has unofficially resumed a spokesperson's role.

•••

Myrlie Evers

In the summer of 1994, I conducted a short phone interview with Myrlie Evers-Williams for *TV Guide*. Home Box Office was showing a documentary on the murder trial, thirty years after the fact, of the man who'd killed her husband, civil rights leader Medgar Evers. Mrs. Evers's story was amazing. After she'd spent three decades trying to get justice in the killing, in February 1994, a Hinds County jury finally convicted Byron De La Beckwith of the crime.

"If I can get the *Times Magazine* to agree to a larger story on you, would you be able to give the time needed?" I asked Mrs. Evers at the end of the phone interview.

"Oh yes, that would be wonderful," she said.

I got the assignment, and was back on the phone to Myrlie Evers in Oregon where she was living, to try to set a date. What we settled on was an appointment to meet in Jackson, Mississippi, over the Labor Day Weekend. A post office was to be named for Medgar Evers. There would be a dedication ceremony. Many of the old-time local civil rights leaders would be present.

On Labor Day morning, 1994, Myrlie Evers, then sixty-one, stood on a platform in Jackson, Mississippi, and cut ribbons dedicating the Medgar Wiley Evers Post Office Building. A church choir sang "He's So Wonderful." Mississippi politicians, black and white, made speeches. Two blocks away, Byron De La Beckwith, seventy-three, who was convicted in February 1994 of the 1963 Evers murder, sat at the Hinds County Detention Center. "I chuckled at the thought that the jail was so close," Myrlie Evers said after the festivities.

She was a handsome woman, tall, with a spark in her chestnut eyes. "I hope he heard everything," she went on. "I want him to understand how much he's motivated me all this time." The journey that brought Myrlie Evers to this sweet moment of justice took her thirty-one years to complete. In June 1963, her husband, the field secretary of the Mississippi NAACP, was gunned down in front of the family home in Jackson. The killing was among the first of that decade's political assassinations and a turning point in the civil-rights movement. President John Kennedy dedicated his ground-breaking civil-rights legislation to Evers's memory. Within days of the funeral, Byron De La Beckwith, a white supremacist, was charged for the first time with the murder. He was tried twice in 1964; both times, all-white juries deadlocked, creating mistrials. Though strong evidence linked Beckwith to the killing, and though he himself dropped hints of involvement, the Hinds County prosecutor eventually dismissed the murder charges.

With the killer free, Myrlie Evers led two parallel lives. She moved to California, where she raised her children—Darrell, Reena and James (now forty-three, forty-two, and thirty-six), took on a career in fund-raising and public relations, and married Walter Williams, a labor activist. Today she lives in Oregon and travels the lecture circuit. All the while she kept constant tabs on events back home, monitoring Beckwith's whereabouts, always seeking a way to reopen the case.

The break came in 1989, when *The Jackson Clarion-Ledger* began investigating the activities of the Mississippi Sovereignty Commission, a secret agency that operated in the 1950s and 1960s. Commission documents pointed to possible jury tampering and official involvement in Beckwith's second trial. With this fresh information in hand, Myrlie Evers pressured Mississippi officials to move for a new trial.

On February 5, 1994, almost thirty years to the hour of the first trial, a racially mixed Hinds County jury found Beckwith guilty of murder. "I didn't realize how deeply implanted this need to clear everything up was," Evers explained later. "When it was over, every pore was wide open and the demons left. I was reborn when that jury said, 'Guilty!'"

This was an interview that meshed because of the pure drama of Evers's story. Conducted in bits and pieces over that Labor Day 1994 weekend in Jackson, on planes to her next speaking engagement, and in follow-up conversations afterward, it ran in the *Times Magazine* three months later on November 29.

Of all the civil-rights widows, you seem to be the only one who has carved out an independent life.

I'm not sure that's really accurate. Betty Shabazz, Malcolm's widow, went back to college and got her doctorate. She's an administrator at Medgar Evers College in Brooklyn. Let's just say that I have not depended on Medgar's name. I'm the only one who's remarried. None of the other widows have ventured off into areas such as politics, corporate America—where you bare yourself to all kinds of criticism.

You are a vice chairman of the board of the embattled NAACP—an organization now in crisis. Benjamin Chavis has been purged as executive director amid charges of financial mismanagement and sexual harassment. The chairman, Dr. William Gibson, has been accused of charging up nearly a half-million dollars in expenses. Do you worry for the association's future?

It will survive. But what will it be? People are drifting away. We need strong leadership, which I hope will include more women at the helm. We need leaders who guard the monies of the association very carefully— and who do not abuse the privileges that come with leadership.

Are you thinking of seeking Chavis's old post?

I'm not the least bit interested in becoming executive director. That's a 24-hour job with constant travel. However, I have been encouraged by some leaders to run for chairman of the board. My husband, Walter Williams, is not well and his health is a big determining factor in whatever I do. I have the financial background, the overall commitment, [and] a forty-year association with the NAACP.

How is it that an organization that has given the world heroines like Rosa Parks and Daisy Bates has so few women in top positions?

I believe that many of the men think of the women as nice decorations and are perhaps not even aware that there's a problem. The president is a woman, but we don't need tokens. Women are mostly on the very soft committees, where no major decisions are made that directly impact the operation of the organization. The women of the association are more than ready to assert themselves and to call the hand of those males who have not guarded the association as carefully as they should have.

On the subject of Byron De La Beckwith—why was it so important to go after him when so much time had passed?

Because Beckwith committed a crime and he still boasted about it. I saw it as a moral issue. A society should not allow murderers to go free. People long for justice, you know.

In the end, the trial had a good effect on Mississippi. A poll before the trial by *The Clarion-Ledger* showed the public very much against trying Beckwith again. Another poll after the verdict read just the opposite. Mississippi has always been known as the poorest state and one filled with racism. I have watched Mississippi try to make progress, try to get accepted. Getting this verdict helped.

What do you recall of the atmosphere in Jackson in the spring of 1963?

The tension. For years, ever since 1954, when my husband accepted the position of NAACP field secretary of the state of Mississippi, we knew his life was on the line. In the spring of 1963, Medgar was leading economic boycotts of downtown businesses discriminating against our people. In the Jackson newspapers, there were editorials calling for "a flow of blood" in the streets, pinpointing Medgar as someone something should be "done" about.

Over the eleven years of our marriage, we had often spoken about the possibility of assassination. But in the spring of 1963 we spoke of it constantly. A dear friend, Dr. Felix Dunn of Gulfport, Mississippi, told my husband of a plan to wipe him out. Dr. Dunn had seen a death list with the names of ten civil rights leaders on it. Medgar was number one. It was a white person [who knew people in the Ku Klux Klan] who had shown Dr. Dunn this list.

In the days before Medgar was killed, there was almost a morbid presence about him. It got to the point where he said, "Take care of my children." The last morning he was at home, he kissed us all and went out to the car and came back again. That night, Medgar went to an NAACP meeting. The children and I stayed home to watch President John Kennedy give a civil-rights speech. We heard the motor of Medgar's car. The car pulled in the driveway. Then, a rifle blast. I ran to the door. Medgar was still alive. Every drop of blood was coming out of him.

Afterwards, I remember thinking, "I'm going to make whoever did this pay."

When did you first hear the name Byron De La Beckwith?

A few days after Medgar's death. The rifle had been left in the bushes and the dew had frozen the thumb print. I knew he was the assassin from the first photographs printed of him. There was a wound on his eye from the rifle's telescopic sight.

Were you surprised by the speed of the first two trials?

Yes. At first, I thought nothing was going to be done. I had lived in Mississippi all my life and could not recall a single conviction of a white for killing an African-American. I recall a meeting with Bill Waller, the prosecutor in the 1964 trial, and I asked him how he planned to address me in court. He said: "You were born here. You know how things are." I told him, "Mr. Waller, if you address me as anything other than 'Mrs. Evers,' I will protest in court because respect is one of the things my husband died for." In court, he called me . . . nothing.

What did you feel when you first came face to face with Beckwith?

Anger and hatred. This was when I went to court to testify during the first trial. Beckwith had this smirk on his face. He was very pleased with the publicity. You could tell from the way he looked at me that I was a nonentity to him. But I stared at him and our eyes locked.

While I was testifying, the Governor, Ross Barnett, walked in—I'll never forget this—and he paused and looked at me, turned and went to

Beckwith, shook his hand, slapped him on the shoulder and sat down next to him. He was sending a clear signal to the jurors that this man was to be acquitted.

Those first few months of widowhood must have been terrible.

I was thirty. I had dropped out of college to marry Medgar when I was eighteen and now I had children, ages three, eight, and nine, looking to me. Medgar had made $6,100 a year and had left me with thousands of dollars of debt. The NAACP said, "If you'll make appearances on our behalf, we'll continue to pay his salary." I did it. Every weekend I was away making speeches. My eldest son began to fear that I, too, would be killed. He stopped talking and he could not hold down his food. And I was suicidal. The only reason I struggled to stay alive was the promise I'd made to Medgar to take care of the children.

It became difficult for the family to have any semblance of recovery as long as we lived in that house. The blood remained on the concrete. The refrigerator still had the dent from the bullet that had passed through Medgar's body. There was nowhere in Mississippi I wanted to live. Medgar and I had always talked about how, if we ever left the state, we'd go to California.

I felt very guilty about leaving. We moved to Claremont, a college town thirty miles from Los Angeles. I enrolled in Pomona College—so that I could get a degree. Only when we arrived there did I realize that Claremont was all white. On the whole, the new environment proved good for the children, though I would have liked a more balanced racial mix. Sundays, I took them to nice restaurants, something we'd been barred from back home. There was satisfaction in finishing my education and having a career. After my graduation, the Claremont Colleges hired me as development director. I ran for Congress in 1970 as a Democrat and won 36 percent of the vote in a traditionally Republican district. In the campaign I did not run as "Mrs. Medgar Evers," but rather as Myrlie Evers. I was beginning to develop my own identity. In the next few years, I would go on to work as director of community affairs for Atlantic Richfield, and as a columnist for *Ladies' Home Journal.*

How did you meet your second husband, Walter Williams?

At the Claremont Colleges. He phoned and asked to show me a like-ness he'd made of Medgar. He was a longshoreman, active in his union, and a civil-rights fighter from way back. We began having dinner and became friends. It's been a wonderful marriage and I'm in awe of the way Walter handles Medgar's memory. In many ways, the marriage has been "Walter, Myrlie and Medgar." For any man to understand that is rare.

You managed to keep on the case, even from California.

I had to return to Mississippi several times annually, to see my elderly parents. Whenever I was there, I inquired, "Have you heard anything about this man?" Beckwith ran for lieutenant governor in Mississippi. He spent some time in prison for attempting to bomb a Jewish leader in Louisiana. After some years, people said: "Myrlie, you're living in the past. Let it go." But the fact that no one had been found guilty made it hard to let go. And Beckwith couldn't keep his mouth shut. I thought, "Keep talking—one of these days you're going to give yourself away."

How did the break in the case finally come?

President George Bush had asked my brother-in-law, Charles Evers, to do something nice for Jonas Savimbi [the Angolan guerrilla leader]. So Charlie invited him to Mississippi and presented him with the Medgar Evers Award for Achievement to Humanity, or something like that. I hit the ceiling. A reporter with *The Clarion-Ledger*, Jerry Mitchell, phoned me about that and mentioned he'd been working on an exposé of the Mis-sissippi Sovereignty Commission. It would later turn out that he had some records of the Mississippi Sovereignty Commission and that he thought that there was enough evidence there to seek a new trial because the jury in the second trial had been tampered with.

It was something to get started with. I called the Hinds County Dis-trict Attorney's office and asked for an appointment. The first meeting was nasty. "It can't be done. This is too old a case to try to resurrect. We don't have the files anymore." That was what the District Attorney, Ed Peters, told us.

Sitting on a sofa, the assistant district attorney, Bobby DeLaughter, held up the case file, which had two or three pieces of paper in it, and sighed, "Mrs. Evers, this is all we have." Well, that's a start, I told him.

And we had Federal, state, city and county officials adding their clout to the demand for a new trial. The Jackson City Council passed a resolution asking for the case to be reopened.

A key piece of evidence, the murder weapon, had been lost. It would turn up in the private collection of a Mississippi judge. How did that happen?

It's really weird, isn't it? I'm not sure that the real story has been told yet. But that wasn't the only missing evidence. The photos from the first trial had disappeared. One day, the District Attorney was called anonymously and told to expect them. We needed to find the witnesses after 27 years—we had a wonderful, aggressive investigator named Crisco, who found people where and when they were still alive. Bobby DeLaughter called me and said, "We have to drop the case without a transcript and we don't have one." I answered: "When do you need it? I have a certified carbon I've been saving for my children."

I was a woman driven. I lived and breathed the case. The hardest part came when the Mississippi Supreme Court was deciding whether or not they would allow a new trial. It took them forever to make a decision. So I went to the press and complained. There was such foot-dragging, but eventually we got that trial.

How was the third trial different from the first two?

The trial was actually held in the same Hinds County courtroom where the other two had been. But in the first two trials, we had only white males on the jury. This time, we had males, females, Caucasians and African-Americans. This time, I was always addressed as "Mrs. Evers." New witnesses came forward, too. A former Klansman named Delmar Dennis testified that at a Klan meeting Beckwith had said that, "Killing that nigger gave me no more inner discomfort than our wives endure when they give birth to our children." There was also a woman who said she was in a restaurant where she heard Beckwith bragging about killing Medgar. She'd been too frightened to speak up before.

The night before the verdict was difficult, because everyone had expected a very short deliberation. By six or seven of the first evening, with no verdict, I thought, "Oh, we're in trouble." Then came the verdict, and I thought, "Yessss...Medgar!"

Rumor has it that Fred Zollo, producer of Mississippi Burning—*a movie that many civil-rights leaders found offensive—is preparing a feature film on your campaign to prosecute Beckwith.*

As I understand it, the movie is a fictional story and will not be solely based on Medgar and myself. He has bought the rights to a book about Medgar's case. It doesn't bother me that Bobby DeLaughter will be the main character, because he deserves so much praise. I am apprehensive, however, about how Medgar and I will be portrayed. Will Medgar come across as someone afraid of his shadow? I certainly will be watching developments carefully. And with legal counsel.

Your second husband is now quite ill. Does that bring back some of the pain of losing Medgar?

This is different. With Walter, there's time for us to talk, to find comfort, to work through the fear and the pain of losing each other. Medgar's death was violent, and there's something about violence that tears out your innards.

In Mississippi, there's a debate on whether all the files of the Mississippi Sovereignty Commission should be opened to public inspection. Where do you weigh in?

I feel it's important to have those files open so that we can see the evil that prejudice and racism breeds. There was information included in the files that helped secure a third trial in Medgar's case and perhaps there will be similar information in opening up some of the other Mississippi murder cases.

Do you ever wonder what Medgar would be doing if he had lived?

He'd be an elected official of the state of Mississippi. He used to say, "The day will come when enough of our people are voting and we will have elected officials and I plan to be one." I'm so proud that Mississippi has the largest number of African-American elected officials in the country. That's a tribute to Medgar and all the others.

And how do you think he would like the person you've become?

After the verdict, my two sons asked me, "Ma, do you think Daddy could have dealt with you now?" I said, "It'd be pretty tough on the old guy, but I think he'd be proud." And he is proud, if there is such a thing as reaching beyond.

POSTSCRIPT:

Since the interview, Myrlie Evers-Williams's life has continued it's dramatic turns. Her much beloved husband, Walter Williams, died of cancer—leaving her widowed a second time. She also did end up challenging the NAACP establishment for the Chairmanship of the Board, a move she narrowly won. *Ghosts of Mississippi*, the film Fred Zollo produced about the third trial of Byron De La Beckwith, was released in the fall of 1996.

•••

John Shalikashvili

I was in Washington in the late winter of 1994 when a press aide to Tipper Gore began telling me of a trip that Mrs. Gore and the Chairman of the Joint Chiefs of Staff, John Shalikashvili, had taken to refugee camps in Goma, Zaire. It was an unpublicized fact-finding mission and both the Chairman and the vice-president's wife had spent time tending refugee children.

The head of the most powerful military force in the world comforting orphans? This was something that defied stereotype.

When I returned to New York, I browsed through General Shalikashvili's Nexis clippings file and discovered a wonderful narrative: a refugee who'd come to America in his teens, who was the first draftee and the first foreign-born officer to become Chairman of the Joint Chiefs of Staff. I called Chairman Shalikashvili's press office at the Pentagon, and made my proposal. They were interested, but no one could see a moment in the near future when he'd have two full hours to sit with a reporter. Eventually, we scheduled two appointments over a period of several weeks. Of course, each session seemed to end just as the general began to feel comfortable with my questions, and thus a third appointment was added. Two things saved us: one was Shalikashvili's willingness to truly participate—he was not about to give up any state secrets, but he was truly attentive and open to whatever was asked. I felt a likable, accessible quality in him that must have been a great asset in his rise to the top of the military. The other was my empathy with what I believe is the general's most central private experience: his immigration. At one point, I asked him the question that ends the interview: Did he consider himself a man of the new or the old world? Shalikashvili's face lit up. It was a question he'd long been considering.

The interviews were conducted in February 1995, and the *Times Magazine* ran the finished piece on May 21 of that year. That interview ran 3,200 words. This version has been expanded to almost 6,000 words.

There was a humorous, self-deprecating quality to John Shalikashvili, then fifty-eight, the first draftee, and the first foreign-born soldier, to rise to Chairman of the Joint Chiefs of Staff. If the image of a four-star general is that of a Patton-style warrior—gruff, laconic, righteous—then Shalikashvili is an iconoclast: witty, thoughtful, accessible through three interviews totaling more than three hours. He fudges rarely, and laughs often, sometimes at the ironies of his own life story.

In many ways, Shalikashvili's narrative has the broad sweep of a David Lean movie. The grandfather of America's top soldier was a czarist general, and his father, Dimitri Shalikashvili, was a Georgian nationalist who fought the Red Army, worked as an officer for the Polish military and, after Poland fell in 1939, joined Germany's Georgian Legion in the hope that Hitler might defeat Stalin. At the end of World War II, the Shalikashvilis settled in Bavaria, living as poor relations on the estate of aristocratic relatives.

The family immigrated to Peoria, Illinois, in 1952 when John was sixteen. He was drafted in 1958, and rose quickly through the ranks. For sixteen years, he held command and staff positions in Germany, Korea, and Vietnam, as well as in the United States. By the 1980s, Shalikashvili (pronounced shah-lee-kahsh-VEE-lee) had become a general, and gained a reputation for political and military smarts. In 1991, Generals Colin Powell and John Galvin picked him to run "Operation Provide Comfort," a military-political effort aimed at saving the lives of half-a-million Kurdish refugees starving in the mountains of northern Iraq. "He has unique qualifications as a combat arms officer and yet he is enormously sensitive to human suffering," says Powell.

When Powell was Chairman of the Joint Chiefs of Staff, he made "Shali" his assistant; he was later sent to Europe as Supreme Allied Commander of NATO. In 1993, Shalikashvili returned to Washington to succeed his mentor as the top soldier at the Pentagon. "When you think that someone who didn't come to this country until he was sixteen could rise to be Chairman of the Joint Chiefs, this is unique in the world," Shalikashvili says with a smile. "Despite all the bad things that we are fond of reciting about this country, it's incredible that a kid can come here and do this."

Former Secretary of Defense McNamara recently declared that the United States should have withdrawn from Vietnam after the murder of Diem. He said, "We were wrong, tragically wrong." As a Vietnam veteran, what did you think when you heard that?

Disappointment. A degree of frustration, because there's an implication—I've not read his book—that these are things that the men who were in leadership positions knew, but did not do anything about.

McNamara told [The New York Times] *that similar mistakes are being made in Washington today. He pointed to Somalia and Bosnia as examples.*

To compare Somalia to Vietnam is factually and morally wrong. Somalia was a totally different humanitarian effort—to save lives. So is America's role in Bosnia. It's unfair for me to sit and try to make judgments on what I have not read. But if the question is, "Can one compare the Vietnam conflict with America's role in something like Somalia or America's involvement in something like Bosnia," it's patently wrong. You can't compare one with the other.

So I don't know why he said it. I happen to disagree with him.

Last November, when Senator Jesse Helms was saying that senior military figures thought Clinton unfit to be Commander in Chief, you took the unusual step of publicly disputing with him. Why?

One of the great things about this country is that we in uniform swear allegiance to the Constitution, which says that he who has been elected president is Commander in Chief. We have a long tradition of not debating whether he's right or wrong. I didn't want anyone to misread Senator Helms's remarks and assume that senior military people were involved in a debate on the Commander in Chief. I was worried about [his statement] being misunderstood by the soldiers, that somehow it was all right for us to hold this kind of debate.

It's your view that President Clinton's "Don't Ask, Don't Tell" policy [on homosexuals in the military] is working well. How exactly is it doing that?

It meets the needs of the services, and I think it properly safeguards the rights of the individual. For right now, we have struck the right balance.

Were there people you served with who you knew were homosexual?

It wouldn't surprise me, but no one comes to mind.

Do you agree with the premise that homosexuals are security risks?

No. Those arguments might have been made earlier when someone out of fear of exposure could have been blackmailed. Those days are probably waning, if they aren't already behind us.

Let me ask about women in the military. The armed forces are a beacon to the rest of society in race relations. Why can't they be the same in creating an atmosphere of tolerance in these other areas?

They are. Some 25 to 26 percent of all our ROTC cadets are women. That's enormous. Point me [out] any other United States institution [in which that is true]. Can we talk about the clergy or Congress or the leadership of General Motors?

But you've made such progress in the racial area, more than the civilian sector [has], and then I read about women in the military academies complaining about sexual harassment.

They certainly have been complaining of sexual harassment in the academies, and any sexual harassment in the academies is wrong. My sense is that we should never condone any kind of demeaning behavior of one person to another, one group to another, but we also need to understand, as we judge, how it compares to [the] same sort of behavior somewhere else. I don't feel apologetic at all.

Have you, during your long career, known military women who were frustrated with their lack of career-progress?

I think so. Particularly early on. There must have been a great deal of frustration, of feeling that you ought to be able to do everything within your abilties. The Gulf War, I think, was a very important point from the standpoint of more women participating in many, many positions than ever before. Women getting hurt, women becoming prisoners—the nation accepted all of that. So a big part of this whole process was how much would the nation accept. In all of that, the Gulf War was a very important step forward because it conditioned the country to what it means to have women in war—and how well they did it! I was very gratified to see that. I think it put aside some fears and stereotypes and concerns that some had about the relationships between men and women and all of us soldiering together. It was a very beneficial experience and it has helped to move us along.

The Speaker of the House, Newt Gingrich, made a statement a while ago on women in the military. I believe he said something to the effect that women were not suited for combat because they tended to get infections and had not been biologically programmed to hunt giraffes. What is your take on his analysis?

I think the issue of women in the military is really almost behind us. Women have acquitted themselves firmly in places like Desert Storm, Haiti, Rwanda. I think we have made the right adjustments as to what units and specialties we think women should be allowed to be in. I think that clearly there are some who wish we were pushing faster. And some who think we ought to slow down. As always, the answer is probably some place in the middle. I feel comfortable with the process.

Have you ever done any thinking about whether or not men are genetically programmed to hunt giraffes?

157

[Laughs.] I really have not thought about it. Giraffes are not one of the animals I would have thought about going hunting for.

As part of the Contract With America, the House of Representatives voted to restrict the number of American soldiers serving under foreign commanders. How do you feel about such limitations?

I think there are aspects of that Contract With America, particularly the one that deals with command and control, that, in my eyes, [constitute] an unwarranted and perhaps even unacceptable infringement upon the flexibility the president must be allowed to retain.

Look, throughout our history, there've been Americans under foreign commanders. We have it today. It is correct to demand that whenever we do so we have a clear understanding that the person commanding is competent, that the rules under which he commands are acceptable to us, that the rules of engagement you give to the soldiers are proper. Another issue that bothers me [in the Contract] is this notion that [one] can legislate when one can extend the [NATO] alliance. It's one thing for the Congress to express the view that the alliance ought to be extended. It's another to argue that by such and such a time, you must admit. . .

Poland, Hungary, the Czech Republic. . .

That's right. This is not for us alone to decide. This is an extraordinary, complex process—one on which the stability, if not the security, of Europe hinges. If you do it on some kind of a time line, you stand in danger of doing more harm than good.

One senses you're not in any great hurry to expand NATO.

I have argued that before we talk about an expansion we ought to have something like what I can modestly say I had some part in [originating], the Partnership for Peace, the development of a relationship between partners and the alliance that would bring them closer to us in a meaningful way, that would allow them to become more like us.

And also not scare the Russians?

Yeah, and it certainly allows the Russians also to come closer to the alliance through the Partnership for Peace.

Are you one of those people who was astonished when the Cold War ended?

I think all of us were. People who gave this much more thought than I couldn't imagine it. What they thought was that the Cold War would ebb and flow. But [not that] the Soviet empire would come to an end. And this is very different from the end of World War II, the last upheaval of a whole political and social structure. Then, there were people who argued [about whether] the war would end in '45 or '46, but they knew it would end and that the world would be very different afterward.

This time, there wasn't anyone who seriously asked, "How do we work with a Europe that is no longer confronted by Communism?" A lot of the problems we are witnessing now are due to this. If it took us ten years to get our house in order after World War II, it is going to take us every bit the same now—if not longer.

Your father, the lifelong anti-Communist, did he live to see the end of Communism?

No, though till the day he died, he dreamed of going back to Georgia. Toward the end of his life, he stopped believing this was going to happen. My mother did live to see the change. She was born in St. Petersburg, fled that city after the Revolution, saw it renamed Leningrad and lived long enough to see it renamed St. Petersburg again.

As a child, did your father speak to you much of his native Georgia?

Oh, yes. My father always thought of himself as a Georgian. He had traveled to Russia, and became an officer in the czarist army. After the overthrow of the czar, there was a narrow window when Georgia was an independent country. He and his brother were on an official mission to Ataturk's Turkey at about the time that Georgia was overrun by the Communists. Eventually, my uncle joined the French Foreign Legion. My father went to Poland. In the early 1920s the Polish Army was looking for foreign contract officers. It was in Warsaw that my father met and fell in love with my mother, another refugee from St. Petersburg.

One of the rumors about you is that your maternal grandmother was a lady-in-waiting to the czarina. True?

I think so. She was German. She'd moved to Russia at an early age and married a Russian officer, my grandfather, who later became a general. As I was growing up, my mother told me vivid stories about court life in St. Petersburg, about Rasputin and about the family's flight from St. Petersburg after the Communists took over. I thought they lived a very exciting kind of a life. Others would think of my childhood as something sad because of all the turmoil. But I remember it as exciting and fun. During the Warsaw Uprising in 1944, I remember moving through sewers because you couldn't get from one side of the street to the other. I remember being bombed in Warsaw and the building collapsing over us. I saw these things not with fear, but somewhat as an adventure. Children can be so resilient.

When did your family come to America?

In 1952. From Germany. We were stateless. I've never been a citizen of any country except the United States, which I became in May of 1958. In June of 1958 I graduated from Bradley University. And in July of '58 I was drafted. [Laughs.] An exciting three months for me.

After all the dislocations of Europe, what was it like to immigrate to Peoria, Illinois?

Exciting.

You may be the only person in modern history to describe Peoria as exciting.

For a sixteen-year-old European, it was an adventure. I think I was expecting wagon trains to be still crossing the Mississippi. There were no wagon trains, but it was still marvelous. Oh, there were some antsy moments of feeling shy and insecure, but everything seemed bigger and wider and cleaner. I liked Americans instantly. There wasn't all this formality that exists in Europe. One other thing about Peoria. Because it was the Middle West, it has its rock-solid value system, this clear sense of right and wrong. And people are not flashy. Not fancy. I feel very comfortable with that.

What the Germans call "solide"?

Yes, exactly.

One of the legends about you is that you learned English from John Wayne movies.

Partly true. I studied English in Germany. Still, when I came here, I felt comfortable saying "Yes" and "No," and not much more. So I went to a movie theater after school, and sat there, and watched movies at least twice. The second time around, the English words began to make sense to me. I must have gone to all kinds of movies. But I remember most the John Wayne movies.

As the son and grandson of professional soldiers, were you always interested in entering the family trade?

I went back and forth about it. At Bradley University [in 1954] I enrolled in Air Force ROTC and then lo and behold, I found that my eyesight was not good enough to be a pilot. After that, I convinced myself that I really didn't want to be in the service. As soon as I graduated, I was all prepared to make lots of money in a comfortable civilian life. But then, I received my draft notice. And it was an absolute shock to my system.

That feeling stayed with me until I went on my first assignment as a commissioned officer. I got sent to a very exciting place—Alaska. We would go on these long-range patrols on skis. I remember an instance where we went up to Point Barrow, the northernmost Eskimo village in Alaska, and with Eskimo scouts with dog teams, went out on the ice cap. Eventually, I came to think, "If life is like this in the military, then it's for me."

Your brother told me that your parents did not want you to have a military career because they did not think that recent immigrants would have much chance for advancement. It appears they were wrong?

Oh, I think so. [Smiles.] But I'm absolutely convinced that they came to this country late in their lives because they were *hoping* that the opportunities would be here for the children, regardless of what we chose to do.

We left Europe in 1952. Europe didn't look very promising. And I think it was this idea that they would take us, the kids, to somewhere where we could do whatever, you know, whatever our potential would take us to.

If you think of my father's background—he was familiar with the military—and all his experience told him that you simply can't progress very far in the military if you were not born in that country, have not attended the right schools, had the right contacts and so on. But I'm delighted he was wrong. And that he so misjudged what's possible here.

During your confirmation hearings for Chairman, a reporter went through your late father's papers at Stanford University and discovered an unpublished memoir he'd written of his World War II experiences. In it, your father casually mentions that after the fall of Poland, he joined Germany's Georgian Legion so that he could fight against Stalin. He also says he was briefly under the discipline of the Waffen SS. Discovering this, and having to answer for it before the Senate, must have been one of the toughest moments in your life.

It was. It probably gave me reason to think about my father more than I had before. He was in no way that kind of man. I think you would have found him to be a remarkably gentle man. But you know, it's amazing how a war like this tosses and twists you and turns you around and what situations you find yourself in.

[During the confirmation hearings] there were two issues I wanted to bring out. I wanted to leave no doubt that this was not an issue of me withholding something. Secondly, while my father's unit was associated with the Waffen SS, he was never himself a member of the Waffen SS. I think what happened was that my father never thought of it as something horrible. If he had, why would he have written about it? Why would he have taken his papers and given them to Stanford University?

You had an opportunity to visit Georgia a few years ago. I believe you accompanied then-Secretary of State James Baker, on an official mission. It must have been both strange and compelling to finally be in the country that your father had always spoken of?

First of all, it came very unexpectedly. I had a job at that time that periodically required me to travel with Secretary Baker. And we were on a trip to Russia, and he mentioned that he was going to go to Georgia and asked whether I wanted to come along. And, of course, I seized on it. It came very quickly. Not much preparation.

It was a very exciting period of time because Edvard Chevardnadze had just recently returned to Georgia. There were elections set for Chevardnadze a couple of months later on in the summer. We arrived in Tbilisi and there was a huge throng of people in the square—while the fighting was still going on in the city. In the distance you could occasionally hear a shot, because Gamzakordia was still being pushed out of the city. So it was kind of an exciting time.

I watched with absolute amazement as Secretary Baker and President Chevardnadze, then Chairman Chevardnadze, threw themselves into this throng of people like two guys campaigning. [Laughter]. They disappeared in that crowd. And I'm sure the security guys went absolutely bananas. But it was obvious that there was a genuine friendship between them, and that the people in Georgia, at least that crowd in Tbilisi, loved them both. For me, it was kind of an unbelievable moment, because, first of all, I had not envisioned that I would go back. I had not envisioned that I would be watching Georgians in that kind of environment.

On subsequent occasions when I would meet with people or had an opportunity to talk to Chevardnadze alone, it struck me that the name Shalikashvili was well known in Georgia, that my father's family had been somebody in that country, and that they were all delighted that I had reached the position in the American Army at that time that I had.

And, of course, subsequent to that, I became the Supreme Allied Commander in Europe. And then Chairman [of the Joint Chiefs of Staff]. But even in those days, when I was the assistant to Colin Powell, and worked out of the office, it was still a very strange feeling to realize that it meant something to the Georgian people that I had accompanied Secretary Baker there.

Another thing that happened to me was that I had been convinced all along that I had no living relatives in Georgia. Yet, a number of Georgians named Shalikashvili came up to me and identified themselves as my distant cousins. I remember one lady who came to a luncheon that Chevardnadze gave for us. She asked whether she could say a few words. And she spoke about me and about my family, and then presented me with a small, little wooden box with rosewood inlay, the kind of box in which, in days gone by, you kept handkerchiefs. And she said that when she was growing up she had an English teacher, and her English teacher was my aunt. This aunt of mine had, on one occasion, given her as a present this little box. And she wanted to return it to me because it was a box that belonged to the Shalikashvilis.

You know, moments like that really touch you. And sort of give you the feeling that you are really home, that after all these years, this woman would have kept that box. It's very special when you realize that you do have roots somewhere.

About Bosnia. In the past, you've asserted that the West overestimates the military power of the Serbs. Is that still true?

Sure. I believe that whenever we have been resolute—NATO particularly—we have been able to have our way. Whenever that was so, the Serbs read it very correctly and acted accordingly. And I am frustrated that we are often prevented from [being resolute], and lately more so than not.

Many members of the new Congress are opposed to using military forces for humanitarian missions. They say that soldiers should fight, not be relief workers.

And there are some in the Pentagon who'd be very happy if I put outside a sign that read, "We only do the big ones." The notion that we exist, first and foremost, to fight our nation's wars is something I subscribe to. But I also say, "In this new world, we cannot deny our government a very important tool to try to manage crises, bring stability to an area, deal with operations that overwhelm traditional humanitarian organizations." But you have to be selective—or you could fritter away resources and capabilities.

After the Gulf War, you were put in charge of "Operation Provide

Comfort," which saved the lives of hundreds of thousands of Kurdish refugees who were starving in the mountains of Northern Iraq. When Powell first gave you that assignment, did it seem possible that you'd be able to rescue such huge numbers?

No, it surely didn't. It was so grim, and we had so few tools at our disposal. And so many were dying every night. We didn't even know where they were. We ended up using satellites to try to locate all the people in this extraordinary, rough, mountainous area.

But all of us who were there sort of resolved that we were not going to rest until we got them out of there. And we set ourselves a time line, where we knew that if we didn't get them out by a certain time, we would lose the majority of them. And everybody—there were some thirteen nations involved in this effort—everybody from the lowest private in no matter what military to the most senior U.N. workers there, were just absolutely remarkable. You had to say to people, "Stop now. You can't work that many hours. Get a rest."

You see pictures of soldiers, marines, holding children. You could tell in their eyes, after having been trained to fight wars and kill, what excitement it was for them to be saving lives on such a vast scale.

I think all of us at one time or another were Boy Scouts or Girl Scouts or something. We all learned to do good and to take our coat off and put it over the water puddle so the old lady can cross the street safely. But very few of us ever have the opportunity to help others on such a vast scale as these operations. And, you know...the young men and women who went to Somalia did every bit the same thing. And folks that went into Bangladesh during the floods. All of them have a source of pride and satisfaction that will last them for the rest of their lives, if they just take the time to reflect on what they did.

And yet these operations are often criticized [because] it's really not the military's job to do that. And I agree. Except in cases where the civilian organizations that exist to do this sort of thing become overwhelmed, either because of the enormity of the crisis, or because it develops so quickly. Like in Northern Iraq...there simply was no one else.

Whoever said, "It's not the thing for the soldier, but only a soldier can do it," is correct.

Do you find it ironic that there are leaders now in the Pentagon who are strong advocates of this kind of military activity and people in Congress who are utterly opposed?

No. I think this debate exists in the military as well. The military is a tool that ought to be at the disposal of the government to deal with those issues. We cannot be there just simply for the day when someone attacks our shores—though that is our principal purpose.

That's what distinguishes this world from the world before the Iron Curtain came down. Because then the threat of a military confrontation was so great that we couldn't take our eye off it. And we had to be extraordinarily careful not to get tied down somewhere because any moment, with little warning, we were facing the potential of having to fight the Soviet Union.

The world is different now. And the world has not only changed in that we do not face that threat to our shores in the same way that we did before, but also that the world has become much less stable. Before, the Bosnias didn't happen because the Soviet Union sat on them. The Rwandas and other things didn't happen because everything was seen in that East-West context. And that's no longer so. We've kind of taken the lid off a lot of these things, unleashed them. And until they run their course we have to be prepared to insure that we don't allow any of this to get out of hand. One of the tools that ought to be available is the military.

The military has defined readiness as the capacity to fight two simultaneous wars in two different parts of the world. With base-closings, troop reductions and budget cuts, are we still able to?

I believe so. But we have always said that we will be able to engage in two widely separated conflicts providing we continue to improve our ability to lift forces and to command and control forces into separated areas of the world. It's not easy to do. It talks to the issue of how many satellites you have to provide you with intelligence, communications. There are enhancements to that force that we said from the beginning that we'd need.

Who do you perceive as the greatest security threat to America?

Always, always, the greatest demon is our own complacency, our sense that the world is safe and that we don't have to worry.

Today, we understandably worry most about our interests in the Middle East and a place like Korea. [But] we need to avoid being too fixated on Iraq or North Korea. I worry about a place like Iran in the years to come. In its support for terrorism, I think Iran is a potential threat to the whole region. Its actions in the Strait of Hormuz recently, all of that leads you to wonder what their aims are. Listening to the rhetoric coming out of Iran, it's hard to conclude anything other than that they are very much opposed to the sort of things we and our friends stand for.

You were decorated with the Bronze Star during your tour of duty in Vietnam. How did you come to win it?

Oh, it was an action where I accompanied some American and Vietnamese troops and we had information about a North Vietnamese command post that had moved into the area. This was at the time of the floods. We had received information that they were holed up on a piece of land surrounded by water, that had become an island, and so our task was to see that we captured them. Which we did. But in the process we had a fairly good-size fire fight. And what I remember of it is—no particular heroic action on my part. Except that we were all in boats and they were on land. And we were trying to make it to that land so we could overwhelm them. And take them prisoners. And as long as we were in those boats we were pretty helpless there. So we had to see how quickly we could paddle and how quickly our motor boats could make it to that island. In the end, we succeeded.

When President Clinton moved to normalize U.S.-Vietnam relations, I take it he asked for your advice?

He surely did. My view was then, as it is today, that that's the right thing to do. For two reasons. First and foremost, to help us gain more information on those that are still missing. I think we gain that information better through dialogue and through constant presence in Vietnam than we do if we stiff-arm each other.

We did that for many, many years. But I have become convinced

167

that we have gone as far with that [stiff-arming] policy as possible, that it is time now to move forward to the next step: a more active dialogue. I think I was right in that judgment. I think the president was absolutely right in making that decision. I am very happy to see that, the other day, the American flag was raised over our Interests Section in Hanoi. I think it's time to move forward with improving the relationship with Vietnam.

Look, we have fought wars with nations before. We have always been of the view that there comes a time when you must move forward and begin to have a more normal relationship. After all, at the end of World War Two, we were very quick in that process with two of our most bitter enemies, Germany and Japan. And today they are our staunchest allies. It was because we moved on and recognized that the world keeps moving forward. And that's . . . the right course. Just as I think we were right for a while with Vietnam, I think we are correct now.

You've told several interviewers that when you retire, you want to open a hardware store in Oregon. Why a hardware store?

Can't you picture me? The idea of being able to have something that you do and still have plenty of time to sit in the sun and read a book and contemplate life. . . . Hardware stores have always fascinated me. Ever since the first time I walked into one of these old-fashioned musty hardware stores where you can rummage and find old bolts and nails. It's a dream. [With a grin.] As a matter of fact, I've talked a number of senior officers into going into business with me.

A final question: do you consider yourself more a man of the New World or the Old?

The preponderance must be New World. The proof of it is whenever I spend any time overseas, I am just delighted to come back to the United States. The strudel might be nicer in Germany, the Big Mac is an awful lot better over here. And I happen to like it better. I like more what this country stands for.

•••

Nadine Strossen

The voice on the phone on a winter's day in 1993 was that of Erwin Knoll, the editor of *The Progressive*, with an idea for an interview: "There's a woman finally heading the ACLU and I had her on my radio show and she's really terrific on feminist censorship and those kinds of issues. Why don't you give her a call?"

Strossen sounded interesting. She was a forty-three-year-old law professor, writer, and legal theorist, and the youngest lawyer, and the first woman, to head the American Civil Liberties Union. Moreover, I owed Erwin a favor. I owed him a dozen favors. (In some ways, I owed Erwin my career. In 1974, he'd sponsored me for a grant from the Fund for Investigative Journalism to expose coercive sterilization practices directed against Mexican-American women. That grant and the subsequent publication of my investigations in *The Progressive* led to the Federal government monitoring informed consent practices for these women and started me on the path of investigative journalism.)

Still, I hedged: "Lawyers can be so boring."

"Nadine is the opposite of boring," he countered.

And of course, she was.

As a young woman, Strossen had no dreams of lawyering. "I had never met a woman lawyer," the dark-haired Strossen explained on a frozen New York winter afternoon at her offices at the New York Law School. "I had never met a woman who was a professional anything, other than teacher. I became vicariously ambitious for the males I knew. I was state champion debater and the only woman on my team. I said to all my male debate partners that they should become lawyers. It never occurred to me that it was a possibility for me."

While a student at Radcliffe in the early 1970s, Strossen became involved in the legal battles for reproductive rights and, perhaps benefiting from some of the early wins of the women's movement, attended Harvard Law School. Once a lawyer, her passions were women's rights and human rights, which brought her to the ACLU. Ironically, Strossen is serving as ACLU president at a time when it is defending free speech from full-scale assaults on sexual literature from both government *and* feminists.

Spend a few hours with Nadine Strossen and one senses her to be the kind of person early feminists were speculating about in countless 1970s discussions of what "women of the future" might be like. She is intellectual, combative, extremely sure of herself, unvictimized. She leads the life she wants to live, passionately, fearlessly.

There's also an interesting kind of glamour to her, born of self-confidence. This is a law professor who goes to work in a shimmering silk outfit and a ton or two of free-form silver jewelry. If some feminists have declared that sensuality and glamour are a piece of their oppression, she insists on declaring it part of her being.

Our conversations took place over the Christmas holidays in 1993. *The Progressive* published the interview in March 1994.

Nadine Strossen, your religious affiliation could almost be described as "First Amendment Absolutist." Have you always been a civil libertarian?

It goes back as far as I can remember. My maternal grandfather was a pacifist and a Marxist in World War I. He was made to stand in front of the town hall in West New York, New Jersey so that passers-by could come and spit at him. Now, as a socialist, he was not oriented as much to a strong sense of individual rights as I am. But he was very much a humanist, an idealist.

My father grew up in Berlin. He was involved in anti-Hitler youth organizations and was arrested and put into forced labor camps. He was liberated by Americans in Buchenwald and went out on one of the very first ships of survivors who went to America. Later in life, he became a committed conservative. When I think about it, I realize I selected

out particular aspects of my family background that were most reso-
nant to me. In my father's case, it was a belief in individual rights, a
kind of libertarianism.

I'm not exaggerating when I say that my earliest memories are of
having a sense of privacy, justice, and free speech. I was constantly arguing with parents and teachers when I felt they were intruding on my rights
or the rights of other people. I was always deeply upset when I saw animals in kids books being treated unfairly.

You're the first woman to head the ACLU. Proud?

Yes. Very proud. And it's a wonderful symbol that for the first time
in the ACLU's seventy-plus years, the top position is being filled by a
woman. From the beginning, women played a very important role in the
organization.... I'm very proud of the fact that in 1920, our founding
mothers included Jane Addams, Crystal Eastman, and Jeanette Rankin.
A lot of our founders came out of the women's suffrage and peace movements. From the beginning, the ACLU took women's rights cases, including those of one of our founders, Mary Dennett, and also Margaret Sanger.
They were prosecuted for distributing birth control information under
"obscenity laws."

*Given the ACLU's history, it must be astonishing to see this con-
temporary call for censorship coming from some feminists... the women's
anti-pornography movement?*

I'm not surprised, Claudia. I guess at this point, I'm jaded enough
to think that threats to civil liberties are going to come from all points
on the political spectrum.

The way I deconstruct this movement is that its leaders are looking for a quick-fix solution to very complex and troubling social problems. There are a lot of women out there who are understandably
frustrated about misogyny and discrimination. Their answer seems to
be: "destroy troubling imagery." Problem is: censorship is never going
to deal with the underlying problems of violence and discrimination.
We have to change people's perceptions. To solve a social problem, we
need *more* speech.

My critique of people like Andrea Dworkin and Catharine MacKinnon is that their call for censorship doesn't protect women's safety or advance women's equality. On the contrary, censorship undermines it.

Moreover—I have to say it—I find the pro-censorship feminists politically naive. And I would put the people wanting to institute "hate speech" regulations on campus in the same category. When the pro-censorship feminists and the anti-hate speech people say that there is a power establishment in this country, from which women and racial minorities have been systematically excluded, they are right. But then they go on to give this new tool to the power structure, this open-ended power to punish or to prevent words that may be subordinating or degrading to women, or hate-speech.

The power structure is going to use hate-speech regulations and censorship laws against the very groups that are themselves the most marginalized: the women, the minorities, lesbians and gay men. Truth is—the hate-speech codes on campus have consistently been enforced disproportionately against members of minority groups.

So you would say, "Why give the power structure more weapons of suppression than it already has?"

Exactly. Look at what's happened in Canada. In 1992, the Canadian Supreme Court adopted the Andrea Dworkin/Catherine MacKinnon definition of pornography as sexually explicit speech that is "degrading and dehumanizing" to women.

Catharine MacKinnon worked very closely with a Canadian women's organization which had argued the case before the Canadian Supreme Court. Given that open-ended standard, the Canadian governmental authorities immediately used their new powers to attack images of lesbian sexuality! The very first prosecution when that new law went into effect was of a lesbian magazine and a lesbian and gay bookstore in Toronto.

There has, in fact, been such a systematic pattern of harassment against lesbian and gay bookstores since this law went into effect that the ACLU's counterpart in Canada, the CCLA, has brought a lawsuit against the government, saying that it is discriminatorily enforcing the law against lesbian and gay bookstores. Whereupon the government has broadened its effort somewhat and has attacked feminist and some campus bookstores.

Interestingly, the Canadian government has also barred two of Andrea Dworkin's books from coming into the country: *Pornography—Men Processing Women* and *Woman Hating.*

Does the mere title "Pornography" make something pornographic?

Well the Canadian authorities probably looked at the contents of the book, which like so many of these anti-pornography tracts contain vivid descriptions of the very material that they are seeking to have censored.

I have heard that Andrea Dworkin had long said that she recognized that her own works might be the first casualties of this law and that was a price that she considered worth paying. I don't know if she said it. But . . . it's indisputable fact that her works are subject to censorship under this law! Her books are *filled* with images and descriptions of vicious, violent pornography.

And that's not surprising. If you look at the tactics of women's anti-pornography groups, their classic technique is to display the most horrific, frightening, horrifying images they want banned. The reason they display this stuff is not because they believe that people are going to look at it and commit a rape, but because they want to sensitize people to the serious problem of violence against women. And I'd like to commend them for that. I believe in getting those ideas out there. However, I vehemently disagree with their chosen means for solving the problems of sexism and misogyny—censorship is not going to help women. More than that, it seems to get a lot of women censored.

And it also leaves room to let some wrongdoing men off the hook. With the MacKinnon-Dworkin approach, you can, analytically, understand them to be saying that a man who commits a sex-crime is himself a victim. He is the victim of the pornography that made him do it.

So serial killer Ted Bundy gets up and says . . .

" . . . Pornography made me do it!" He said it to try to get out of the death penalty at the last minute. He saw it as a mitigating factor. And under state law, it would be a mitigating factor. If you could show that you were driven to a crime by some external factor, that can reduce the level of the offense and the penalty. That's why, when the Senate, last year, considered the Pornography Victims Compensation bill, some Senators voted against it because they felt it would displace responsibility from some perpetrators of crime and put it on pornography.

So you oppose the anti-porn feminists tactically and substantively?

Right. And more than that: I do not see all pornography as conveying unmitigatedly misogynistic messages.

You look at it yourself... sometimes?

I do. I find some of it physically beautiful, the way one might find paintings of nudes physically beautiful.

You know, what you see in a particular image is so subjective. Take the kind of image that feminists might find objectionable... one that might convey a woman being raped, a woman not involved in voluntary sexual activity—if you read Nancy Friday's books of sexual fantasies from thousands of women, she says that a significant theme is women being turned on by images of rape. Not real rapes, of course. The way she explains it, in a society where many women still believe it is bad for them to want sex, these images are acceptable to them.

Obviously, I'm not going defend the actual rape of a real woman for the purpose of creating a pornographic picture. But many supporters of MacKinnon and Dworkin do not just say that pornography causes rape, but that it *is* rape.

So you're a woman who's unafraid to say that you are a consumer of sexual materials?

Absolutely. I do look at *Playboy*. I consider the imagery beautiful and often erotically stimulating.

What else? I liked Madonna's book. I thought it aesthetically pleasurable to look at, funny, brave, feisty. I got a good laugh out of it.

There's something intellectually provocative about some pornography. In hotels, they sometimes now have this soft-core porn. At night, when I'm done giving a speech, I don't mind turning on the Playboy Channel or The Red Shoe Diaries. [Laughs.] I mean, what's the alternative? My husband isn't there. I do a lot of traveling and I'm glad the hotels have this stuff.

How do you feel when Big Sister is telling you what you can enjoy and can't?

Furious. And I've always been that way. What I read, what I enjoy, how I spend my time, should be my decision as a human being—so long as I'm not harming anyone else.

There's always this hypocrisy at the bottom of all calls for censorship. Because those who advocate censorship are themselves the most massive consumers of, and in some case, creators of, materials that they think are too dangerous for others to see. Dworkin and MacKinnon have probably seen more pornography than most men we know. The Meese Pornography Commission, they steeped themselves in the stuff. And they went to Times Square and looked at everything—and then said, it was much too dangerous for anyone else to look at.

Another thing, there has always been a kind of elitism and classism involved in censorship. Certainly, it's been true of pornography. And movements to censor have always been associated with the invention of a new mass medium that makes this material more widely available. You know, when "gentlemen" could see pornography through expensively produced editions, it was just fine. But then it became widely available through magazines and worse yet, films, and now it's going to be available to everyone on...

On CD-ROM...?

Right. On computers. My husband, who is a technology buff, brought home one of those things. I did not find it erotic. It's unconvincing at this point. But it's interesting.

I keep worrying about all those people who are going to trade herpes for eyestrain and VDT headaches...

[Laughs.] Right. "Honey, I can't look at the computer now...I've got a headache." A new meaning to an old excuse.

The anti-pornography feminists would say that your ideas on sexual literature are the end-product of your oppression as a woman.

I find that deeply insulting. *That* to me is degrading and dehumanizing. It's saying that "you are less than a human being. Your feelings are not really your own. By the way, your ideas are not really your own—and your body is not really your own." Well, what's left?

I was in a debate some months ago with Kathleen Mahoney, a Canadian anti-porn activist, who argued the case in which the Canadian Supreme Court accepted the MacKinnon-Dworkin definition of "pornography." And she actually told me that individual liberties and a belief in civil liberties is a male idea and that anybody who has that idea is essentially a male. I was furious. Can you believe that? I've had my own ideas about freedom long before I was taught by any man or read a book by any man. I consider it the height of insult to suggest that I'm not thinking for myself.

How do your civil libertarian friends react to your pro-porn position?

A number have said that I'm going too far in saying I'm pro-pornography. They say that I should just say, "I'm pro-free speech." Well, *that* goes without saying about all expression. My point is, "we don't make a disclaimer when we defend any other kind of art." Some porn is good, some is bad. Why is it that we have to make this disclaimer when we are talking about sexual expression?

Frankly, I think I get that reaction because the term "pornography" has become so demonized in our culture. It's come to mean, "any sexual speech that I don't like." It's important to reclaim the language—and people shouldn't have to be defensive about speech on sexual topics, which is the literal meaning of the word "pornography."

Speaking of sexual literature, you had a recent op-ed piece about Senator Packwood's diaries. You said he had the right to keep them private.

There's an important principle here: material that we turn over to one person or organization for one purpose may not therefore be seen by any other person or organization for another purpose. The notion that you let one person see them for the purpose of transcribing does not mean that the diaries are open to the world.

This is a point that the U.S. Supreme Court unanimously recognized in the closest case to this issue, which is a case involving Richard Nixon's diaries, which he also kept on tape, which also included a combination of personal events and public events. They were also transcribed by a government employee who was working in his office. These were tapes like the ones Packwood made, where Nixon recorded his impressions of events. The Supreme Court held that they were private.

Packwood won't win this one—will he?

I think he will. In the courts. I think ultimately he has a good argument. He may have lost his case at the Federal District Court level, but I think that ruling was incorrect and I hope it will be overturned on appeal. If not, it creates a dangerous precedent not only for the Bob Packwoods, but for all of us, for anyone who treasures privacy.

Now, in the legislature, in the Senate, I think he's pretty much dead. And frankly, I wouldn't have been surprised if he decided to resign. I'm glad he didn't because it would have set a very bad precedent if the Senate had been allowed to walk rough-shod over his privacy rights. I also hope he persists with his legal claim, despite the initial setback in the lower court.

You'd better elaborate.

Packwood's privacy rights were violated by the incredibly open-ended fishing expedition approach of the Senate subpoena—which was not limited to material relevant to the sexual misconduct and intimidation charges. The Senate can't say, "We want license to rummage unfettered through these diaries on the chance that we might find something that would lead to other charges." That's not the way things are supposed to be in this country. They can't search your house hoping to find evidence of a crime—and then charge you with a crime. The charge has to come first.

In terms of the First Amendment, there was an attempt to overturn his election on the basis of statements made in his campaign. And our argument was, that kind of punishment for statements made in a political campaign violates the core political principles about the government not being in the position of censoring political speech.

I'm sure he's not going to run again and he may be forced to resign, but we can't have the government deprive him of his speech.

For someone who's legal career started in the campaigns to legalize abortion, how are you feeling about the recent Supreme Court decision to make right-to-life protests at abortion clinics illegal under the RICO laws?

I am opposed to rulings that would limit the rights of anti-abortion activists to express their views in a peaceful, non-obstructive way. This new ruling is dangerous to all political activism because it poses the threat of enormous financial costs to people who are expressing controversial political opinions. This same kind of law could be used against any political demonstrators including those in favor of abortion or civil rights or even civil liberties.

If this law had existed in the 1960s, we know it would have been used against Dr. Martin Luther King and the sit-in demonstrators.

OK, on another subject, give us your assessment of the state of civil liberties during the twelve years of Reagan-Bush?

Reagan and Bush systematically appointed individuals to the Court who have a very narrow view of human rights—and as a result, we've seen decisions that have cut back on human rights across the spectrum: everything from freedom of speech to freedom of religion to rights of people accused of crimes to reproductive rights. We have fewer constitutional rights now than we did before the first Reagan election.

Abortion? It's harder now to get an abortion than at any time since the early 1970s—that's a frightening reality that the Supreme Court dealt us.

Civil rights? The civil-rights division of the Justice Department was coopted by people who were anti-civil rights.

After the 1988 election, the acronym ACLU became something dirty, "pornographic," if you will. George Bush accused Michael Dukakis of being a "card-carrying member" of your organization—which he implied was a dirty, awful and unpatriotic outfit. It was an interesting sign of how far the spectrum of acceptable political discourse had moved. In the 1950s, you couldn't be a "card-carrying" Communist.

Actually, George Bush's ACLU-bashing campaign had a positive effect. Tens of thousands of Americans wrote in and said, "I want to be a card-carrying member of the ACLU." That kind of surge is always true in an emergency, but when the excitement passes, there's a dip in interest.

In some ways, the Clinton election was not good for the ACLU— in that our members and friends had an exaggerated sense of how much better things would be under Clinton. To be fair to Bill Clinton, he's been very good on reproductive freedom. It seems as if his judicial appointments are going to be good, starting with Ruth Bader Ginsberg. But he has been a deep disappointment in reneging on campaign statements on some civil liberties issues. In the category of broken promises, there's gays in the military. The Clinton administration is actually in court arguing that Keith Meinhold should not be in the military.

I take it you find Clinton's "Don't ask—don't tell" policy on gays in the military appalling?

Yes. This administration is in court, basically, defending the old Bush policy. It's not a step forward, it's a step backwards, which makes it easier to challenge in court.

The Clinton notion says that you can exclude people from the military because their sexual orientation *makes other people uncomfortable*. In other words, we have a policy based on the complete suppression of your free speech rights. "You can be who you want, but you better not talk about it." And second, our new policy expressly caters to the prejudices of other people. The administration's policy sort of says, "'Other People' will be uncomfortable around gays, because they hate gays and for that reason, we are going to suppress your sexual orientation." Now, this is surrendering more openly to naked prejudice. The old policy at least had the fig leaf of national security. In the old days, the rationale was that gays were "a

179

threat to national security because of the threat of blackmail."

On issues like the death penalty, there's no way to tell the difference between Clinton and Bush.

You dislike Janet Reno?

As a leader, I don't admire her. I have to say that quite candidly. She's the chief law enforcement authority and she has used that platform in ways that are at worst counterproductive and, at best, ineffective. [In her] testimony before the Congress on TV violence she said the various measures that are being proposed to restrict violent imagery on TV are constitutional. And they are not constitutional! And to have our top law enforcement officer making that kind of pronouncement, I find deeply distressing.

On the positive side, she's said she's against mandatory minimum sentences. Let's see how effective she'll be at raising those concerns.

A final question: do you ever wonder if the Bill of Rights could pass Congress today?

Every now and then someone does an opinion poll where people are told what the Bill of Rights is. The respondents always seem to say, "Let's get rid of that." That's why Roger Baldwin, the principal ACLU founder, said, "No fight for civil liberties ever stays won." I'm afraid it's more true than ever.

•••

MEDIA PHREAKS

Richard Dreyfuss

*T*his interview started out as a *TV Guide* interview—though it was never published in that form. Richard Dreyfuss had given a speech some months earlier in which he'd denounced television as evil. When a publicist proposed to *TV Guide* that they run an interview, in hopes of promoting a documentary series the actor was narrating, the *TV Guide* editors went for the idea and urged me to focus on Dreyfuss's speech.

Thus I arrived at Richard Dreyfuss's hotel at the specified hour, and there was Duddy Kravitz at the check-out desk. "Hey, Richard Dreyfuss," I announced. "I'm Claudia Dreifus."

"Yeah . . . yeah," he shrugged. "Listen, I can't do this. I've only got this afternoon to look at some apartments in New York. Then I've got to go catch a plane. Sorry."

Don't lose your cool, I whispered to myself, and quickly tossed out a counter-offer: "Can I go with you while you look at places? We can talk in the car."

So for the rest of the day, Richard Dreyfuss, a real-estate broker—she thought I was the actor's cousin—and I drove from Riverside Drive to Central Park South, checking out expensive sub-leases, doing a half-assed/half-hearted interview in the patches between. Like Mae West, the good interviewer "likes a man what takes his time." This was the definition of a bad interview.

Somewhere in the middle of it all, I found myself asking the L.A. actor the obvious: "Hey, why are you looking for a place in New York anyway?"

"I'm coming East till August to do a play about torture in Chile."

"You know, I was in Chile two winters ago, covering the transition to democracy," I said. "It's an interesting place."

And suddenly everything changed.

Now I was a real person, whose ideas and experiences mattered; not just a hated member of the press. We talked Latin American politics for the rest of the afternoon. Might as well. The interview wasn't going to happen anyway. I accompanied Dreyfuss in his limo as far as Kennedy airport and somewhere on the Van Wyck Expressway wangled a commitment for another appointment when he returned to New York.

The second interview session happened not long afterwards in the actor's suite at his Central Park South hotel. We had a room-service supper and plenty of time to schmooze about television, politics, Chile, and more politics. We also tried to figure out if we were related, since Richard looks frighteningly like my late father, Henry Dreifus. (We're not. His family hails from the neighborhood of Minsk/Pinsk. Mine comes from Germany.)

In this more relaxed atmosphere, the raw interview material that developed was fascinating.

The legendary Italian interviewer, Oriana Fallaci, once told me, "You need complicity to create a good interview." Richard Dreyfuss was now offering me that.

With Dreyfuss in town for *Death and the Maiden*, we met socially for the occasional supper. He wanted to talk with torture victims. I knew some. Richard, in turn, was quite helpful as I prepared for a *Playboy* interview I was doing with William Safire; he knew Safire's work quite well and was able to feed me some interesting questions.

Hanging out with Richard, I began to perceive the reasons for his reticence about the public realm. I'd had friendships with film actors before—Donald Sutherland and Rip Torn had been pals—but Dreyfuss's fame was different and frankly, unbearable. Both Rip and Donald could, when they wanted, walk the city streets and not be recognized. But Richard couldn't. Wherever he went, the assumption that he belonged to everybody but himself was relentless.

How does a person stay within themselves under such pressure? As I got to know him, I could see Dreyfuss had a strong need to live as near a normal life as possible. He wanted to do what actors do—watch people instead of being watched all the time. Nor did he need the affirmation of seeing his face everywhere. His films did enough of that. The hot glow of the star-making machine really did nothing for his life. Richard Dreyfuss certainly didn't want to be any more famous than he already was.

One way Richard coped was to minimize his press contacts. It was self-protective, and even if I was on the other side, I had to respect it. Nevertheless, his anti-media ways ended up costing me. By the time the interview was completed for *TV Guide*, a big snag had developed: Dreyfuss's personal publicist refused to permit a photo shoot with the actor unless the magazine gave him approval rights on the pictures. Not surprisingly, the *TV Guide* refused to surrender editorial control on its visuals and killed the story. I then gave the piece to *The Progressive*, which ran it, illustrated with a drawing, in May 1993.

This interview was conducted during December 1992 and January 1993.

You are an actor who has maintained a consistent sense of public citizenship throughout your career. When you are not campaigning for candidates, you're front and center for reproductive rights issues. Do you ever get flak for your activism?

Yes, and I hate that. There are those Uriah Heep-type people who are always knocking actors for being political. Why don't they criticize people who *aren't* political?

I've always been political. I was political before I was famous. I'll probably be political after I'm famous. "Political" only means that you're interested in being a good citizen.

I've read that when you were younger you dreamed of holding elective office. What happened to that dream?

It disappeared. When I was a kid, the thing I wanted most was to be a Senator. That dream disappeared partly because of the corruption of politics. Elective politics is so much held hostage by the requirement of money for television ads that it's an impossible profession for anyone with ideals.

All a Senator does all day, and I've been around some, is ask for money. What do they want the money for? So they can buy ads for television and stay elected. They don't exercise any governance, they raise money. Surely, you've noticed that there aren't a lot of Wayne Morses in the Senate anymore. I think this is part of the reason why.

Morse was one of the two members of the Senate who voted against the legislation that began the Vietnam War. Is it true that for a while in the 1960s you considered becoming his legislative assistant?

We talked about it. I admired him tremendously. But he died before any of that could happen.

You're aware that in many ways, you're considered the cinematic face of the sixties generation?

Yeah, and we're all, the entire generation, going bald.

Do you miss the 1960s?

I miss the vitality of the 1960s. I miss the innocent beliefs of the 1960s.

Was it just because you were young then?

To a certain extent, it probably is. I can remember the 1960s. I can hardly remember the 1970s. I can remember the 1980s because I had my children then.

What do you remember about the 1960s?

I remember that we all felt connected to the world around us, even if we weren't activists. You knew your world was a large world. You felt that you were the center of the universe but that your parameters stretched out and encompassed all kinds of things and people. That's what I remember about the 1960s. That [world] shrank and shrank over time. So that by 1980, we basically perceived our world as a circle surrounding only ourselves.

I think the people who have been the most frustrated and unhappy these last few years are those 1960s remnants who've been thumping around hoping that other people's circles could become wider. The fact is that 1960s people's circles are still wider. They're connected. They just don't see others stretching out beyond themselves enough.

But you know, I can look out at the world and see that it might happen again. Something might be out there over the horizon. One of the things that is going to happen in the next few years, as the cycle swings back, is this: [Americans] are going to have to start behaving better. And from what I feel and hope, the cycle is beginning to turn. When people say they are sick of seeing the homeless on the streets, they are not saying they want to take machine guns and shoot them; they want something done about it. People are not becoming David Dukes; they're becoming impatient more with the lack of common sense—whether it's with the Republicans or the Democrats, or whatever party.

In **The Big Fix** *in the 1970s, Moses Wine, your character, looks at movie footage of times past and weeps. He feels that the generation failed. Do you agree with that, you personally, Richard Dreyfuss?*

No! I feel that we succeeded. Because we ended the war.

We slowed and stopped an execrable and bitter war. Without us, the Vietnam War would have gone on. And it would have gotten worse. You know, I was a conscientious objector during the war, and I'm proud of that. I'm proud of having been against the Vietnam War. I'm proud of who we all were then.

Perhaps there should be a monument in Washington to those who stopped the war?

I like the wall that's there already. I'm very impressed with it. It says everything. The American soldiers who were killed in Vietnam are part of the 1960s generation, too, and what happened to them should be remembered.

It's no secret that you were addicted to cocaine for the better part of the 1970s and that you went through a difficult personal struggle to free yourself of it. As an ex-addict, how do you perceive the government's official "war on drugs?"

I feel it is an insincere, unfocused, misdirected waste of time and money. We have not gotten anywhere with the real problems and the real solution, which is jobs. Give people training and employment. Give people something to live for. People who are connected to their work, with jobs and ambitions and hopes for their children, do not displace that with drug obsessions. Drugs become central to people who have nothing else.

Is it hard for you to go without drugs?

Well, if I didn't have three kids, I think it would be tough. The knowledge that I am a parent makes it a lot easier—because the demands are so no-kidding-around.

Few of those "Just Say No" ads talk about the reality of the attraction of drugs, particularly to people in terrible emotional pain.

I do. I talk about that a lot. When people see an addict going through withdrawal on television, they misinterpret it. It's not physical pain they are going through—it's desire. It's intense desire.

There are some who say that the drug plague could be slowed by legalization. Agree?

I used to be against legalization. Now I don't know how I feel about it. Still, I believe it's a psychological gesture of enormous import to legalize drugs, and if you do, it could be the death knell of our national character. The idea sounds good: "We'll make it available and you'll get it if you need it. We'll put everything in balance. It will be licensed like alcohol."

But are we strong enough to handle that? I'm a history buff and I know there are cultures that have gone down because of alcohol.

I think you have to think about this: should we have billboards for cocaine?

So you're against legalization?

I fear it.

Speaking of addictions, last year you gave a speech to the Magazine Publishers of America in which you complained that "TV is the crack cocaine of our lives." You later advised reporters to "throw all the TVs into the sea." What is the root of all this anti-television zealotry?

I don't mean to sound hysterical about it, but people do respond to any criticism of television as if one is attacking religion or Mom or the old Pontiac in the garage. What I was saying in that speech is [that] the country should organize a blue-ribbon commission something like the Kerner Commission on Civil Disorders, to give some serious thought to the role television plays in all our lives.

No, really, it isn't my intention to talk about television in the same way a vampire does about a silver cross. What I want to do is ask people to think about television in a serious way, to study television because it does have an impact on national life that we are not paying attention to. Truly, you could name almost any aspect of American culture and sooner or later it comes back to TV in some harmful way: politics, education, entertainment, culture, news. It's there and it needs to be examined.

You'd better prove that.

OK, take politics. About the only pressure on politicians nowadays is [having to raise] money for television advertising. That one fact has completely changed American political life. What a politician looks like on television, what he or she sounds like in sound bites, how much money the politician can raise for advertisements.... The ferocity and viciousness of those negative political ads have completely overwhelmed political debate and obscured our ability to know and understand public issues.

Another example? Education. The decline in our educational system is a fact. I'd like to raise the question: Is there any correlation between how television broadcasts images, how people perceive them, and the decline in our educational system? Should there be a discussion of this? I think so.

Wait a second. There are many social critics who say that television has brought greater citizenship into millions of homes by making public hearings, trials and events instantly accessible to the public in a way that was never true before.

Well, I'm not sure about any of that. Even the "instantaneousness" of news can be a problem.

I think American politics has been corrupted beyond recognition by the influence of television. What television is harming is the ability to reflect. The public's reaction is so immediate—we react not just overnight, but within the hour, to a CNN poll on a specific issue—that a civil leader has no mobility. This paralyzes politicians.

What do you watch?

I don't watch anything in particular. I just *watch*. It's like a new thing, the grazing that people do—that's what I do. It's an aspect of our culture that there are intelligent people who sit in front of a TV set with a remote control and just don't watch anything.

Now, I'm not saying that everything on television is bad. My kids watch *The Simpsons*, and I approve of that. That show's writers are very good cultural commentators. Very rarely have we seen anyone, except maybe a few daily newspaper cartoonists, who are as current with where people are as they are.

So my point is not that there's no good stuff on TV. My point isn't against the substance of television. It's against the medium of television. Television has an unexamined psychological impact on the brain. It has tendrils snaking out into the culture that are poisonous, and we should discuss it.

I'm not saying we should boycott television. You can't. Boycotting television is like boycotting the air we breath. So my intention is not to shut my mouth and close my eyes until television goes away.

That sounds as if you'd like to regulate television more, perhaps censor it?

No, no, no. I'm absolutely and unequivocally opposed to any kind of censorship. What I've been saying is that there are as many TV stations as there are atoms in the air, and there are as many hours, and there's no one regulating it or the advertising. We regulate driving far more than we regulate television. We monitor our schools more.

Until we start to be responsible for television, it will careen out of control, against the walls of our culture—bumpity, bump, bump—and will inflict damage.

What have been the more interesting moments of your television-watching life?

When I saw Oswald killed. November 24, 1963. It was extraordinary. To this day, it seems unbelievable.

Peter Arnett's coverage of the bombing of Baghdad during the Gulf War. President George Bush didn't want the CNN reporters to stay in Baghdad, but even he watched what they put out. Perhaps that is what television does with singularity: show you history at the very moment that it is happening.

On the other hand, since television has become the prime source of news for most of us, it scares the hell out of me when television news submits to government restrictions and censorship—which they admitted doing during Grenada, Panama and especially during the Gulf War.

Ed Morrow would never have stood for this. I don't understand why the press accepts these kinds of limitations now. It's not that the institutions have changed; governments will always try to limit news from getting out. But it seems like people in the press have changed.

What news do you watch?

I don't really get my news from television. I watch CNN and I click through the various network shows. But the truth is I get most of my news from newspapers and magazines. I'm a print person.

How do you like movies when they get quasi-newsy? For instance Oliver Stone's dissertation on the Warren Commission, JFK?

Well, I found the reaction against it amusing.

Me, I've always doubted the Warren Commission. The killing of the president of the United States and its aftermath created a wound that has festered for thirty years; [we] never had closure.

It's not a *small* thing to distrust the Warren Commission. It's a big deal. It's a big deal because for 150 years we believed, at [different] levels of certainty and trust, that the government was on our side and was going to tell us the truth. This was the final blow. And then the Vietnam War put the nail in the coffin, whatever side you were on. It created a permanent suspicion from both the Left and the Right towards the government. Permanent suspicion.

Back to movies: You along with certain other male actors—Dustin Hoffman, Al Pacino, Robert DeNiro—revolutionized the world of enter-tainment during the early 1970s. Before, film stars were tall, blond, Anglo-Saxon and Ken-doll handsome. Then you guys arrived on the scene and the idea of the movie star was transformed to include someone who might be short, dark, and brooding.

I know what you're talking about. Around 1976 or thereabouts, I remember saying to my brother, "What I'd like to do is reserve a banquet room and invite Al Pacino, Bobby DeNiro and Dustin Hoffman"—none of whom I knew then—"to a party. I would raise a glass and say, 'I don't know exactly what it is that we've done, but we've done it. Here's a toast to us!'"

Do you think that one of the things your career has added up to is advancing the image of Jewish men in the American story? You were always such a consciously ethnic star and your films had the most open, unam-biguously ethnic themes, from **Duddy Kravitz** *on.*

I looked around one day in the industry and noticed, "Gee, no one else is admitting to being Jewish. I will." I always liked to be different. When I first started acting, the first jobs I had were Irish and I would have gotten away with being Irish had I wanted to. But I said I was Jew-ish, which is what Barbra [Streisand] did. And Jeff Chandler didn't. And Cary Grant and everyone else [didn't].

You're talking about changing the nature of what a movie star is. After you guys broke through, movie stars weren't just tall Waspy cow-boys but short, soulful, ethnic types.

Not so. It's true that I'm not Gary Cooper, but there have always been two traditions in the American cinema. One of which is John Wayne and Gary Cooper. And the other is James Cagney, Edward G. Robinson and Spencer Tracy. And that's who I am. And so is Dustin. There will always be Robert Redford and Kevin Costner, which is a classic Ameri-can thing, and there will always be guys like me.

The mythology of American movies is a broad spectrum. You can get everybody in. You can get Arnold Schwarzenegger and Danny DeVito, and you figure it out. They're both movie stars. Categorize them. I can't. Nor should you have to.

You seem such a political man. Have you been able to combine your art and your politics much over your career?

In a sense, that's what *Prisoner of Honor* was all about. I took *Down and Out in Beverly Hills* not because I wanted to do a piece on homelessness but because it was the only job offered to me at the time.

For the most part, I feel the need to separate those two parts of me. My goal is not to create movies that are political. On one hand, I'm an actor. On another, I'm a citizen.

I used to say the best life is, "to do a comedy, then do a drama, then do a vacation, but don't do anything twice." One of the things I've tried to do in my life is not play the same character twice. Now, I've done that, but mostly, I've tried not to. Actually, when I think about it, what's wrong with repeating yourself? That's how Gary Cooper and John Wayne became icons.

Do you think you're an icon?

Hardly.

An anti-icon?

I hope not. Talk about the sound of one hand clapping.

I don't know what I am. I have never been able to get out of me. I have no idea what my style is, what my celebrity is. I have never, for twenty years, been able to feel it from the outside.

Earlier, you spoke of the pleasures of idealism experienced by the 1960s political generation. Do you feel sad that your children aren't coming up in such an idealistic world?

I'm most concerned that my children will have a life of freedom and health. Who they are within the world is more up to them than anyone else. I can help my children be people of fine character who know the difference between good and evil. Politically, what I'm responsible for is to make sure they can breathe in and out and do that without secret police listening in.

Do you feel that we boomers are a successful or a failed generation.

I don't perceive my world through the filter of a generation. I am an American, not just a member of the postwar baby boom. As an American, I think that we have been changed and harmed by this series of events that has altered our optimism and our certainty about the future and out of which came what once would have been impossible—the Vietnam War and the Kennedy assassination.

On the other hand, when I said before that I finally feel the possibility of change, I'm not being glib. I'm saying that the change we've hoped for for twenty years might be possible.

We've all walked around and said, "When will they have enough? When are they going to feel it? When are they going to get connected? When? When?"

Well, we're beginning to wake up from this torpor, this belief that we can't prevail.

It has nothing to do with Democrats. It has nothing to do with Republicans. It's that people look out at homeless people and say, "I don't want to shoot them." Ten years ago, that's what I was told I would think—that I would want to shoot them. People are beginning to say, "I want to do something, finally."

POSTSCRIPT:

Some months after the last curtain went down on *Death and the Maiden*, Dreyfuss's production company, Dreyfuss-James Films, began assembling a movie about one of the most corrupting moments in recent American history. The film, *Quiz Show*, about the 1950s television production scandals, starred Ralph Fiennes and Rob Morrow, and was directed by Robert Redford, but it had Richard Dreyfuss's mark all over it. The film was full of Dreyfussisms, and many of the ideas he plays with here are really key elements of the movie. At the end of the day, Richard Dreyfuss, producer, expresses himself through film in a way that allows his previously separate identities, actor and citizen, to merge.

•••

Esther Dyson

*E*ach year Esther Dyson, futurist, philanthropist and venture capitalist, who has become one of the most influential figures and certainly the most influential women in cyberspace, brings together some 500 cybernauts for her annual PC Forum. The 1996 site was a posh desert resort in Tucson, Arizona, where, each morning, they gathered, hundreds of the computer industry's elite, huddled in small groups, swapping shop talk, making deals. In one corner, Michael Kinsley, editor of Microsoft's new on-line magazine, *Slate*, chatted with Bernard Vergnes, head of Microsoft's European operations. In another, Jim Barksdale, president of Netscape, talked *sotto voce* with Steve Case, chairman of America Online.

How Dyson makes her living is hard to classify. She is the editor and publisher of the widely respected newsletter *Release 1.0* (and of its Eastern European cousin, named with the double pun *Rel-East*). She is chairwoman of the Electronic Frontier Foundation, an industry-financed civil liberties watchdog group. She runs EDventure Ventures, an investment fund that plugs Western dollars into Eastern European technology startups. And she manages this conference, which is to the computer world something like what the Cannes Festival is to film.

Dyson comes from a famously brilliant clan. Her father is the physicist and author Freeman Dyson. Her mother, Verena Huber-Dyson, is a mathematician. Her brother, George, is the world's leading expert on the kayak. At fourteen, Esther began studying Russian; at sixteen, she was at Harvard; at twenty-five, she was reporting for *Forbes*; and by thirty, she was analyzing technology stocks for Wall Street. In 1982, Ben Rosen, now chairman of the Compaq Computer Corporation, asked her to help him put out his *Rosen Electronics Letter*, a pioneering publication about new technology, which the following year he sold to Dyson, along with PC Forum. Now, thirteen years later, *Release 1.0* circulates to 1,600 computer industry leaders attracted by its thoughtful inquiries into thorny issues like intellectual property. "What I try to do," Dyson says, "is find worthy ideas and people and get attention for them. I meet a lot of people, read a lot of stuff and try to promote new ideas."

I met with her at the beginning of 1996, and *The New York Times Magazine* ran the interview on July 7, 1996. Some weeks later Dyson signed a million-dollar contract for a book she is writing, one of whose central ideas is that in the future the value of intellectual property will be much reduced.

Microsoft's chairman, Bill Gates, is rumored to have once denounced you as a "socialist." Why?

There was some misunderstanding. He thought I was going around saying that intellectual property *should* be free. Actually, as the Web expands, the big effect will be that intellectual property is likely to lose a lot of its market value.

Let me explain. In the past, there was a relative shortage of creative work. There was a limited amount of content and people had a limited amount of time, and both were pretty much matched at current price levels. Now [since the Net became popular], there's much less cost associated with the distribution of content. If you put a book or a magazine up, all the costs that are attributable to paper, printing, inventory, holding publications in stores, go away. The other thing that is happening is that everybody can get up on the Net, sing their own songs, write their own poetry. You no longer need a publishing house to get a book published. So economics would say that since the supply of content is increasing, and the costs of duplication and distribution are diminishing, and people have the same amount of time or less, we are all going to pay less.

The idea of copyright will still be important because it is the law and it is moral. Second, a content producer will still want to control the integrity of a work. Even if I get no royalties, I want to make sure that my work isn't dumbed down and sold under someone else's name.

Whenever I talk about this, content producers go nuts. All I'm saying is that you need to figure out how to be paid for producing content because the business models are going to change.

If intellectual property is to have little monetary value, how will writers, artists, and composers make a living?

They'll get money for performances, readings, for going on line and interacting with their audiences. The free copies of content are going to be what you use to establish your fame. Then you go out and milk it. Also, a lot of creators will get paid by audience gatherers rather than the public. Content will be sponsored somewhat in the way network television programming is today.

I see this trend manifesting itself in my own life. Like everyone else, I get lots of free information on the Net. I also get offers to subscribe to stuff and my attitude often is, "Why should I pay to get more when I have too much already?" Now, I do pay for really special stuff. I also pay when I want to support work of a particular creator. Future scenarios on this are obvious. A consultant will write a book, hand it out for free and then charge higher fees for his services.

But a consultant isn't an artist. What will happen to the producers of literature?

Some of them will write highly successful works and then go out and make speeches.

What if they are shy?

Then they won't make any money.

I kind of like the way things are heading. If content is free or almost free, it will no longer be worth millions of dollars to promote the Jackie Collinses of the world.

Why?

Because what she produces is no good.

That may be. But millions buy her work.

Only because she's famous. Ideally, content will have to stand on its merits because the content becomes advertising for something else, rather than something that is advertised for. Thus, the content will have to be good. The good writers will get sponsored. The bad ones . . . maybe they'll be more useful in some other line of work. Listen, we're all facing this. For writers and artists, the ones who are going to survive economically are those who are most committed, those who are the best and those with other sources of income.

You are currently working on a book tentatively titled "Release 2.0: Second Thoughts on the Digital Revolution." Will you be getting an advance from a publisher or will you just post the whole thing up on the Net where anyone can take it for free?

I certainly want the book to make money. Content may have declining value, but it hasn't hit zero yet. It may be free on the Net, but people will still pay for it in a convenient form, which is a book with a cover and photographs. On the other hand, I do intend to post chunks of it on the Net. Whoever my publisher is, they'll have to feel comfortable with that, because my purpose is to get ideas out.

In many ways, I see the example of how I work as representative of the way things are going for creators. The newsletter I publish, *Release 1.0*—which costs $595 times 1,600 subscribers—breaks even. But the PC Forum, which is a kind of one-time performance each year, generates about $1.5 million in revenue, and participation is open only to newsletter subscribers. So the money-making part of my business is really an offshoot of the content production. Also, I do other things: consulting, speeches, which come to me because of my writing. In other words, I get paid for my activity rather than my products.

Why is your conference, the PC Forum, such a motive-power in the computer world?

Why do we have sexual reproduction? Because you get better offspring when you mix genes. And this conference is the greatest gene-pool mixer. The critical mass of the industry comes together and looks at the future. I try to take the core of the industry and put new viruses into it. I try to provoke people to think, to meet new ideas and new people. The result is that parts of deals often start there, trends are previewed. At the 1989 PC Forum, I got Lotus to announce Notes nine months before it was actually released. That really helped launch the product and the idea of groupware. Three years ago, we held a conference called "Content Is Key," with the idea that content, and not just tools, moves the world. It didn't single-handedly create the situation where people are now paying billions for content companies, but it helped the truth become recognized. I'm always considered a crackpot because I'm early with ideas. But that's O.K.

Do you use Windows 95?

No, I use Xywrite for a word processor, Eudora for E-mail and Netscape as my Internet browser. As for Windows 95, I gave my review copy to my stepmother and father. There's no compelling reason for me to make the switchover. My old stuff works. If I were starting over with a new computer, I'd get it loaded with Windows 95, and I do suppose in the long run, I'll move over to it. Right now, a switch would be complicated. Besides, it's not that easy to install, which reminds me of a joke: Why did God need six days to create the world?
Because he had no installed base.

Give me your prophesies on what the newspaper of the future will look like.

If you're looking twenty to thirty years from now, they will probably be printed out on local printers by whoever wants one. People will still want their news, but a lot of the traditional newspaper will disappear.

With electronic distribution, there's no real reason for recipes and foreign coverage to be stuck together in one big wad of paper. Instead, the newspaper of the future will be customized to a consumer's needs.

Stock prices and classifieds will probably drop off first—and this should happen in a very few years. After that, data-intensive items will go—like local movie listings. These are sections that are so much more valuable when they can be electronically searched, filtered and graphed.

It's really stupid to print out thousands of apartment listings for thousands of people. Just put them on line and let people select what they want by neighborhood and price range. As for investments, I want all the stock prices covered and filtered. I want to be able to call up all the securities that went up 10 percent in the last two months.

Many social critics worry that the new technologies will become as much of a social problem as television is—do you share their fears?

Television is a medium. The computer is the same. Television is a reflection of our social problems, as well as a creator of them. Now, television as a medium, beyond what it carries, encourages passivity. The Internet, beyond what it carries, encourages fragmentation. Some of that is great. People can find each other. The bad part is that it can encourage isolation from reality.

So what is real and what is virtual among the Net-aratti? Recently, there was a headline in the New York Post that read, "MY WIFE'S A CYBERSLUT! NEW JERSEY MAN SEEKS DIVORCE FOR COMPUTER ADULTERY." Do you think this woman was really an actual adulteress?

Oh, what is infidelity? Is it when some guy puts his thing into some woman? Or is it when his attention is taken away from the person to whom he owes loyalty?

But isn't cybersex really just metaphoric sex?

No, I think it's real. You can engage in emotional infidelity on the Net. You can be disloyal on line. With these people, I don't know what their marriage contract was. . . . If it was based on trust and exclusivity, she has betrayed him.

200

Tell me about growing up in 1950s Princeton?

Two of our neighbors were Nobel Prize winners. A third developed color television. As children, my brother, George, and I played on the derelict remains of one of the first computers, which was on the grounds of the Institute for Advanced Studies, where my father worked. Mrs. Hans Bethe [wife of a key architect of the A-bomb] was my godmother. Edward Teller [father of the H-bomb] came to the house often. I have these memories of him pouring excessive amounts of chocolate sauce over his ice cream while declaring, "My doctor says I shouldn't do this, but I never pretended to be an honorable man."

Were there any traumas in this idyll?

When I was 5, my mother ran off with a mathematician, though my father says I was quite philosophic about it. He claims I said, "Oh, who needs a mother once the milk is gone."

I had a huge amount of diverse experiences because my parents were divorced. Two years after my mother left, my father remarried and we settled into a traditional two-parent-family situation. My mother moved to Berkeley, where she had bohemian friends. She had a lover who was a computer programmer, and he was our favorite. The second computer I played on was his. He'd let my brother and me play with his punch cards. We'd try to read them based on the codes, which you could figure out.

Incidentally, my mother taught mathematics at the University of California in Berkeley at the same time as Ted Kaczynski [under Federal indictment as the Unabomber]. For all I know, my brother and I ran into him when we played tag in the math department elevators.

I'm fascinated by the Unabomber, whoever it was. Number one, he's a maniac. Number two, he's asking valid questions: Is technology bad? On the other hand, his manifesto is an example of a freelance writer who wasn't very good, but then, his writings are what got him caught. Interestingly, he could have put his manifesto on the Internet without going to *The New York Times* or *The Washington Post*. It was broadly distributed on the Internet anyway. I keep thinking that if he were even remotely plugged in, he could have been spouting all his stuff on the Net and that might have kept him from getting all bottled up inside.

Various legislators have proposed a number of new laws aimed at keeping criminals and terrorists from using the Net. Will these help?

They didn't catch the suspected Unabomber by tapping any lines. As head of the Electronic Frontier Foundation, I am troubled by most of these new laws, ostensibly aimed at criminals and pornographers but restrictive of *everyone's* freedom.

There are two specific items here—encryption and freedom of speech. Last year, Congress passed the Communications Decency Act, after very little debate. It was censorship, pure and simple. Fortunately, last month a Federal appeals court ruled the law unconstitutional. God bless those judges. They came in knowing little about the Net, but they opened their minds and said that the Internet was more like a soapbox than television and much more democratic.

As for encryption, the government keeps trying to do what governments naturally do: control people. They would like to ban encryption [which scrambles and unscrambles information on computers] to make it easier for law enforcement to listen in on people. In principle, all they want to do is stop crime. But the fact is encryption is defensive technology against big government, big business, big crime. I'd rather have defensive technology than leave the power to snoop in the hands of people I might not trust. Basically, the intelligence community wants this.

A couple of years ago, you visited the CIA headquarters in McLean, Virginia, and found people there to be quite uninformed about the new technologies. Were you surprised?

Mitch Kapor [founder of Lotus] and John Barlow [a co-founder of the Electronic Frontier Foundation] and I went down there. Barlow said they wanted to re-engineer and change their act. It was like talking to a bunch of middle-level managers who knew what the Net was but had no concept of how decentralizing it was. They said, "Do you think if we put our CIA information on the Net, people will appreciate us?" We said: "Your content isn't good enough to survive on the Web. You're the people who didn't understand what was happening in the Soviet Union."

What did they want to do—have a CIA home page?

Sort of. They were well meaning. But they had no sense of what they were trying to do. They wanted to be part of the Internet community and be on line, without having a sense of what that involves.

It's funny, as a kid, I grew up thinking that the CIA was very smart and very powerful. You know, I wanted to do a lot of things when I was a kid: marry Prince Charles, be a famous novelist, and I also thought I would make a very good spy—which I still think. But there was never anyone I ever wanted to spy for, including the CIA.

Did they ever ask you?

No. Well, once, after I had been going to Russia for about two years, an analyst for the CIA did, in fact, call me. It was a person who'd never been to Russia. She came in and asked one or two really stupid, uninformed questions. I said, "Gee, I wondered why it took you so long to call me." Because I had the impression they would call after I'd gone there twice. Anyway, I said, "Look, why don't you take these newsletters and read them and then call me back." She never did. I'm sorry, it was really a waste of my time and this person knew nothing. And she would have learned a lot about Russia by reading my newsletter—because it really is full of information.

It's no secret that you're high tech's most obsessive Slavophile. How did Russia and Eastern Europe become your personal passion?

I studied Russian in high school and at home. My father had always taught us that Soviets were bad but Russians were good. So I didn't grow up with the typical American thing of "those Red commies." Twenty-five years later, I visited Russia for the first time during *perestroika*. The minute I landed, I felt this "separated at birth" thing for the place. It was chaotic. Nothing worked. I wanted to help. And I think I've been able to. I get to Russia nearly every month and I do a lot of free consulting, teaching Russians in high tech how business in the West works. I give talks on business strategy, try to help people connect with their counterparts in the West. It's exhilarating work. The companies are not privatized state industries but start-ups. The people who staff them are not Soviet apparatchiks but programmers and physicists.

I also have a small venture capital fund that invests in Eastern European high tech. For years, I was urging my Silicon Valley friends to invest in Russia and Eastern Europe. Eventually, several friends raised a million and a half dollars for me to invest for them. This is a for-profit fund. Its goal is to make a profit by doing good things.

Has it been an advantage for you to be female in the mostly male world of high tech?

I'd say so. From the beginning, I was noticeable. I also had a psychological advantage because the thing that happens to most men in this business is that they start to compare themselves with Bill Gates and they feel inadequate. Obviously, I never had that problem. Also, in the computer world, I find, being a woman, you are not so pressed to conform. There's a broader range of character traits that are acceptable.

Are you sure? People in the computer business are always buzzing about your private life—or the fact that you don't seem to have one. Do you think they'd bother if you were male?

No. They'd say, "He's a bachelor," and move on. Or if he were gay, they'd move on even faster. But I feel this comes with the territory. When I was having this relationship with [publishing magnate] Bill Ziff, it was a relief to me when a magazine printed news of it—once something is in *Business Week*, it loses its magic.

What's your advice for the millions out there who are Internet-phobic?

If you're over 40, unless you're looking for a job, you are not going to die as a failure if you haven't used the Internet. People should not be made to feel socially inadequate if they are not wired. The important thing to remember is that this is not a new form of life. It is just a new activity.

•••

Cokie Roberts, Nina Totenberg, Linda Wertheimer

For the 14.7 million listeners of National Public Radio, Cokie Roberts, Linda Wertheimer, and Nina Totenberg are the Three Musketeers: gutsy, witty, informed reporters who break stories from inside the Washington political machine. As a troika, they have succeeded in revolutionizing political reporting.

Twenty years ago, Washington journalism was pretty much a male game, like football and foreign policy. But along came demure Linda, delicately crashing onto the presidential campaign bus; then entered bulldozer Nina, with major scoops on Douglas Ginsberg and Anita Hill; and in came tart-tongued Cokie with her savvy Congressional reporting. A new kind of female punditry was born.

Today, the three are expanding their audiences by branching out into television. Roberts, in addition to her NPR wake-up stint on *Morning Edition*, is the co-host with Sam Donaldson of ABC's *This Week*. She is also Ted Koppel's frequent understudy on *Nightline*. Wertheimer anchors NPR's flagship broadcast, *All Things Considered*, and is a frequent guest on Sunday morning news talk shows. And Totenberg, NPR's legal affairs correspondent, does commentary and reporting for ABC.

In real life, these broadcasting Musketeers are the closest of friends, sharing vacations, theater subscriptions, everyday advice, and general emotional support. They have husbands who, in varying degrees, participate in the friendship. Cokie Roberts is married to Washington pundit Steven Roberts, with whom she has two grown children, and together they write a syndicated political column for New York Daily News Features; Totenberg is wedded to Floyd Haskell, a former Senator from Colorado; and Wertheimer's husband, Fred, is chairman of Democracy '21, an organization fighting for campaign finance reform.

One morning in the fall of 1993, in Roberts's cramped office at ABC News in Washington, the three reporters ruminated about the pains and pleasures of their breakthrough careers. While Cokie knitted, the four of us dished. The interview was published in *The New York Times Magazine* on January 2, 1994.

Getting the women together for interview had been a near impossible task. "You'll never be able to this carry this off," Nina Totenberg insisted when I first suggested that we do a group interview. "It's impossible. The three of us are never together. Besides, all you'll get is a jumble of voices."

"Listen, I did a group interview for *Playboy* once with three top Sandinistas and they had much bigger egos than any of you. Plus it was in Spanish."

Totenberg seemed momentarily intrigued.

But she was right. Getting everyone in one room at the same time was a logistical nightmare. After endless rounds of phone calls, we finally settled on a late October Monday morning at the Washington Hotel Westin Ana. I took a special room so that we'd have privacy and had a huge breakfast brought in. There could be no excuses to break up this hard won moment. No telephones could ring. Whether the women wanted coffee or crumpets, everything was perfect as pie.

Everything but Robert Packwood. The morning of the interview was the morning the world learned of Senator Packwood's very interesting sex-and-legislation diary. He was to go before the full Senate that very day, explaining how he had become the Frank Harris of parliamentarians (and why no one should read his literary production).

Thus, we did the first interview session under conditions where the women's hearts and heads were elsewhere. Nina Totenberg actually stared out the window in the direction of the Capitol. We barely got an hour's worth of taping done. And little of it was worth printing. As soon as was minimally decent, the three tore out the door and headed for the city and their story.

It was the ever-organized Cokie who later dragooned her two friends into giving me another hour and a half at her office. Most of this piece comes from that second session.

Today the Senate discusses what to do with its most famous diarist. Do any of you stand a chance of making an unsolicited appearance in Senator Packwood's little memoir? "Today I placed my hand on Nina

Totenberg's knee..."

Nina: Not unless he's been fantasizing.

Linda: This is part of being older. I mean, I would say that in the last ten or so years any member of Congress that came after me would be somebody with an asterisk by his name that said "senile," "demented."

Cokie: The Members of the House—they're just babies! They're soooo much younger than we are. They call us "ma'am." They see us as dowagers.

Nina: Speak for yourself, Cokie!

As young girls, whom did you dream of being?

Nina: Nancy Drew. She was perfect. She could do everything, from perfect dives off a diving board to finding the bad guy.

Cokie: And she had a racy blue roadster. As for me, there was never anybody I wanted to be. I suppose I expected my life to be like my mother's. But I did not have some special heroine.

Linda: Well, your mother counts: Lindy Claiborne Boggs, your father's closest counselor and then a Congresswoman herself, counts as a heroine. In my own case I wanted to be Pauline Frederick, the NBC correspondent to the United Nations. I remember watching television in 1956, and there was Pauline out on the steps of the United Nations when the tanks were rolling into Hungary. I was thinking, "I didn't know women could do that." And in fact, they couldn't.

When did you conclude that they "couldn't?"

Linda: In 1967, after working for a couple years at the BBC in England, I went to NBC in New York for a job. And there this "gentleman" informed me that "women are not credible on the air." He then offered to introduce me to a woman at NBC whose career he thought I should emulate—she'd been a researcher for ten years—and I just started yelling at him. It was in neon: "This Is the Only Job a Woman Can Have!"

Cokie: I had a very similar experience in that same time frame. In 1966 I left an on-air anchor television job in Washington, D.C., to get married. My husband was at *The New York Times*. For eight months I job-hunted at various New York magazines and television stations, and wherever I went I was asked how many words I could type.

I was told quite explicitly that women would not be hired to do the kinds of jobs that I was looking for, that women's voices were not credible, were not authoritative to deliver the news, women could not be writers at news magazines because men would be working for them and men could not work for women.

It took me eight months to get a job in New York. The discrimination was just blatant. And the trouble with it was that each time you have these experiences you would go home and think you were crazy. And I was married. I'd go home and say this stuff to my husband and he really thought I was crazy.

Nina: It was blatant. You were constantly thrown in the position of feeling like you were asking for favors when you applied for a job. Two experiences come to mind. The first was in 1965. I called *The Quincy Patriot Ledger* because I heard there was an opening, and this male editor said to me, "Oh, we don't hire women." The Civil Rights Act had recently passed. I'm not sure I knew that women were covered. It was so much the way things were that I wasn't outraged.

Ten years later, I was a somewhat accomplished journalist. I'd won prizes. I'd had jobs for a long time. And I was looking for another job. I had lunch with the bureau chief of a distinguished chain of newspapers. This man looked at me and without a moment's hesitation said, "But, Nina, we already have our woman." I felt the rage well up through my gullet and I just shoved it back down again. What could I do? Throw my food in his face?

Cokie: One other thing—while these men were saying we couldn't have the jobs, their hands were on our knees. We were having the experience of what now we call sexual harassment, but they didn't have a term for it then. But it was "The Works." It was the full gamut.

Nina: There were a couple of instances that were truly awful, but most of the time if you just moved away about a foot, they got the message and there was no scene. That's all you ever wanted, to avoid a scene.

And did you get the job?

Nina: No. But you weren't getting the job anyway.

Cokie: Probably the reason he was having lunch with you to talk about the job was to see . . . you know, how. . . . Well, it took us all a long time to figure that out. And I was married at twenty-two and thought that a wedding ring was protection. Ha!

Twenty-five years later, along comes Anita Hill. Given your own experiences, you must have empathized.

Nina: Well, since Anita Hill was my story, I should answer that. Many, many years earlier, I had been aggressively pursued by a supervisor. That may have helped in talking to Anita Hill. But other than that, I just thought it was a good story, as much about the Judiciary Committee as anything else.

Cokie: I do think, though, that in some ways women of our age were less sympathetic to Anita Hill because what happened to her didn't seem so bad as compared to what happened to us. I mean, it was just talk. And she had the job. So when the hearings happened it was a very interesting moment in our offices, where the young women were truly appalled and the older women were basically saying, "Ahhh, that's nothing, babe. Let us tell you the way it used to be."

Since we're talking history, how did you three meet?

Linda: Cokie and I went to school together at Wellesley, but we didn't know each other there. She was in the class ahead of me, and from a famous family. Everyone said, "Oh, she's the daughter of the House majority whip, she's Hale Boggs's daughter."

Nina: I was the one who drafted Cokie for NPR. That must have been 1977. Linda and I were there already, and there was an opening for another reporter. I had heard that Steve Roberts and his wife were back in Washington after living overseas for a few years, that she was looking for work. So I called him and he brought over her resume. And I remember Linda saying, "Is that Cokie Boggs?" The rest is history.

Cokie: When I came in for an interview Linda and Nina were there, greeting me and encouraging me. And it just made all the difference in the world. NPR was a place where I wanted to work because they were there.

Nina: NPR had quite a few women on staff. It was, and still is, a shop where a woman could get considerable visibility and responsibility. NPR's wages were at least a third lower than elsewhere in the industry, and for what they paid, they couldn't find men.

Linda: Cokie joined me over on the Hill covering Congress. The hilarious thing was that I had spent years trying to develop a beat in Congress, working really hard, trying to understand what the talk meant, how the monster actually worked. I thought I was good at it. Then Cokie arrived, after living in Greece for years, and I had the feeling that she was born to understand Congress.

Cokie: We were a great team. Tip O'Neill always said to me, "I give youse girls from NPR first shot at everything."

How did the tag "Three Musketeers" get pinned to you?

Cokie: Oh, how does any of that get started? It's basically, "they all look alike." We were three women who were very good friends. We socialized together, sat together in the office, had our desks close together. We were all the same age and people just didn't distinguish between us.

Are there qualities that any of the three of you envy in the others?

Nina: I envy Cokie's tact. . . . Linda and I started a union at NPR. During negotiations we all had roles: I was the Screamer, Linda was the Rational One, Tactful Cokie closed the deal. We don't do this anymore because the NPR boys have become quite good at negotiations.

Cokie: Well, I envy Nina's guts. Sometimes when we're all sitting together at the office we see Nina working the phones, and Linda and I just look at each other and say, "Dear God. . . . " I also envy Linda's incredible persistence. I mean, when she goes in to a live event, she can tell you every little detail down to the mortar in the cracks of the building she's about to sit in.

Linda: I would say I envy Nina's courage, and Cokie taught me a great deal about not blowing up. I have an awful temper.

Has Cokie ever been rude to anybody?

Cokie: Oh, sure. Let me think. When John Tower was up for Secretary of Defense and was running into confirmation problems about his alleged womanizing and drinking. There was concern about him having his finger semi-on the button. So Senator Tower went on the Brinkley show. It was live, and it was remarkable because he came on and took the pledge not to drink. David was away, and Sam Donaldson, who was hosting, said something like, "Well, Senator, it's not just alcohol, you know. There have been charges of womanizing." So Senator Tower says, "I'm a single man. I do date women." And then he says, "What is your definition of womanizing, Sam?" And then, basically because I'm sitting there in a skirt, he turns to me and says, "Cokie, do you have a definition of the term?"

Linda: And Cokie said, "Well, I think most women know it when they see it, Senator." I watched that and thought, "Ohhhhhhhh, my God...." It was one of those moments. I had a similar one with the sportscaster Red Barber. We were on the air and he said something to me about how many really fine women there are at NPR. And then he said something like, "Speaking of the other gender, do you think Winning Colors is gonna be in trouble with the muddy track at Pimlico?"

Cokie: This is an attempt to sabotage.... A total sandbag job.

I don't get it.

Cokie: Well, that's the point. [Laughs.] You're live on the air, and you've got the world's sports expert on with you. You're a girl, right? And he just segues from this gracious thing to asking you a totally impossible question, like, "What is 4,852 times 900,848—and tell me right now."

Linda: And I suppose he didn't think I had any idea who Winning Colors was. Well, I just started laughing. "I'm really rooting for the filly, Red," I said. "But I think we've had a lot of rain, and you know, Pimlico is really going to be muddy, no question about it." Hah, hah. I always read the racing news in *The New Yorker*. The bastard didn't get me!

Well, Linda, perhaps the late Red Barber could have traded notes with Ross Perot on their dislike of you?

Cokie: Linda spoke vicious truths to Ross Perot.

Linda: Yes, I asked him about some history and he got very upset.

Cokie: He went nuts! I heard the broadcast while driving down Sunset Boulevard. I had been interviewing somebody and I was driving back to my hotel, and there on the radio was Ross Perot barking at Linda, "This is a classic setup. Is this a radio program? You're not just somebody calling in? Whoever you're trying to do a favor for, you've done it, and I'm sure you had a smirk on your mouth as you got me into this." It was a riot. I almost had a wreck!

Nina: Here's Linda's thoroughness again. Linda had covered the tax bill, in which Perot had succeeded in getting himself a multimillion dollar loophole of the kind that he was condemning all over the country. So she had him dead to rights because she'd been there when it happened. He went ballistic.

Ross Perot didn't much care for you either, Cokie.

Nina: In the beginning he loved her. He wanted her to run for vice president.

Cokie: Oh, that was just a rumor. I had written an op-ed piece that talked about why he was having the effect he was having. And I had heard from people in his organization that this was the best description of the phenomenon they had seen. But then I had him on *Nightline* and he again talked about us not asking him questions that he wanted to be asked. The whole interview became just unbelievably testy, and it just got ruder and tenser and awful. We just sat there thinking, "Is he gonna get up and leave? Is he gonna throw the chair? Is he going to strangle himself on his microphone?" The next week he gave his comment about not minding reporters, just female reporters, "They're all trying to prove their manhood."

Actually, you three have been charged with proving your womanhood. The conventional wisdom has it that with the increasing number of women in the Washington press corps, you have changed the nature and content of political reporting.

Linda: Well, we were interested in the range of issues that have defined the role of women in politics.

Cokie: This was more true in covering Congress than on the campaign trail, because you're covering issues on an ongoing basis. During the 1990 budget-agreement talks, when the budget negotiators from the Bush administration and Congress were all holed up at Andrews Air Force Base, our male colleagues would ask them, "How many MXs are there still left in the budget?" And I'd ask, "Are mammograms still covered?" In the 1988 presidential campaign I felt that had there not been so many women on the campaign bus, Gary Hart's womanizing wouldn't have been a story. Hart's behavior was something that a lot of us had talked about in the prior election. We'd wondered at what point Gary Hart's relationships with women were a story. Then the 1988 race came around and it looked like he might become president. Because there were a lot of women talking about this as an issue, that might have had the effect of sending *The Washington Post* and *Miami Herald* out on that story.

Do you ever wonder if it was a mistake to politicize the private lives of politicians? Bill Clinton was rumored to have a Gary Hart-ish sexual life, yet he's turned out to be quite supportive of women's rights.

Cokie: So's Bob Packwood.

Has Bob Packwood's story long been known in Washington, as Gary Hart's was?

Nina: In a way. I've run into female staffers who ran Senatorial offices ten years ago, who would, as a matter of course, instruct newcomers not to be in a room alone with him. If you were a woman on Capitol Hill, you knew who was a bottom pincher and who wasn't. If you were a female reporter you still had to interview everybody, but there were certain Senators you knew to sit far away from—or dress like a nun with.

Cokie: The point is that ten years ago no one would have thought Packwood's behavior with women was a story.

Nina: Cokie and I did *Nightline* recently with Dianne Feinstein. Senator Feinstein was the only member of the Senate we asked who would go on the program about Packwood. And she felt very strongly, as she said on the air, that there was absolutely a direct connection between Anita Hill and Bob Packwood—that the Packwood disciplinary proceeding would not have happened without the Thomas-Hill hearings.

Your friendship sounds so idyllic. Do you ever get angry at one another?

Nina: Oh, we have been angry, but it never lasts long.

Linda: Mostly there's a lot of cooperation; there were plenty of times when one of us would have to go somewhere and the other one would cover. I'd go to a news conference and then come back and say, "Here's what happened, and the cut of tape you want is there." And we just had that kind of trust. And we also had the capacity to divide up the work without getting competitive.

Not even a wee bit competitive?

Cokie: Whatever competition there is . . . is pretty healthy. I mean, there have been lots of primary nights when we'd sit there at three o'clock in the morning exhausted, trying to outwrite each other. And if the other one had not been there, you wouldn't have done it, because at moments like that you're so tired that all you want to do is go to bed.

Nina: Our beats do overlap, but we manage it. Cokie and Linda both cover Congress and the political beat. And I certainly trample on their turf. If there's a big confirmation battle over a Supreme Court nominee, there's no question it's my story. And they've always deferred to me on that. Totally. And if I'm covering a political story, like a presidential campaign, I have no expectation that I'll get first dibs.

Is the friendship something like . . . a three-way marriage?

Nina: It's a much more forgiving situation than a marriage is. But like in a marriage, we have a friendship that's matured over the years.

Cokie: Linda and I basically had the same job for a very long period of time. And we worked together at the Capitol, we worked together on the campaigns, and we worked together at public television. And I think it's remarkable how we did not get angry with each other. The strength of the friendship through all of that, I think is quite something.

Linda: And whenever there have been stresses on the friendship, it's not been professional. It's been because somebody's had some kind of personal problem and we've had to adjust to provide the support.

Cokie: We've had life situations in the course of our friendships that have...you know, brought us closer together but have also caused each of us to be in need of more support at different times. For Nina it was Anita Hill. We've lived through the deaths of Linda's parents, the death of my sister...

In closing, how do you feel when you meet younger women in journalism who haven't any idea how rough things used to be in the "bad old days"?

Nina: Murder comes to mind.

Linda: I think what happens now is that the young women get the first job, and the next job, and achieve some level of success. But at some point they hit a wall and they find out that until and unless a substantial number of mostly white men die, they may not be able to move up. It's a shock to their systems.

Cokie: On one hand you always have to fight the feeling of saying, "Just you wait, my pretties..." You don't want to be the Wicked Witch of the West, but you do know that they will run into sex discrimination as they proceed in their journalistic lives. Still, you're proud they don't have to fight as hard as we did. We opened things up—for them.

•••

John Sayles

Within the world of the cinema, John Sayles manages to do what so many others find impossible: call his own shots by writing/directing/financing/editing movies on hidden corners of American life. In an industry where *Twister* is the money-cow ideal, Sayles somehow manages to make wonderful small pictures on themes that the rest of movieland ignores. His classic *The Return of the Secaucus Seven* focuses on a group of sixties activists at midlife, still grasping for their ideals. *Baby, It's You*, Sayles's only major-studio Hollywood flick, shed warm light on the big American secret—social class. *Matewan* concerned a West Virginia coal miners strike. *City of Hope* was a brawny meditation on modern urban politics. *Lone Star*, Sayles's 1996 masterpiece, is about immigration and the Southwest border. In addition to directing, Sayles writes novels and short stories, including the 1991 *Los Gusanos*, a broadly drawn epic about Miami Cubans who, like the characters in *The Return of the Secaucus Seven*, are desperately clinging to their ideals in an atmosphere of betrayal.

Sayles met me on a sweltering July 4th afternoon in 1991, in an Italian restaurant in Poughkeepsie, New York. Long based in Hoboken, New Jersey, he and his companion, Maggie Renzi, had recently moved to a farm in upstate New York so he could work in an atmosphere of serenity.

The restaurant site for the interview had been picked because Sayles is an insistent guardian of his own privacy and would not meet in his home. Or even near it. However, over pasta and Diet Cokes in a public place, John Sayles—tall, darkly handsome—was ebullient, open, and giving.

The Progressive published the final interview that November.

John Sayles, you're really one of the only directors around who's telling certain kinds of stories.

. . . Or who's getting to.

How do you feel about being one of the few who "gets to" make movies about coalminers, sixties activists, academic lesbians, and urban politicos.

Well, it's unconscious. I'm not consciously saying, "This is what THEY are doing, so I will do something different." I'm a writer. I write stuff and then I realize, "This doesn't really fit into any genre." Usually, when I have to pitch a script to a potential backer, I have to tell the story. I find I can't say, "This is a cross between *Rambo* and *Missing*." My pieces tend to be between genres. They tend to be about characters, about situations, rather than say, "an action-adventure-police" story. So the stories that I happen to be interested in telling are that way.

How is it that you manage to be a man with a sixties consciousness who is directing?

Well, I think I've been very lucky. For one thing, my bread-job has been a very lucrative one. My bread-job was writing movies for other people. So even when I first started and was getting "scale," my bread job was ten thousand dollars a movie. Most people's bread-job is waiting tables or teaching in some form, where you make a base pay of ten thousand a year! I can write a genre picture and do three or four of those a year— so even when I was just getting scale, I could make fifty thousand dollars in one year. It only took me two years to get up enough money to do *The Return of the Secaucus Seven*. I financed that picture myself.

I financed *The Brother From Another Planet* myself. I was one of the major investors in *Matewan*. So rather than make that one independent film and have to sit around for another five years till someone gave me the money to do another one, I've been able to put myself back into the game by financing my films myself.

So when there's a story you want to shoot, you'll write a TV movie and then, voila!, you've got seed money?

Yeah. Or I'll doctor a script [for someone else]...and that's fun as a technician. It's not something that you're going to put your soul into, because it's somebody else's story. When it's done, at least I have the money to get my own film started. With *Lianna*, we started needing to raise a budget of $800,000. We ended up making it for $300,000, of which I put up $30,000. Now, most people I know, when they start to make movies, they don't have $30,000. Thirty thousand is as tough to raise as three million, if you're talking people into it. So that's one thing: I've had that economic advantage.

About **The Return of the Secaucus Seven:** *were you yourself active during the sixties?*

Certainly. But only as a foot soldier. I was at events with thirty thousand other people, on marches and things like that. I went to Williams College.

Williams? I had the impression you came from a grittier background, that your family was more blue-collar.

It's a long story how I went there. I really didn't know if I wanted to go to college, but I ended up there. I knew I really didn't want to be in the Army, whether there was a war or not. When the anti-war stuff happened, I would occasionally participate. But student politics always seemed a little strange to me. That wasn't where the problems were happening. Certainly, not at Williams College. It was an elite school, but in a funny way. It wasn't very competitive. It may be competitive to get in there—which I didn't know. I sort of had a guidance counselor say to me, "Here's two places I want you to apply to—Williams College and Colgate." I hadn't applied anywhere yet.

I ended up feeling like if I went to Colgate, they'd want me to play serious football and I had played much too serious football in high school already. So my place of education was accidental. Williams was the kind of place where, when the black kids took over the administration building, the first thing the college president did was make sure they had enough food.

Were you involved in a march on Washington where a deer got killed en route—"Bambicide" as you call it in The Return of the Secaucus Seven?

No, but we did on a couple of marches get stopped by cops on the general theme of "I know where these guys are going—lets stop them and search for drugs." Well, it's a funny thing. The people that the film is based on are not so much people I knew in college, but people I knew afterwards when I was living in East Boston. I knew a lot of people who were involved in the little city halls there—a bunch of people who had known each other in the sixties.

No doubt you saw The Big Chill, *which many critics noted was about a group of ex-sixties types getting together for a long week-end reunion—just like* The Return of the Secaucus Seven.

It's a different movie. It's called "The Big Chill" for a reason. It's a film about people who have either lost their ideals or are realizing that they never had them in the first place.
Secaucus Seven is about people who are desperately, desperately trying to hold onto their ideals. That's a very different group of people. "Chill" people are more upper middle class. The *Secaucus* group are more lower middle class—some of them are probably the first people in their families who went to a four-year college. And they've chosen to be downwardly mobile. The movie I think *The Return of the Secaucus Seven* most resembles is a Swiss movie, *For Jonah, Who Will Be Twenty-Five in the Year 2000.* That was the precursor.

Come on, admit it: surely you felt a bit...cribbed by The Big Chill. *The structure and the idea seem so similar: a group of ex-sixties folk get together for a long week-end and wonder what they did with their lives.*

No. I actually didn't have any big problem with it. I thought it was more thoughtful than the usual Hollywood movie. It's very much about people who do exist. It's just that they weren't my friends. It was not a rip-off. There's too much thought, and too much feeling in that movie.

He [director Larry Kasdan] sees the world differently.... It was more, "Here's what happens when the people *I know* get together for a three day weekend."

But again, we come to the original question, you're about the only bona fide member of the sixties generation making movies—how come?

I don't think I'm the only one. DePalma, Scorsese, they were very much of that moment and then they grew into doing different things. Wasn't one of DePalma's first films, *Greetings*, about the draft? Besides, I keep running into these people who used to be in the Weather Underground who are producers now.

As a director, I get very few offers to direct anything. The offers I get are from independent producers who are so out of the loop that they think [my involvement] will help them get their movie sold. And they don't know. If there's a list of preferred directors, I'm probably not even on it.

You're often compared to Spike Lee. Fair?

Well, he's doing things that nobody else was interested in doing for a long time. But he's been much more successful at getting out to a large audience than I am. He's doing pretty much what he wants to do and still reaching some kind of mass audience. It's not the mass audience that something like *Terminator II* reaches, but he's working on studio budgets now, and that's a real achievement; to be able to do that and still make the movie you want to make.

Something we talked about before, that I'm the only one making these kinds of movies. However, I find that in this country there's a real suspicion of content—sometimes, a real resentment of content. Some of it came out of the *auteur* theory. There is a whole raft of movie critics who basically feel like, OK, what we treasure a film director, an *auteur*, for, is their ability to put their stamp on any material. The minute you're talking about that, you're automatically talking about *style*. On the other hand, there's a much smaller group of people who only care about content and whether you're politically correct or not.

I'm sure that Sam Goldwyn, Sr., said a lot of intelligent things, but the one that we always quote is "If you want to send a message, call Western Union." [Cinematographer-Director] Haskell Wexler and I were talking about this once. He said, "All films are political." I agreed. I said, "*Beverly Hills Cop II* is a political film." If you look at it, it's about attitudes about women and violence and it says a lot. But nobody would look at the director of *Beverly Hills Cop II*, and say, "Hey! That's a political film." Because those are mainstream values—so no one notices them.

So I think that one of the reasons why I am one of the few people making those kinds of movies may be that if you're working in the mainstream media, if you're going to story conferences, what almost always gets sacrificed is *content*. Because they distrust it. Because it is almost always considered secondary to making this great arcade-like ride that the people are going to pay money to get on.

What I like [to ask myself of] moviemakers is, "Are they doing well what they set out to do?" That's why I like "The Naked Gun" movies. They do that well, and they work hard at it. Actors I like tend to be people who have some talent and who work at it. Like Tom Hanks. I see that with directors—Sidney Lumet. He's made a lot of impressive movies and is still trying. There are quite a few people. I like the Coen Brothers movies, I think they are very good writers. Especially for people who give as much attention to visual stuff, their scripts are very literate. Most movies seem very badly written.

You're still telling stories like no one else—and you're constantly breaking formulas. In Matewan, *the good guys lose and the community is shattered. That's against the Hollywood formula of happy endings for the protagonists.*

In *Matewan*, the hero does not pick up a gun, and that was a problem that most mainstream moviegoers had with it.

It was, "Now wait a minute, the hero really is a pacifist. He's not going to turn out to be a guy who's a great shot and who takes his gun off the wall. In so many Westerns—[for instance] *Shane*, that's the tension of the story; this guy has decided he's a pacifist and there's this thrill in the audience when he finally straps his gun on one more time. It's a difficult thing to fight.

When we were creating the film, it was hard to create a guy who is telling people something that might get them killed...we gave him a speech. He said, "Look, the way things are now, the coal owners are just waiting for a chance to trounce you. Yes, if you pick up the gun, you'll give them that excuse. If you do that, the war is going to start and you're going to lose."

And they do—and that's what happens in Matewan. *But to change the subject, you've just published a novel about Cuban-Americans in Miami,* Los Gusanos. *How's writing a book different? It must be a place where you have total control. After all, as the writer, you're God.*

Well, I don't have to worry about how we can afford extras. In *Los Gusanos*, I do the Bay of Pigs invasion and I don't have to worry about how we get the tanks and the extras—all those practical things that make a movie difficult. What you don't have in a book is all the fun of a collaboration, and I do think movies are collaborative, *auteur* theory aside.

You wrote Los Gusanos *between movies. How did you keep your concentration?*

Well, as far as research went, I never left the novel. Thirteen years ago, I had an outline, which I pretty much kept to.... What I did was write the first few chapters and then I couldn't go on without much more research. So I did movies, and research while I did the movies. Whenever I'd run into people who were Cuban-Americans, I'd talk to them and that got filed. There were two long Writer's Guild strikes and during them I got to work on fiction. And then finally after I finished *Matewan*, I took a year off and finished it. That was twelve years after I started.

But you know, nothing I've done has been a career move. Every project, from the movies to the novel, was something I wanted to do, and that's the move. It's not, "How do I get myself to the point where I am going to be in the Hollywood system?" I never thought, "If I take a year off, I'll lose where I am." Being a fiction writer is a nice net to have. I like writing much more than being a writer. If I have to spend two years when I can't get a movie off the ground, well, I can always write novels.

About Los Gusanos. *I had this feeling that one of the things that appealed to you about Cuban-Americans was their commitment to a cause?*

To me, the important spectrum in *Los Gusanos* is not Right wing or Left wing. Because most of the people are right-of-center. It's between "believers" and "cynics." A lot of what I'm dealing with is how do you still act once you know too much to be a true believer, to be a narrowly focused, almost religious believer.

I'm interested in commitment and how we still have commitment. I have a character in the book who was in the Lincoln Brigades, and I have a lot of respect for those guys. In this nursing home in the book, you have this guy who's a veteran of the Lincoln Brigades right next to this guy who was in the Bay of Pigs. My question is how do you keep commitment once you KNOW. How do you not get cynical?

*You ask the same question in many of your films. What kind of movies did you see as a kid—***High Noon?**

Mostly Westerns and comedies. I only liked color movies. I watched a lot of TV, too.

Were your folks movie buffs?

Readers. They really encouraged us to read. Both of my parents were teachers and then my father became a school administrator later on. And both of their fathers were cops. I think the main way my parents were influential is just that they encouraged us to read a lot and they didn't lay any big trips about, "This is what you are supposed to be or do." Enough people in my family did things that they didn't like and they didn't want us to do that. I wanted to be a pitcher for the Pittsburgh Pirates.

When I got out of college, it was a bad time to get a job. I ended up working in nursing homes and factories, because that was something I had done before. If I had gone into anything else that paid a little more, they would have said, "You know, you're signing up for the long run. We want people who will be here for fifteen years and be happy about it." I wasn't interested in that. I worked as an orderly because it definitely was not a career decision. But what was good about it was that the minute the day ended, I was no longer an employee.

So in the entertainment industry, when I went into it, I was only interested in it for the work. I wasn't interested in it for getting a big house.

All I was interested in was, "I think it would be really great to make movies. This is the kind of story-telling that I really like. How do I get to do that and do that on my terms?"

At first, I worked for [B-movie mogul] Roger Corman, and it was really fun. It was the equivalent of working in a hospital. You didn't have to take that home. Nobody took themselves that seriously. They worked hard. Nobody fought about, "What does this movie mean?" What you knew was that every ten pages, or every fifteen pages, you were going to have some kind of animal attack and it's meant to be fun.

You seem so nonchalant about what you do—as if it's as natural as breathing air. Most film directors I've met are religious about their profession.

I'm *not* nonchalant. I'm interested in the stuff I do being seen as widely as possible—but I'm not interested enough to lie. There comes a time in any story when you say, "I know how to make this more popular." But then, it's bullshit. I have worked on movies that were basically fantasy movies—where you try not to say things you don't believe in and you can do it because the whole thing is really about the genre.

For instance, *Alligator.* If you read the script, other than being a monster movie in the classic Japanese tradition, it is about how social problems start in the lower classes and nobody is really dealing with them until they start eating the rich people. *Battle Beyond the Stars* to me is about death, but finally it is just "The Seven Samurai Go to Space." That's what was handed to me to write and that's why people watch it. That's what Roger [Corman] gave me to do. *Battle Beyond the Stars* is about how these different creatures [who] are not human beings feel about death.

The important thing to me is the conversation. The important thing is to get that moment when someone in the audience thinks, "I have never spent time with the people in this movie," and then they realize that because of the movie, they have.

So that conversation is what I'm ambitious about, being a part of that. To a certain extent, so many mainstream movies are just consumable items. They aren't things people can remember and apply to their life. I think, in general, consciousness is a real important thing and that's one of the reasons why I'm glad I work in the consciousness industry. I think in a cumulative way movies do have an effect and if you don't like the effect that they are having, maybe you can do something to counteract it. At least, you can be part of the conversation.

•••

Dan Rather

Interviewing a figure as legendary as Dan Rather is daunting for a fellow journalist. He knows all the twists and turns. He uses them himself. Thus in the summer of 1995, when the *Times Magazine* sent me over to CBS's studio's on West 57th Street to try to fish out an in-depth with him, I felt at a great disadvantage.

We sat around his office above the set for the *CBS Evening News* for four or five sessions. And the material was flat. Part of the problem seemed to be his likable tendency to be a "gentlemen" when talking about those who'd betrayed him. The other part was that he was just too much in control there in his roost. One day, in desperation, I threw my hands in the air and declared, "Dan, this isn't working. There's too much mask here. We don't see the real you."

Not long after that, one of Rather's assistants called with an invitation. Would I like to join him for a drive through certain parts of Texas which had great emotional importance to him? We could do the interview on the road, in the car. He'd be away from the office. Relaxed.

It was a marvelous offer.

Dan Rather, then sixty-three, had just barely survived his year as co-anchor of the *CBS Evening News* with Connie Chung. He survived the budgetary slashings of CBS's chairman, Laurence Tisch, and the ratings dive that the news program later suffered.

"I guess some of this comes from being born during the Depression," Rather said on the August 1995 morning when we drove through southeast Texas in a pickup truck. "Also, I realized pretty early on that while I had skills, there were an awful lot of other people with better skills. All that may have given me strong survival skills."

These words were being spoken at a time when Rather's survival skills were likely to be tested once again. A couple of days later Tisch announced plans to merge CBS with the cash-poor Westinghouse Electric Corporation. This move convinced many CBS staff members that there might be still more cuts in their future.

We were talking on a blazingly gorgeous morning a full month before Rather would begin his fifteenth season as the *CBS Evening News* anchor and managing editor. Our goal was to visit the places of his childhood, to do an interview free of the formalities of his New York life.

We dashed to Huntsville, the site of Rather's alma mater, Sam Houston State College. Then it was on to the oil town of Wharton, his birthplace. Finally, we drove to Austin for dinner with Mrs. Dan Rather, the artist Jean Rather, then fifty-nine.

Between stops, there were gawkings at cattle, an encounter with a highway patrolman who pulled us over for driving without seat belts, and constant trips to pay phones as Rather sought updates on the pending CBS-Westinghouse merger.

The New York Times Magazine ran the interview on September 10, 1995.

David Letterman did a Top Ten list the other night about the CBS-Westinghouse merger. Among his predictions: The current CBS brass would be replaced by a "whole new batch of weasels," and your next co-anchor would be a coffeepot. Can you work with a coffeepot?

The real question is, "How will a coffeepot feel about working with me?" [Laughs.] Actually, I'd prefer a refrigerator. But I'm not sure I'll have a coffeepot or a refrigerator because I'm not yet convinced we'll have Westinghouse. And if we do, we may not have Westinghouse for long. . . . As we speak, the deal is a long way from finished. The thing to look for in whoever winds up with CBS is whether they have taken on so much debt that they have to squeeze CBS News down further to help service [the debt].

That's what happened when Tisch took over the company eight years ago, isn't it?

Uh-huh. And now we are in 1995. And this is a much bigger deal.

Andy Rooney recently said: "Larry Tisch did all the wrong things with CBS.... He turned the best broadcasting company in the business into one of the weakest and got even richer in the process." Agree?

[Slowly] Mmmmm...I'm going to have to say I'm not going to answer that question. What I will say is that there's real concern about what effect one merger after another, each one bigger than the last, will have on the news. Everywhere. Not just at CBS. When we were purchased last time, much of what Wall Street said needed to be done with CBS was wrong. Now, I understand that CBS needs to make a profit, but we also are, in some ways, a public trust.... When the new buyers talk about "increasing margins," it makes me nervous. A recent *Wall Street Journal* article quoted someone from the new potential ownership saying that more layoffs are inevitable.... At CBS News, we're down to the bone, past the bone, and we've been there a long time.

A lot of CBS News people are praying that Ted Turner will buy the network. Are you a member of the "Waiting for Ted" camp?

Well, I like Ted Turner and respect many of the things he's done with CNN. Now, I do have concerns. Turner already has the infrastructure of a worldwide news-gathering operation. If he were to take CBS, the danger is, that might gut CBS News, perhaps leave around it some of the trappings of what it once was, but wipe out the depth of our talent.

This could happen anyway?

Well, with any potential new management, you don't know. It's true, somebody else might get hold of CBS and gut us anyway. The last time the company changed ownership, what we first believed turned out to be several area codes away from what was true. The picture that was painted of the new ownership [then] was that it would bring in a new era of aggressive expansion and leadership in news. You can make a case that we had a critical moment in 1988—when the *CBS Evening News* on the flagship CBS station in New York was moved from 7 P.M., where it was strong, to 6:30, where it would be weak. What was put in our place at 7 was a game show, *Win, Lose or Draw*. When that happened, I knew the tide had turned against news. I, among others, fought as much as I could. "We can make more money by buying this syndicated program, and we decided we want the money," we were told by management. And we said, "If this is only about money, it's a short-term gain and long-term loss. If you move the *CBS Evening News* from where it is doing well, the signal goes out to our affiliates that they can move the news to any time they damn well please. They'll move it to terrible time periods." Which they did. Affiliated stations began playing the "Evening News" at 6:30, 4:30, 5—it was Death Valley. The signal from the top was, "Go for the buck." Now, this move was not Larry Tisch's idea, [but] he approved it. I'm now thinking, whoever winds up owning us, if they want to make a bold move for all of CBS News, they should put the news back at 7 at every owned and operated station.

You made headlines earlier this summer when Connie Chung was removed as co-anchor. At the time, she said she refused a smaller role because it was "inappropriate for the only woman on the three major network news programs to have anything less than coequal status."

This is not and was not a gender issue. Connie has often said, and rightly so, that she didn't come into the job because she's a woman. And she didn't lose it because she was a woman. It was a business decision to try it, and it was a business decision to stop it.... There was a time when some people thought having two anchors would make us more flexible, give me a chance to get out in the field more—and it was thought that it might improve our ratings. After two years, basically, the same people who decided to do it realized that our ratings were poorer than when we started out.

When did you first hear that Connie Chung might be leaving the "Evening News"?

Word was beginning to get around that Connie's agent was negotiating... [I figured] she'd probably sign a new contract, would stay on with CBS and be a central star and probably would continue to be a dual anchor. I'd been told [by the CBS brass] fairly recently that the intention was to continue. I left New York for Austin [after the Friday broadcast] to give the commencement address at the University of Texas... I thought, "They may very well say to me, 'We want you to work at CBS News, but we want you to go off in a different direction.'"

So you thought you, not Chung, might be pulled from the anchor's chair?

The thought occurred to me. Television, after all, is a young person's game. You can count on one hand the people in television, in news and entertainment, who are front and center who are over fifty-nine. There's Angela Lansbury and Dan Rather. Also, there had been this business with the Oklahoma City bombing coverage. [Immediately after the explosion, Chung was sent to the blast site; Rather was told not to go there. Eventually, he did join the coverage team.] Afterward, I said [to management], "We have to work out something so that we don't have this situation develop again." If something like that breaks, I want to be on it. Not to the exclusion of anybody else. My feeling was, I love this job, but I can't, I won't, go through this again. [Being kept from the story] chewed me up inside. It was like trying to swallow barbed-wire-wrapped ball bearings.

I got off the plane, my beeper was going off. I was told, "Somebody is calling around the newspapers saying that Connie is trying to get out of her contract." Of the things that I've read, the one that strikes me as having the strongest possibility of being true is that Connie and her agent made a decision that they wanted to put heat on CBS to get what they wanted by way of contract resolution. And in order to get what they wanted, this writer quotes someone as saying that they made a conscious decision to pursue a "scorched earth" strategy.

On screen, the two of you always looked miserable together—as if you'd been pushed into the video version of a shotgun marriage.

231

People have said that to me. But I never felt that. I never had any personal problems with Connie, which surprised me, in a high-pressured situation every day for nearly two years. Now, it has been suggested—and I think this may have some merit—that the [on-air] dynamic between us changed in about late February or March [of 1995].

Was that about the time of her "just between you and me" Kathleen Gingrich interview?

Yes. That's a wee small answer, yes. I spoke up for Connie at the time. What I felt privately was something not to express publicly. So, looking back on it, I did begin to notice a change in our on-screen dynamic in late February or March.... Also in March, I learned of some meetings that had taken place before the November 1994 elections—discussions about what the election coverage would look like. I didn't know the exact details of who said what to whom. But in March I was told—and did confirm—that there had been meetings at which [Chung's agent] Mr. Geller and the person for whom he was working sought, at the very minimum, to have a much larger role in election-night coverage—at my expense. Now, there are differing versions of what happened. What stuck in my mind was Mr. Geller saying to somebody, "You know, it's time for Dan to step aside." It's a rough trade and I understand that, but I didn't take kindly to that.

What would you have done if that argument had been successful?

I would have said to my employers, "Well, do you have anything else besides anchoring for me to do?" If I am able to do something in journalism, I'd be OK.... You know, I was supportive [of Chung]. I worked hard to make it work. I gave much more than I got. And happily so. I was protective and defensive. I gave it everything. I believed it would continue indefinitely, until I found out about election night and what had happened in secret. Until it was made very clear to me that there was a push on, not for me to share, but to give up.

Most of the reportage on l'affaire Connie Chung painted you as the heavy. Of the three network anchors, you seem to be a lightning rod for personal attacks. Do you have any insight on why that is?

I have no idea where that comes from. The best I can come up with is that I've been around a long time. Sometimes, there's been envy, jealousy, wonderment, "How did a guy as dumb as Rather get where he is?" My answer is, "I got in early, stayed late, worked hard, cared a lot and God smiled on me. And by the way, I might not be quite as dumb as you think I am." Another thing; I think it sometimes peeves some people when someone from the bottom breaks through. My background is Texas and poor. There was a review of a book about education in *The Wall Street Journal*, and the headline was, "Dan Rather and Other Enemies of Civilization." The review said, more or less, that television news was incredibly literate before I was on the air and concluded that we should shut down all teachers' colleges. I had attended Sam Houston State teachers' college. It hurt. The truth is, I got a wonderful education at Sam Houston State teachers' college and afterward at CBS, where I was trained by masters—Charles Collingwood, Eric Sevareid and, by extension, Edward R. Murrow himself. I met Murrow. But he left CBS just about the time I got there.

Now, I know I'm not Ed Murrow. [Smiles] Every morning, when I shave, I say, "Boy, what a wreck you are. And I'll tell you one damned thing, you're not Ed Murrow, and Ed Murrow you're never going to be." But that doesn't mean I can't practice the lessons that these guys taught me.

Tell us what the late Charles Collingwood taught you about men's haberdashery?

When I first came to CBS, Charles said, "If you want to make it here, young man, dress British and think Yiddish." And he certainly taught me the British part. "You should buy at least one tailored suit," he said, and then he took me to his tailor on Savile Row. He showed me what traveled well. I should have remembered his advice many years later when I was at *60 Minutes* doing a story on drug dealers. We had an informant in Wyoming who said he'd only talk if I came into town in complete disguise. So I dressed up in biker clothes—jeans, a T-shirt, with sleeves rolled up to my shoulder, a pack of cigarettes stuck in the sleeve and a phony tattoo. I thought I was completely unrecognizable. But on the plane, I sat down next to an African-American businessman, who looked me up and down and declared: "Dan Rather, is that you? You look bizarre!" Moral of the story? 'Tis better to dress British than Biker.

Or sing off-key. **TV Guide** *recently accused you of "conduct unbecoming a network news anchor" because you sang "What's the Frequency, Kenneth" on the David Letterman show with the rock group REM.*

Oh, that was so ridiculous. Everyone knows I can't sing in a bucket with a lid on it. I laughed when I read that. What does "conduct unbecoming an anchor" mean, anyway?

It means you're not being grave enough for a guy telling the country about Bosnia.

Verrrrry interesting. Conduct unbecoming an anchor is "selling out." You know, most of the time I'm accused of being too grave. All this comes under the heading of "Either way you go, you're going to catch it." If you read the news in a deep baritone, they are going to say, "God, he's stuffy." If you let any part of your other self show, it's "conduct unbecoming an anchor."

Can you envision Ed Murrow singing with REM?

Yes, I could. Ed Murrow, you know, was roundly criticized for sitting down and just talking to Marilyn Monroe! That was his equivalent of singing with REM.

The REM song is actually about your 1986 assault, when one of the people who attacked you said, most oddly, "Kenneth, what's the frequency?" What I recall about the coverage at the time was that there wasn't a lot of sympathy for you. It was played as, "Well, weird things always happen to Dan Rather."

And as with so many other things, I shrugged my shoulders and thought, "This is what comes with the territory." Who knows what it was about? A lot of people get very badly hurt in assaults. I came away lucky.

When Michael Stipe [lead singer of REM] was in New York last, I did talk with him about why he wrote this song, which I like a lot. He said that one of the themes he thinks about is the surreal and unexplainable things that happen. He remembered this as a kind of crazy, surreal experience of the kind a lot of people go through.

Speaking of the surreal, do you have any insight on why a journalist with Diane Sawyer's reputation would participate in something like her "interview" with Michael Jackson? According to newspaper reports, the singer was able to alter his appearance on the videotape and choose the format.

With this kind of program, the problem is a servility to ratings. Listen, Michael Jackson can produce a 42 share. Dyn-o-mite! There isn't an executive in television who doesn't lust for a 42 share! And once we get ourselves into that obsession, we are all very close to making that mistake. Even the best among us.

How do you rate your competitors—do you ever envy them?

They are all very decent, classy people—Peter, Tom and Bernie Shaw. Peter has a sense of elegance about him, which I greatly admire. Tom has a steadiness and unflappability that I especially admire. Bernie has a terrific tenaciousness, but with it, an ability to make it no big deal most of the time. It doesn't even show. Each manages to get less criticism than I do. And I do envy [that] ability. Both Tom and Peter seem to be at ease in every social situation. I'm not. I'm not a big Hamptons party guy. I'm not even good at big New York parties.

Do you ever watch **Murphy Brown?**

I do. I know people like that.

Which one is you?

Some of each. Mostly Murphy. First of all, she loves the news. Secondly, she's vulnerable. Thirdly, when she's on a story, she is focused and unstoppable. In most of the characters, I see some part of myself. Jim Dial—he also loves the news and is so very serious about it. There are times when he doesn't talk, he announces. It's the common fate of anchormen. "Heeeeeeey, I'm hooooooome, everybody!" When I do that, my family cracks up.

Now the best movie about television, I think, was *Network*. I saw that in the 1970's and thought, "Paddy Chayefsky's got it." He understood then the real danger of everyone worshiping at the temple of the ratings. I think he was trying to say, "Realize where this is going to lead—unless something dramatic and profound happens."

To return to your colleague David Letterman. Does it trouble you that the atmosphere at CBS is so demoralized that even he is making jokes about it?

No, I'm pleased and relieved that we have David around to keep alive whatever humor he can. I know that sometimes it's gallows humor. But at least it's humor.

•••

Samuel L. Jackson

*D*oing a Q and A with a movie star can be the best or the worst of the interview experience. On one hand, actors are potentially great interview subjects—readers are interested in them, their job makes them story-tellers, they lead interesting lives, they work, for the most part, with words. On the other hand, a lot of movie stars aren't actors, but celebrities. The truth is that celebrities often have little to say. "I'd like to direct... I think I'll do a comedy... I'd like to work with Speilberg, blah, blah, blah."

Now Samuel L. Jackson, the lanky Bible-quoting killer in Quentin Tarantino's *Pulp Fiction*, the avenging father in *A Time to Kill*, is the kind of movie-star subject who breaks these rules. Here is a vivid guy, full of great, great stories and willing to give himself fully to the interview process. In fact, interviewing him was a lot like an acting improvisation. If I asked a question, he considered it, played with it, and gave a gut-answer. We cooked.

In fact, we finished most of the interview in one morning session around a lot of coffee in Jackson's publicist's office in the Westwood section of Los Angeles in March 1995, with the rest by telephone that April. One-shot interviews that really work are rare. But as I say, we were cooking.

As the piece was being prepared for publication in the film magazine *Premiere*, the editors and I had a tough job selecting which material to include. This version of the interview includes some of the material that the magazine had to cut for space considerations. *Premiere* ran the piece in their June 1995 issue.

A lot of people wondered what you silently mouthed to the camera when you didn't get the Best Supporting Actor on Oscar night [in March 1995].

What do people think I said?

"Shit!"

I did say "shit." I was disappointed! Though, in the days before the ceremony, I tried to guard myself against too much optimism, I began to think that "maybe...maybe." Just about everyone I ran into said they'd voted for me.

But they also said, "Landau's gonna get it because of the sentimental vote. He's been nominated often and has never gotten it." Still, the more people talked to me about this "sentimental vote," the more I thought, "Morgan Freeman has been nominated four times and nobody's ever given *him* anything." Enough people told me that they'd voted for me that I began to think that maybe justice would be served in some kind of way here. I was kind of hoping against hope that this would be the time. I made this bet with my friend Dolores Robinson, who used to be Wesley [Snipes's] manager that I would not be sitting there applauding and smiling like most losers—that I would react in an honest kind of way. So when I didn't get it, yeah, I thought, "Shit!"

The part you didn't get Oscared for—Jules, the Bible-belting hitman in Pulp Fiction, *how did you create his look?*

Well, as you may already know, the Jeri-curl wig was a total mistake. Quentin has this fascination for the blaxploitation period of films. So his idea was to have me in a big Afro.

But on the day of the studio test, the girl that they sent to get the wigs brought back these Jeri-Curl things. And when I put one on, it fit the look. I had already grown big sideburns and this Fu Manchu mustache because they were part of the look I remembered from those films. Ron O'Neal in *Superfly* had those same sideburns and that mustache. The Jeri-Curl brought the character right into the 90s. It gave Jules a kind of street look and it also gave an image that goes along with that fire and brimstone thing that he does. I've seen a lot of preachers with hair like that.

Was Jules raised in a religious family? One sensed he might have had a daddy who was a preacher.

Well, according to the biography I made up for him, he did go to church and Sunday school. Because that's what I did when I was a kid, growing up in Chattanooga, Tennessee. If I stayed up late on Saturday, I had to go to Sunday school the next day. Now, Jules, he was a consummate professional. And a stickler for detail. He had this God-complex. He was the person who controlled life and death in most situations. That's why John Travolta's character just stood back and let Jules do everything.

Do you ever wonder what Jules did after he left the restaurant on that sunny California morning?

Well, he actually does exactly the thing that he says he's going to do. He goes on this trek. He starts traveling around the country, the world, wherever. And getting into these adventures and meeting people. Now, that doesn't necessarily mean that he stops killing people, 'cause that's what he does. When he's out trying to find the true meaning of why he was saved, he still can fall back into the same things that he was into before. But not necessarily with the same kind of purpose. So if he runs into danger or a sticky situation, he can extricate himself in all the [same] ways. But not with the same intent.

You almost didn't get to play Jules. How come?

This is a very long story and a very big lesson for me. You see, I had met Quentin years ago when he was casting *Reservoir Dogs*. The day of my audition for that movie, I was supposed to read with Harvey Keitel. And Harvey wasn't there, and I ended up reading with Quentin and Laurence Bender and I was kind of like, "*Who are these guys?*"

Consequently my audition was not so great. And I didn't see Quentin again until the Sundance Festival that year, where they were showing *Reservoir Dogs*, and where he said to me, "How'd you like the guy who got your part?" So I told him, "I loved the movie, but you'd have had an even better film with me in it."

Two years later, when he was putting together *Pulp Fiction*, Quentin called and said he wanted to have dinner with me. Over dinner, he spoke about this new script and this character he was writing with me in mind. Not long after, I got the script from Danny DeVito with a note that read, "If you tell anybody about this, three guys from Jersey will show up and kill you." The script killed me. I mean, I was *blooooownnnn* away. To know that somebody had written something like Jules for me. I was...over-whelmed...thankful...cocky...you know, this whole combination of things that you [feel] knowing that somebody's going to give you an opportunity like *that*.

Not long afterwards, people called and said they'd like me to read Jules aloud so they could "hear what he sounds like." And to me, that sounded like, "Just come in and we're gonna read through this stuff so we can kinda see if there needs to be something done to it, but the role's yours." So I went in. I didn't learn it. I didn't do any of the things that I do as an actor to prepare, to show somebody who this character's going to be. After that, I went to New York to do *Fresh* for Laurence [Bender], the producer [of both films]. And while I was in New York I started hearing rumblings of, "I think we're going to cast this other guy as Jules." Another actor had come in, auditioning for another part that didn't have that many lines. He'd asked if he could read Jules as his audition.

Clever move!

Yeah. [Laughs.] And he rocked the house. And all of a sudden they're thinking of casting *him*! And I'm going berserk on the phone to L.A. Number one, nobody had told me that the reading was an audition. Number two, if somebody tells me they've written something for me, why am I auditioning for it, anyway? So my manager and my agent, they're calling Danny DeVito, Harvey and Bob Weinstein, they're calling Laurence, they're calling Quentin. Finally, there is a new audition set up for me in L.A. on a Sunday. Now mind you, I'm in New York shooting a film. And I fly from New York on the Red-Eye. I'm scrambling. I'm doing all the stuff I need to do. I'm breaking down the speeches, you know, into beats. I'm kinda doing autobiographical stuff for myself so I can figure out why Jules is here, why he's in this space. Meanwhile I'm learning these speeches. And when I finally get to Jersey Films that Sunday, nobody's there. I mean *nobody*. But the door is open and there's a note saying, "Come over and sit down." They come back eventually and ha! Laurence is introducing me to this other guy, Paul, one of the other producers. And Paul is saying, "Ohhhh nooo noo. You don't have to introduce me to this man! I know him. I love your work. It's my pleasure to meet you Mr. Fishburne." So I'm like, "BOOOM! Oh my God! They don't even know who I am!" But I'm together, I'm cool. I've got it down and am ready to go. We go in the room. Everybody's there: Laurence, Danny, Quentin, Paul, the casting agent. And they've got this guy there who's a reader—doing the John Travolta part. So when we start to do the scene, we're like halfway in the scene and this guy misses a line. And I'm looking at him and I realize, "He's so caught up in watching me, that he's lost." I'm thinking, "*I'm kicking ass. I'm kicking some ass!*"

With this audition, did you feel, "I've been hanging around for too many years. This is my last chance."

I don't know if I felt that. I just wanted this role so badly because it would allow me to soar as an actor. Anyway, there I was, doing this great audition. Then we get to the last speech in the film. The one in the restaurant. And I had worked on this thing, worked on it on the plane. So as I was sitting there, something happened that made me change *everything* I'd thought about doing on my way in there. And I did it the way that I do it in the film now. When I finished doing that speech, you could hear a pin drop. A half-hour later everybody said, "The job's yours."

Now, I saw Laurence again when I got back on the *Fresh* set and he told me that nobody was in that office that Sunday because the other actor had come in again, and done this great audition again. They had all gone to lunch to figure out how they were going to tell me I wasn't getting this role. But Laurence said, when I did that last speech, they finally saw the end of the film. They had never seen how the film was going to end until I did that speech. And that's what sealed it.

It was a valuable lesson for me. Now if somebody tells me they're writing something for me, I know I cannot *not* do the things I've always done to make sure that I get a job. I'm still being tested as an actor. Nothing can be taken for granted.

There's a different kind of story about how you won "Best Supporting

Actor" in 1991 at Cannes for Gator, Wesley Snipes's crack-crazed brother in Jungle Fever. *In that go-round, you were convinced you weren't going to win anything.*

Yeah, the night before Spike left for the Cannes Festival, we went to a Knicks game and Spike kept insisting, "You're gonna win something!" And I said, "Spike, they don't give Supporting Actor awards at the Cannes Film Festival."

In the next few days, I kept roaming around New York like I always did, doing auditions. One afternoon, I phoned my agent to see if I had any call-backs. "I think people from the AP are looking for you," she said. "You won some award at the Cannes Festival." Again, I said, "No, they don't give Supporting Actor awards at Cannes." And she answered, "No, no, Sam, they *created* an award for you." And I was like, "Oh, that's great, but do I have any call-backs?"

Did you?

No. Not then. Later.

How did you prepare to play Gator?

I smoked a bunch of crack. [Embarrassed laugh] No, I knew who he was. In a very literal sense. Yeah, I spent my time doing some of that junk and hanging out. But the easy part was to do the drug part of the role. The hard part is dealing with the manipulative nature of a person you love coming into your life and doing bad things to you—abusing trust. I spent more time dealing with that than I did with the drugs.

Was it true in your own life?

Oh, sure. Yeah. I've abused people and abused their trust. Done those same sorts of things. But that was the human element that was needed to make that character totally believable. I could have made him a cartoon-junkie. But because of the way I actually treated my relationship with Wesley and Ossie and Ruby, people felt that character in a very real and tangible way. I mean people were constantly telling me that Gator was their brother, their cousin, their son, their husband. Gator's someone who's been through a lot of people's lives.

The first time you met Spike Lee you were acting in A Soldier's Play, *in New York. He was an NYU Film School student and he came backstage and declared that one of these days he was going to be a great film director. Did you think him a wee bit over-the-top?*

No. Because I wanted to be a great actor. This was somebody else who had a dream. After we met, I went to NYU and looked at his student film and I saw he was serious. He said when he got ready to make a film, he was going to call me. And sure enough he did. And sure enough, I still had to audition for him. Even the last time Spike wanted to hire me I had to audition for him. I refused, actually. This was for *Malcolm X.*

Is that why "X" is one of the few Spike Lee films you're not in?

Pretty much. And that was right after *Jungle Fever.* I kept asking him, "Why do I have to audition?" He kept saying that the studio needed to see it. I didn't believe it. And I didn't like the feeling. I didn't do the audition. Consequently, I'm not in "X." My wife, LaTanya Richardson, is. We would have played husband and wife in the film.

But there were other things, too. While Spike was casting that film, they asked me to come in and read with all these other people who were auditioning 'cause Denzel wasn't available for reading. So I read Malcolm's part off-camera while they taped. And later Spike told me who he wanted me to play and I was, "Sure, I'd love to do it." This was going to be great. I was going to get to work with my wife. And then, like all of a sudden, it was, "OK, now it's your turn to read for me and not only do I need that, but everybody on this movie is making scale except Denzel." Well, I was not going to work for scale. No way. I don't fault Spike for this. I mean, it's his job to try and get me for as little money as he can. But Spike's like the rest of the producers in Hollywood, he's out to make money for Spike. And that's fine. But it's not, "uplift the race" and "I'm on the black man's side."

If movie stars are archetypes, what do you represent?

Me? Sam Jackson? Gosh. Well, a lot of things. I mean I'm a father, a husband, a son. I'm a friend to a lot of people. To many of my friends, I represent the hope that there's still a chance for them to become the things that they want.

You mentioned your wife, La Tanya. Why do you think your marriage has lasted twenty-five years?

A willingness to fight through all the things that will let you say "fuck it." She refers to it as a "Villa in Hell." She thinks I actually had a space reserved for her and our daughter, Zoe, in this Villa in Hell for a very long time. I was mad. I was crazed. I was not happy with who I was. Consequently, she and our daughter paid a lot of taxes for me doing crazed things to myself that transferred to them.

When exactly was this?

During the years in New York, when I was watching people do things I thought I should be doing. And torturing myself for it. For instance, when I was understudying Charles Dutton on Broadway in *The Piano Lesson.* I was watching the show every night and being, like, "Oh my God, I want to do this play! I don't want to sit back stage and wait on something to happen to Charles so I can do it." And by the time he was nominated for a Tony for that role after I'd done it, I was like ARRRRGGGH! Bugged!

They paid for that. I was staying out. Not coming home. I was, you know, drinking, drugging, womanizing, doing all these things to make myself feel good about myself except the one thing that I should have been doing—working harder to get a job. I should have been putting myself in a healthier acting-situation by getting *my own* job. So she went through that period.

Why did she stay?

Well, she always says to me that I have now grown into the man that she always knew I could be. And she held onto that.

Do you think that's true?

I don't know. I'm basically a good person. I try to be very fair. I try and treat people the way I definitely want them to treat me. I just needed to find a peace that I could live with, where I would know I was giving myself the best opportunity to be the best that I could be. And until I found that, I was not a very easy person to be with.

How did you finally get off drugs?

Rehab . . . like everybody else.

Was that difficult?

You're in there. You're locked up. You can't get drugs. And once you figure out it's easier to take hold of your life than to escape from it, you're on the road. I hadn't faced a lot of stuff. I had used drugs for twenty-something years, from high school into my late thirties. Gosh, I mean, I used to wake up every morning and smoke a joint first thing, and my wife would say, "When are you gonna face the world?" I'm like, "I am facing the world. What the hell are you talking about?"

Ever miss the drugs?

Heck, no. I used to hate going to AA meetings because, you know, the alcoholics always seem to be kind of bent out of shape because they can't have a drink. But that's only normal, because they're sitting at home watching television, "Hey, have a beer! We're having a great time!" But when I started going to Narcotics Anonymous meetings, people are so grateful to be clean, mainly because it is such a misery to constantly chase a high.

Considering that your career has been booming these past five years, has all that transformed your marriage into . . . a Villa in Heaven?

We still go through things. We don't go through *those kinds* of things. Interestingly enough, when *Pulp Fiction* started to garner all this attention, my wife actually said to me that I was living her dream. From the time she was a kid she'd always wanted to be an actress. And I came into this business late in life as a senior at Morehouse College. And these were things that she'd always visualized for herself: the envy, the limos, the offering of the roles. For a moment she was bothered by it. But when she saw *Pulp Fiction*, she called me on location and said that after seeing Jules, she realized I had done something she couldn't do.

She knows so much more about the acting process than I do. She used to tell me that I was this very bloodless actor. I was smart. I could read the script, analyze it, break a character down. But I never invested any of myself in it. I could use the right facial expression. I could do the right vocal inflection. But she never believed it. And until I let all that other bitterness and all of that stuff go, I wasn't able to do that.

Let's talk about another emotion: anger. In Amos *and* Andrew, *you played a wealthy African-American who is the personification of internalized seething anger. Is that part of your own personality?*

I have that, yeah. You know, I grew up during segregation in the South. And that was a survival mechanism. You couldn't even show it sometimes. There were times when things happened that were so awful that I would have loved to have leaped across and wrapped my hands around the person's throat. But you just stood there and showed nothing.

In Chattanooga, Tennessee, as a kid, I saw signs that said, "No niggers and dogs." I remember when I was four or five, I whistled at a white girl from our porch. My grandmother, my mom, my aunt, everybody was out of the house, snatching me up, everybody was hitting me. Because I could have been killed for that.

Did they hide you? That's the sort of thing that got Emmett Till lynched.

No, they didn't have to hide me. It was just a little white girl walking down the street. We actually had . . . PWT living in our neighborhood, if you know what that is. Poor white trash. If they were in my neighborhood, they weren't regular white people anyway. The people across the street were the kind of people who, when it rained, came out with a bar of soap and everybody would stand under the rain gutter and take a shower. I mean, we had running water and a telephone and that kind of stuff. They didn't have that. But even a little girl like that could have gotten me killed.

My family wanted me to learn a lesson. There were lots of things that I could not do, that I knew I couldn't do. Places I couldn't go. And I spent a lot of time in the movies, even then, because my mom loved the movies and I'd go to the movies with her.

Segregated theaters?

Yeah, there were two black movie theaters, The Grand and the Liberty.

We'd see the same films that were shown to whites, but they'd be edited sometimes. Like when I saw *A Band of Angels*, with Sidney Poitier. There's a scene where he slaps Rhonda Fleming because she's black and he knows it and he's become a Union soldier and he comes back to the house and she's sitting there pretending to be the white mistress of the house, and he slaps her. Now, that was a big thing in the South. I mean, we heard about this scene! But when it got to my movie theater, you saw the argument start and the next thing you know she's sitting there in the chair. But you never saw him hit her.

You were raised by your grandparents?

Pretty much. My mom was in Washington, working till I was in the fourth grade. And my father was never there. His story was that he'd been in the army and my mom tried to get money from him for me and he got out of the army rather than pay money for me. My most vivid image of him was when I was in the fourth or fifth grade and my mother had moved back home. It would be late at night and the phone would be ringing and she'd end up crying. He'd get drunk and call her. I didn't even really know what that was about. He blamed her for his army career being ruined because she wanted money for me.

I saw him another time, when my daughter was just an infant. My wife and I were on a tour for the Negro Ensemble Company and we were in Topeka. And my father's mother lives in Kansas City, and we'd never met. But she'd always sent me Christmas cards, birthday cards. She wanted to make sure that [my daughter] knew I had another set of grandparents. So we took the train to Kansas City on her birthday—and my father was at her house. We talked for a while about his not paying for me while I was a child. He was pretty flippant about it. And he started telling me about all these brothers and sisters that I had, and I said, "I don't have any brothers and sisters. I'm an only child."

And the most bizarre thing was, we went around the corner to these people's house, and there was this sixteen-year-old girl there who has this baby, and he's, like, introducing this baby to me as my sister! And I'm looking at him, thinking, "This is stupid, it's crazy. You're still doing the same thing." He finally passed a couple years ago. When he was dying these doctors called me to find out if I wanted to have him put on life-support. I said, "He has a sister in Kansas City, call her and see if she wants him kept alive. If you're asking me, I don't have an opinion."

In **Fresh,** *you played an absentee father. Did you use anything of your own father in that role?*

No. I thought more about myself and my daughter. My father never wanted to be a part of my life—and in some ways, I'm still trying to figure ways of being part of Zoe's life. I mean, she loves me and we do some things together, but sometimes I don't know how to approach her in certain kinds of ways to find out what's going on. She's thirteen. So it's kind of like you ask her what's happening and she goes, "Aw, nothing."

You're a New York actor who's recently moved to Hollywood. Was it a tough transition to make?

No, not at all. See, I always told myself that I would not come to L.A. unless they summoned me. In New York, I used to go to my agent's office and say, you know, "Hollywood call?" "No, Sam, not today."

And one day, after *Jungle Fever*, after I got that special prize at Cannes, I said, "Hollywood call?" And my agent said, "Interestingly enough, yes they did." And I came out here and I had lunch with people and did that whole thing that they say you do. And when I came to L.A. the first time, I had a job, *White Sands.* And then the next thing you know, they summoned me back here to meet the people at Paramount who were doing *Patriot Games*, and then, *Amos and Andrew*, and *Loaded Weapon*. Now the reason we moved here was not because of *me*. It was because my wife got a television series, and we had to move here so she could go to work every day. Unfortunately, the series was canceled very soon after we got settled. My daughter was already in school here and we weren't going back to New York because we don't jerk her around like that. We ended up staying.

Are L.A. people real nice to your wife now that you're a star?

Yes, they are. If she tells them who her husband is, they look at her differently for some reason. She gets considered in another kind of way. We've done a film together—*Losing Isaiah*—even though they didn't know she was my wife until later. But yeah, people afford her another kind of respect. She enjoys it in a certain kind of way. In another way, she resents it because they're not dealing with her [as an] individual. But once they see her abilities, then it's all gone away. Most people are pretty amazed that she's married to "this actor." Whoever they think I am. And they also find it pretty amazing that we've been together twenty-five years.

To change the subject back to this year's Oscars—before the actual ceremony, there was a big controversy concerning your Pulp Fiction *work. There were quite a few critics who thought it strange that Miramax pushed John Travolta for Best Actor and you for Best Supporting Actor. Wonderful as he was, you had more lines than Travolta and your role was completely central to the plot. What happened here?*

Ummmm. I don't know. I'm not trying to be diplomatic about it. I'm just saying that I don't know. I honestly do not know. I mean, I won the Best Actor award from the Texas film critics. As I understand it, I actually won the Best Actor award from the L.A. film critics until they took another vote. Same thing happened in Chicago and in New York. I mean I actually came in second in both categories in New York. Best Actor and Best Supporting Actor.

So I don't know. Whoever makes those kinds of decisions, or wants those decisions to be made, started to make them. They involved me in the process at a certain point. Everybody called and the way the conversations were directed, everyone wanted me to accept the fact that I should be in the Supporting Actor category. To the point that it was presented to me as, "If you allow us to push you for Best Supporting Actor, it's pretty much guaranteed you'll get a nomination. But if we put you in the Best Actor category, then we can't say that it's a lock."

Now, at the time, my thinking was, if I'm going to lose anyway, I'd rather lose Best Actor than Best Supporting Actor. But they said there was no guarantee that I would even be in that mix.

Do you think that's a failure of imagination on their part?

Quite possibly. They could have been hedging their bets. People said all kinds of things, [that] they didn't want to split the *Pulp Fiction* vote between John and me. They said exactly what I just said to you, that there was no guarantee that I would even get a Best Actor nomination if that's what they went after, but I was pretty much a lock to get the Supporting Actor nomination. I mean, I could have made a stink, yeah, but what good would it have done?

What I know is that people are going to see this film, and they're going to see this film forever. And there's nothing that can be done to change the work that I did. People can look at this film and judge for themselves what it is. In a totally fair world, we'd all be nominated for Best Supporting Actor because it's a totally ensemble performance film. But it's not a totally fair world, and that's how things fall out.

When Miramax took a "For Your Consideration..." ad for you in **The Hollywood Reporter,** *they ran you photographed with Travolta. Now, I know he's a terrific guy, very sweet, but doesn't that say, "Sam Jackson doesn't have enough visual recognition on his own?"*

Yeah. Interestingly enough, the same thing happened when I watched television ads for *Pulp Fiction* [before the Oscars]. The ads said, "Pulp Fiction, nominated for seven awards, including John Travolta, Best Actor; Uma Thurman, Best Supporting Actor; Quentin Tarantino, Best Director. Pulp Fiction." And it goes off.... The public perception of what's going on is the same as yours. I mean, there's a lot of outrage, especially in the black community, about that very same thing.

There are people who said this was some kind of unconscious racism.

Well, yeah. It looks that way, tastes that way, smells that way. "Quacks like a duck, it must be a duck." But, you know, you let it go, and you go on. I can't carry that around. 'Cause if I did, I couldn't work. I'd be crazy.

I mean, there are all kinds of examples to support that very same theory. If you go back to *Jurassic Park*. There were people that called me wanting to know where did they sell my action figure? All these little black kids went to see *Jurassic Park*, but they couldn't go in and buy the Smart-Ass-Doctor-Who-Ran-The-Whole-Fucking-Park's doll. Meanwhile, they did have a doll for the fat guy who stole the embryos!

In closing, you're a full-fledged movie star now. Were there moments when you thought, "This is never going to happen"?

I don't know. Over the years, I've always known that becoming a movie star is, I guess, kind of rare. It's like being a college basketball player and all of a sudden you're a senior and there are only 300 jobs [in the NBA] for these 30,000 kids who are coming out of school. Are you good enough to be one of the 300? Or you go into the work force and you play basketball for your job's league, or some intramural league, or you go to some semi-pro league and continue to try and get better.

What if you hadn't made it into the cinematic NBA?

Well, I would have told myself that I was *almost* good enough, that I'm still good enough to play better than most of the people in the country. And I will take the option probably that some of those other guys took; I'd go to Europe and take the money that they have there.

To return to your audition for Pulp Fiction. *Have you ever wondered what your life might like now if you hadn't gotten that part?*

I'd probably be pretty angry. But I also have this great facility to let go of things. That wasn't always true. But it's true now.

•••

POETS

Arthur Miller

In the summer of 1993, a special made-for-TV production of Arthur Miller's much underrated family drama about the Depression, *The American Clock*, was aired on Turner Broadcasting. To note the event, *TV Guide* asked me to do a quick 1,800 words with the man they were happy to label "America's greatest living playwright." After a half-dozen tentative commitments that ended in cancellation, Miller finally agreed to see me on a bright summer morning at his East Side apartment. From the first question on, the session went beautifully. So often in interviewing, the instant personal relationship between journalist and subject will determine the quality of the piece. In this case, I think he liked my questions. I mean, not only did he answer, but he sang, told jokes. He was a totally terrific subject.

Now I knew from reading Miller's clips that the one subject that would absolutely end the encounter was his second wife, Marilyn Monroe. In the few interviews he gives, Arthur Miller tries to redline her as a topic of discussion. And really, what could one ask about La Monroe that would be new?

But as we began talking, a question seemed to organically develop from the conversation. Was Marilyn really a victim? Or was she quite savvy about the role of women in society? (I've always sensed the latter was true.) So finally, at what seemed like a good moment, I sprung my Marilyn question. The answer, while reluctant, proved fascinating.

We met in New York City on July 19, 1993. *TV Guide* published the interview on August 21. Some material has been added here from the transcript of our conversation that was not included in the earlier version.

Your new TV movie, **The American Clock,** *centers on the survival of an American family during the 1930s Depression. Yet it seems a very contemporary story.*

Unfortunately, it is. You know, I wrote *The American Clock* in 1972 . . . a prosperous time. Everything was going to go on forever. And I'd heard *that* before, during the boom years of the 1920s, when I was a kid. I thought we'd eventually be getting what we've got now. I knew there'd be a limit to this everlasting . . . happiness.

You knew from experience we'd eventually get an economic downturn.

Well, the seventies reminded me of the twenties. Nobody *then* thought the prosperity would end, either. As one of the characters in the teleplay says, "Most Americans thought they were going to get richer and richer into the indefinite future." I thought it would be good to remind people that what goes up also comes down.

We're supposedly in a boom now.

It's a depression for an awful lot of people. Millions of people in this country now are in as much of a depression as existed in the thirties. But it's very uneven. In the 1930s, the unemployment, the poverty, the homelessness was a much more generalized condition. Poverty was as horrible in Detroit as it was in New York or Los Angeles. In the 1990s, Detroit is in a depression, but parts of the sun-belt are not. Still, where it's bad, it seems as bad as anything in the Depression.

When you were writing The American Clock, ***what was your mood?***

I was trying to rediscover my youth, in a way. The years of the thirties, and a different spirit in the country. In the 1970s, when I was writing this, the basic feeling in the country was, "Well, I'm all right Jack." And the thing was to get a new lawnmower—and ever the right colored car. People, I thought, were becoming more and more separated from each other. There was no society left. It was all goods and the brass ring.

We were thrown together in the thirties. There was no question that society existed. An idiot knew that. And it felt that there was a kind of humor. If you notice the songs of the 1930s, the pop songs are the most cheerful songs ever written in this country. "Life is just a bowl of cherries. . . . " Remember that? I wanted it on this program, but I couldn't get permission. [Sings] "Life is . . . just a bowl of cherries. Don't take it serious. It's too mysterious." Stuff like that. Some of the best standards were written in that time, and the movies were terrific, because things hit bottom and people started relaxing and saying, "We're all going under—so what else is new?" I tried to give that feeling in the play.

People shared trouble. That's vanished now.

You get the feeling from the play that events were so destructive that people were just crushed by them.

The family, yeah. But they were thrown together. In the 1970s, you got the feeling that there was no society. Margaret Thatcher said it in Britain, but she could have been talking for Reagan. She said, "There is no society. There are only individuals."

And why do you disagree with that?

Because it dehumanizes the human being, it makes all against all. It throws us into an arena where the objective in life is to tear the guts out of whoever's in front of you.

The American Clock *is very frank about what an economic downturn does to ordinary people. It has a kind of gritty populism that's very rare on television. How is it that Ted Turner decided to broadcast this particular story?*

I have *no* idea. I think airing it was mainly the idea of the producer, Michael Brandman and Steven Speilberg's production company, Amblin. They made the project happen. Turner may certainly have approved of the thing. I've met him once and he's certainly no run-of-the mill guy. He's an original.

You say in **The American Clock** *that the nation was saved when people's faith in themselves was finally restored. In your masterwork,* **Death of a Salesman,** *Willie Loman's great flaw is that he has too much faith in himself . . . an unreal faith.*

That's the irony.

Are you torn about that?

Well, I'm torn about people having an empty faith that things are going to get better all by themselves. I think that empty faith is destructive because it wastes a lot of lives. This neglect of social problems is costing us. That's my view of the thing.

Change, improvement, reform doesn't automatically happen. It happens because the people and the leadership sit down and say, "Well, this is what we want. Now how do we get it."

With its disturbing message, could you have done **The American Clock** *at any of the major networks?*

Never! They are afraid to do anything that disturbs. The way they disturb is by shooting a lot of people or showing rape on the screen. That's their idea of "disturbing" people. And you know, it's such a waste! There are terrific things you could do on television. It could be a great thing.

When you watch TV, what do you like?

I tune in the news, CNN . . . McNeil-Lehrer. I sometimes see the programs before and after the network news—and they are appalling. I don't even know the titles of these things. They are full of the most obvious kind of primitive dialogue. The producers of these shows are practically sticking their fingers in the audience's eye—to show them what they should see. It's abysmal, the level of the work.

Who do you think writes this stuff?

Some very nice people. Yeah, sure, I'm sure they are. What happens is that the taste of the leaders of the industry is what we've just been describing. They say, "That's what the people want." My answer is, "That's what *they* want." It doesn't mean that we're a nation of philosophers who want to flock to high art. But I think if they allowed the writers at least the freedom that you have in the theatre—with also the responsibility. You're asking me, "Who writes the stuff?" I can't give you one name. They can't take any responsibility because the writers aren't given any.

When CBS did *Death of a Salesman* a few years ago—with Dustin Hoffman and Volker Schlondorff, they asked me to say a few words at a dinner honoring everyone in the production. I said, "All I'm going to tell you is one man wrote this, one man directed it, and one man stars in it—and there's never been a conference about this."

And this is unusual?

It never happens. In general, they are not going to give anybody like me responsibility for something. I'm sure you're a little amazed at the remark. Can you imagine going up to a writer and saying, "You write something and we'll put it on the air." Consequently, those artists are not taking responsibility for what they are doing. They say, "Oh well, it's a way to make a buck." And gradually they convince themselves, "Oh, it's not as bad as it could have been." But the possibility, the potential in this country, is terrific.

Now, I thought *Death of a Salesman* was extraordinary use of the medium. That was proof that you could do a play on television. No line was added or taken away—and yet it worked. This had the depth of a film, but it still had the language of a play. Dustin's performance is very good and Malkovich . . . they were all very wonderful.

Of course in some parts of the world, they do television with the same care that they do theatre. The Swedes do that. Ingmar Bergman has done one film after another that started out as a television show—and that is good enough to be judged as a film. The same thing is true for some of what we see on English televison. In both those cases, it's not commercial television.

We're cutting public television Federal funding in the U.S.

And you know, I can't believe that the American people value so little the culture of this country. Maybe they do. But after all, public television does do a lot of stuff that nobody else is going to do—the operas, the concerts.

And no one but Arthur Miller is going to get CBS to do something as serious as **Death of a Salesman** *in primetime.*

And only then because of Dustin Hoffman!

You mean, even Arthur Miller couldn't have gotten that onto the air?

No. Of course not. I mean, how many Eugene O'Neill plays have you seen on CBS?

See, they've done their best to separate anything that an adult over sixteen would be interested in from the rest of the pop culture. And they're saying, "There is no audience for that culture." Of course there is. I have plays that are fifty years old that play more now than they did when they were first out. All over the country—and the world. The public's there.

There are often good things on television. Have you ever seen **The Simpsons?** *That's the most profound piece of social commmentary in current American life.*

I think I've seen it, yes. And it goes over, it's popular. So there you are. So there is an audience for good shows that are well-written.

So again, what do you watch?

Basically, anything to do with news events. *60 Minutes*. That's beautifully done. In a few minutes they manage to encapsulate very complicated stories and it's not easy. There's another one, *48 Hours*, I see. Television does that kind of stuff marvelously. They probably do that better than anybody.

I tell you one of the problems with me is that the older you get, the less patience you have. A lot of the acting I see on television is delayed-acting. Everything is slowed down beyond belief. It just seems to be very deliberate, as though the whole machine were running through a fixed serial. It's hard to watch it. Because you're way ahead of it. TV has a way of telling the story, very, very slowly, and pretty soon you're saying, "Why am I sitting here looking at this? I know what's going to happen next."

In the 1940s, when television first came out into the world, were you hopeful about its potential?

I'll tell you a story. In the forties, I used to write for radio because it was a quick way to make a dollar. And during World War II, someone at NBC said, "We want you to look at something that we think is going to be more important than radio in the future." And we went into this room, which had a thousand lights along the walls and ceilings. The heat in there was not to be believed. They had a camera. And on the table, they had a bottle of ketchup. And there was a screen.

And then he said, "I'll show you.... This thing can be sent into every home in America."

And then he turned the camera and on the screen I saw this bottle of ketchup and I said, "You mean, we are now going to *see* the ad?" We had ads on the radio all the time.

"That's the idea. You're going to see the ad!"

I was so shocked that this would be brought into your living room. It was hard to imagine in that time: The intrusion into my space of somebody's product. I said, "Are they going to allow this?" The force of this thing, and the power of it, just blew my mind.

They said, "We don't know how to use this dramatically at this point. Would you work on it?"

So I wrote some things. Experimental scenes. But that bottle of ketchup always stuck in my mind as what this television thing was about. Because those guys were certainly going to bring that bottle of ketchup into your home—and the rest of it was incidental. And that's what it's about with television.

You've said elsewhere that you just hate all the violence on television.

Of course, I hate it. I think the networks are doing it for the worst reason. It's the easiest way to fasten the attention of the audience without having anything to say in the program. Anyone who's creative knows that. I see violence on TV that I wouldn't believe they could show. I don't know if people watching violence imitate it, but it sure doesn't help. That's for sure.

Both Congress and the administration are threatening to legislate against television violence. Good idea?

It would be best if they didn't. Because the next thing they will do is censor politics and opinions. I'm against censorship. But that doesn't mean that citizens can't protest [against] this stuff. If the program has no humanity to it at all, if all we are going to be treated to is the blood and gore, then we have good reason to object to it.

You know, I've seen some of these non-fiction cops-in-action shows that are so often objected to. They're actually fascinating. And even they are not as violent as the fictional stories. I saw one. They busted into a narcotic den, pulled out the people, searched them and put them into police cars. No one was batted over the head and shot because that rarely happens in real life. I didn't see anybody getting their eyes gouged out. I can't say that the cops were gentle, they were scared—but nobody had his head pushed through a window.

Forgive me, I must ask you a question here about Marilyn Monroe. Please don't answer it if it makes you uncomfortable. From your auto-biography, Timebends, *Monroe seems very different from the person we've read about in the exposés. She seems, for instance, very savvy about the difficult relationships between men and women in the 1950s. She's very open about her sexuality, not guilty, almost a feminist. Your recollection of her shows her as much less of a victim than is popularly assumed.*

She was a victim. And she wasn't.

Meaning?

She did understand these things. That doesn't mean that you can't be victimized too.

It's been suggested that had she lived into a time when there was feminism that she would have been happier...

It would have been different, I'm sure.

For her...?

Yeah.

What do you think she'd be like now, in this era?

I have no idea. I don't.

This is something we've sincerely wondered about.

There's no knowing that. She was not scheduled to live that long.

Well, I thank you for your grace in putting up with yet another obnoxious journalist.

You're not obnoxious. You're all right. You know, I was a journalist myself, recently. I interviewed Nelson Mandela for the BBC.

What's he like as an interview subject?

He's really a great man. He's the real goods. He's not a public relations creation.

And being on the other side of the process—that must have been fascinating?

I wasn't good at it. I thought I should let him talk about his early life, his childhood. Nobody ever lets him go into it. And I found it interesting, but... well, first of all, he talks very slowly. On television, all right already, you want to hear things a little quicker.

There was actually some fascinating material. You know, he was the son of the chief and he was raised to be a king. And it was instructive as to what made him what he is. Because he comports himself like a king. He reacts like a king.

But when you were doing the interview, were you saying to yourself, "Oh, I'm not getting good material?"

Yes, and I didn't want to interrupt his train of thought.

Did the experience give you some sympathy for interviewers?

Oh, yeah. I never had any illusions about myself. The only reason I did it was because the idea was interesting. And he had not wanted to be interviewed on television. But I wasn't Mike Wallace enough. I was too kind to him. Not that he needed unkindness. You had to edit him more than I did or it doesn't work. You can't let him go on and I did.

He's never trying to be fascinating. He's trying to tell you how it was.

It's fun to be a journalist, isn't it?

I've done journalism before. I'm not good at it. I work from the inside out, not the outside in. There are other people who do it better. You do.

So you're saying that journalism vs. fiction is the difference between Method acting and technique acting?

See, if I can't find a form, I can't write it. Very often in journalism you have to find a specious form—anything that will hold it together. It's better if you find a real form. But sometimes you can't.

And you can find the form easier in fiction?

I do that all the time. I talk to my characters four times a day for months!

You ask them what their lives have been like?

I do. It's not the same as sitting in a room with somebody and having two hours to do it—as we have.

No, it's certainly not the same. But one more question: If somebody gave you a network to run, what would it look like?

I would hope that I would find a lot of comedians and put them on.

Comics? Why?

Because that's the best thing you can do on television. I love all the old comedians—I saw David Letterman once, I didn't think he was funny. He was just being . . . mildly ironical.

I hear *Saturday Night Live* is good, but I can't stay up that late. If they'd do a *Saturday Morning Live*, I'd watch it.

You could record it on your video-player.

Are you kidding? Have you ever tried to use one of those things? No, I like jokes. It's like, someone asks Hennie Youngman, "Now that you're old, has aging affected your social life." He says, "Oh definitely. Now when I go out, if I'm not in bed by eleven o'clock, I go home."

That's funny! I like that kind of stuff. I'd tune that in.

●●●

Toni Morrison (Chloe Wofford)

ineteen-ninety-three was one hell of a year for Toni Morrison, the genius American novelist and poet. She won the Nobel Prize for literature and became the first African-American and the first North American female writer ever to do so. Several weeks after returning from Stockholm and the joys of the Nobel ceremony, her Grand View-on-Hudson, New York home burned to the ground.

With the Nobel as a news hook, I had wanted to interview her immediately after the ceremony. But the fire and the destruction of all those dear artifacts that make a home—her books, the paintings of friends, manuscripts, drafts, her clothing—proved so devastating that I held off several months before phoning her.

Morrison rarely gave interviews. She'd done nothing around the Nobel except a perfunctory press conference and a few telephone interviews. After waiting a decent interval of several months, I asked novelist Russell Banks—a fellow client of my literary agent, Ellen Levine, and a pal of Morrison's from Princeton—to put in a good word.

Banks's pitch apparently helped. Ms. Morrison invited me to Princeton to see a performance she was staging with choreographer Jacques Demboise and novelist Alice Byatt. This creative troika had created a gorgeous dance-drama starring children from Princeton and from a homeless shelter in nearby Trenton. After the performance, we talked. She didn't think she was up to an interview. Moreover, Morrison believed that there were people at the *Times* who disliked her work. "I think I have a problem at the *Times*," she said.

"I don't know," I answered. "But this is a Q and A. What you put into it is what will appear. More than other forms of journalism, you can maintain a kind of control over copy. I mean, even if you don't trust me, there won't be a lot of room for journalistic interpretation."

When Toni Morrison arrived at the staid Princeton, New Jersey restaurant in a brilliant silk caftan and with salt-and-pepper dreadlocks for our first interview in the summer of 1994, all heads turned as we moved to a table. Princetonians in khaki stared.

Since her house burned to the ground the previous Christmas, Morrison had been living in this very Anglo-Saxon American town. "Princeton's fine for me right now," Morrison, then sixty-three, explained as we sat down to lunch. "I have wonderful students and good friends here. Besides, I'm in the middle of a new novel and I don't want to think about where I'm living."

The new novel was tentatively called "Paradise." In writing it, Morrison said she had been trying to imagine language to describe a place where "race exists but doesn't matter." Race has always mattered a lot in Morrison's fiction. In six previous novels, including *Beloved*, *Song of Solomon* and *Jazz*, she has focused on the particular joys and sorrows of black American women's lives. As both a writer and editor—Morrison was at Random House for eighteen years—she had made it her mission to get African-American voices into American literature.

As a luncheon companion, she was great fun—a woman of subversive jokes, gossip and surprising bits of self-revelation (the laureate unwinds to Court TV and soap operas). The stories Morrison liked to tell had this deadpan quality to them. Like fellow Nobel winner Gabriel García-Márquez, she could recount the most atrocious tale and give horror a charming veneer. One suspected that Morrison long ago figured out how to battle the cruelties of race with her wit.

She grew up Chloe Anthony Wofford, in the rust-belt town of Lorain, Ohio. Her father, George, was a ship welder; her mother, Ramah, a homemaker. At Howard University, where she did undergraduate work in English, Chloe Anthony became known as Toni. After earning a Masters in English literature at Cornell, she married Harold Morrison, a Washington architecture student, in 1959. But the union—from all reports—was difficult. (As open as Morrison is about most subjects, she refuses to discuss her former husband.) When the marriage ended, in 1964, Morrison moved to Syracuse and then to New York with her two sons, Harold Ford, three, and Slade, three months old. She supported the family as a book editor.

Evenings, after putting her children to bed, she worked on a novel about a sad black adolescent who dreams of changing the color of her eyes. *The Bluest Eye* was published in 1970, inspiring a whole generation of African-American women to tell their own stories—women like Alice

Walker, Gloria Naylor and Toni Cade Bambara.

"I'm not pleased with all the events and accidents of my life," she said over coffee and a cigarette. "You know, life is pretty terrible and some of it has hurt me a lot. I'd say I'm proud of a third of my life, comfortable with another third, and would like to redo, reconfigure, the last third."

This luncheon was the first really in-depth interview that Toni Morrison gave out after her Nobel Prize. We met in Princeton and in New York City several more times over the summer of 1994, and the *Times Magazine* ran the interview on September 11.

When you went to Stockholm in December to collect the Nobel Prize, did you feel a sense of triumph?

I felt a lot of "we" excitement. It was as if the whole category of "female writer" and "black writer" had been redeemed. I felt I represented a whole world of women who either were silenced or who had never received the imprimatur of the established literary world. I felt the way I used to feel at commencements where I'd get an honorary degree: that it was very important for young black people to see a black person do that, that there were probably young people in South-Central Los Angeles or Selma who weren't quite sure that they could do it. But seeing me up there might encourage them to write one of those books I'm desperate to read. And that made me happy. It gave me license to strut.

You've said that even after publishing three novels, you didn't dare call yourself "a writer." How was that possible?

I think, at bottom, I simply was not prepared to do the adult thing, which in those days would be associated with the male thing, which was to say, "I'm a writer." I said, "I am a mother who writes" or "I am an editor who writes." The word "writer" was hard for me to say because that's what you put on your income-tax form. I do now say, "I'm a writer." But it's the difference between identifying [with] one's work and being the person who does the work. I've always been the latter. I've always thought best when I wrote. Writing is what centered me. In the act of writing, I felt most alive, most coherent, most stable, and most vulnerable.

Interestingly, I've always felt deserving. Growing up in Lorain, my parents made all of us feel as though there were these rather extraordinary, deserving people within us. I felt like an aristocrat—or what I think an aristocrat is. I always knew we were very poor, but that was never degrading. I remember a very important lesson that my father gave me when I was twelve or thirteen. He said, "You know, today I welded a perfect seam and I signed my name to it." And I said, "But, Daddy, no one's going to see it!" And he said, "Yeah, but I know it's there." So when I was working in kitchens, I did good work.

When did you do that kind of work?

I started around thirteen. That was the work that was available; to go to a woman's house after school and clean for three or four hours. The normal teenage jobs were not available. Housework always was. It wasn't uninteresting. You got to work these gadgets that I never had at home—vacuum cleaners. Some of the people were nice. Some were terrible. Years later, I used some of what I observed in my fiction. In *The Bluest Eye*, Pauline lived in this dump and hated everything in it. And then she worked for the Fishers, who had this beautiful house, and she loved it. She got a lot of respect as their maid that she didn't get anywhere else. If she went to the grocery store as a black woman from that little house and said, "I don't want this meat," she would not be heard. But if she went in as a representative of these white people and said, "This is not good enough," they'd pay attention.

What role did books play in your childhood?

Major. A driving thing. The security I felt, the pleasure, when new books arrived was immense. My mother belonged to a book club, one of those early ones. And that was hard-earned money, you know.

As a young reader, when you encountered racial stereotypes in the classics of American literature—in Ernest Hemingway or Willa Cather or William Faulkner—how did you deal with them?

I skipped that part. Read over it. Because I loved those books. I loved them. So when they said these things that were profoundly racist, I forgave them. As for Faulkner, I read him with enormous pleasure. He seemed to me the only writer who took black people seriously. Which is not to say he was, or was not, a bigot.

It must have been fulfilling, in 1970, to see your name on the cover of The Bluest Eye.

I was upset. They had the wrong name: Toni Morrison. My name is Chloe Wofford. Toni's a nickname.

Didn't you know that your publisher, Holt, was going to use the name?

Well, I sort of knew it was going to happen. I was in a daze. I sent it in that way because the editor knew me as Toni Morrison.

So you achieved fame misnamed?

Tell me about it! I write all the time about being misnamed. How you got your name is very special. My mother, my sister, all my family call me Chloe. It was Chloe, by the way, who went to Stockholm last year to get the Nobel Prize.

In your acceptance speech you spoke against "unyielding language content to admire its own paralysis"—language that "suppresses human potential." Some of your critics thought you were using the Nobel ceremony to advocate politically correct literature.

You know, the term "political correctness" has become shorthand for discrediting ideas. I believe that powerful, sharp, incisive, critical, bloody, dramatic, theatrical language is not dependent on injurious language, on curses. Or hierarchy. You're not stripping language by requiring people to be sensitive to other people's pain. I can't just go around saying, "Kill whitey." What does that mean? It may satisfy something, but there's no information there. I can't think through that. And I have to use language that's better than that. What I think the political correctness debate is really about is the power to be able to define. The definers want the power to name. And the defined are now taking that power away from them.

Which authors influenced you when you began writing?

James Baldwin. He could say something in a phrase that clarified all sorts of conflicting feelings. Before Baldwin, I got titillated by fiction through reading the African novelists, men and women—Chinua Achebe, Camara Laye. Also Bessie Head and the Negritude Movement, including Léopold Sédar Senghor and Aime Cesaire. They did not explain their black world. Or clarify it. Or justify it. White writers had always taken white centrality for granted. They inhabited their world in a central position and everything nonwhite was "other." These African writers took their blackness as central and the whites were the "other." After I published *The Bluest Eye*, I frequently got the question, "Do you write for white readers?" The question stunned me. I remember asking a white woman at Knopf, "What do white people mean when they say, 'I know you did not write that book for me, but I like it'? I never say, 'Oh, Eudora Welty, I know your book was not written for me, but I enjoy it.'" This woman explained that white readers were not accustomed to reading books about black people in which the central issue is not white people. In my work, the white world is marginalized. This kind of ground-shifting seems much more common to black women writers. Not so much black men writers. Black men writers are often interested in their relations with white men. White men, by and large, are not powerful figures in black women's literature.

When you began writing, the best-known black literary voices were male—Ralph Ellison, Baldwin, Richard Wright. Did you make a conscious effort to change that?

When I began writing I didn't write against existing voices. There had been some women writing—Paule Marshall, Zora Neale Hurston, though I hadn't read Hurston yet. When I began, there was just one thing that I wanted to write about, which was the true devastation of racism on the most vulnerable, the most helpless unit in the society—a black female and child. I wanted to write about what it was like to be the subject of racism. It had a specificity that was damaging. And if there was no support system in the community and in the family, it could cause spiritual death, self-loathing, terrible things. Once I did that, I wanted to write another book. By the time I wrote the third one, I began to think in terms of what had gone on before —whether my territory was different. I felt what I was doing was so unique that I didn't think a man could possibly understand what the little girl in *The Bluest Eye* was feeling. I did not think a white person could describe it. So I thought I was telling a tale untold.

There's a boom now in black women's literature. Terry McMillan makes bestseller lists. Bebe Moore Campbell's **Brothers and Sisters** *is a Book-of-the-Month Club main selection. Is the book world changing?*

Yes. This means there is now such a thing as popular black women's literature. Popular! In 1992, there were four books by black women on the bestseller lists—at the same time. Terry McMillan's, Alice Walker's and two of mine. Now that's exhilarating!

When I was a book editor, I had to worry about all the books I was publishing by black authors being lumped together in reviews. Black authors who didn't write anything at all like each other would be reviewed together. Their works were understood first of all to be black, and not, you know, history books or novels.

Back to your Nobel. What did you do with the $817,771 that came with it?

Put it away for my retirement. And then, of course, the minute I did that, my house burned down. So, suddenly, I needed it and couldn't put my hands on it. [Sighs] It's probably just as well. Because if I hadn't done that, I would have taken the money and rebuilt my house and it would have been like most of the money I've ever had—as soon as you get it, there's this big hole waiting for it.

Did the fire seem like some kind of mystical leveling for flying too high?

No. In the two years around the Nobel, I had a lot of bad luck, a lot of very serious devastations. My mother died, other things. The only thing that happened that was unexpected and truly wonderful was the Nobel Prize. So I regard the fact that my house burned down after I won the Nobel Prize to be better than having my house burn down without having won the Nobel Prize. Most people's houses just burn down. Period. When I think about the fire, I think I may not ever, ever, ever get over it. And it isn't even about the things. It's about photographs, plants I nurtured for twenty years, about the view of the Hudson River, my children's report cards, my manuscripts. There were some months when I wouldn't talk to anybody who had not had a house burn down.

That must have been a limited circle.

Oh, I don't know. You'd be surprised how many people had their house burn down. The writer Maxine Hong Kingston and I traded information. She had her whole house burn down. Right now, I don't want to think about where I live because I'm working hard on a new book. And I am getting deeper and deeper into the book. And I can feel myself getting vaguer and vaguer and vaguer. Pretty soon I will be like someone looking through water—everybody will look to me as if I'm in a tank somewhere.

I read that your two sons didn't particularly like growing up with a writer for a mother.

Who does? I wouldn't. Writers are not there. They're likely to get vague when you need them. And while the vagueness may be good for the writer, if children need your complete attention, then it's bad for them.

You wrote your early novels while holding a full-time job and raising your sons alone. How did you keep the responsibilities from silencing you as a writer?

It wasn't easy. But when I left Washington, I really wanted to see if I could do it alone. In New York, whenever things got difficult I thought about my mother's mother, a sharecropper, who, with her husband, owed money to their landlord. In 1906, she escaped with her seven children to meet her husband in Birmingham, where he was working as a musician. It was a dangerous trip, but she wanted a better life. Whenever things seemed difficult for me in New York, I thought that what I was doing wasn't anything as hard as what she did. I remember one day when I was confused about what I had to do next—write a review, pick up groceries, what? I took out a yellow pad and made a list of all the things I had to do. It included large things, like "be a good daughter and a good mother," and small things, like "call the phone company." I made another list of the things I wanted to do. There were only two things without which I couldn't live: mother my children and write books. Then I cut out everything that didn't have to do with those two things. There was an urgency—that's all I remember. Not having the leisure to whine. Not paying close attention to what others thought my life should be like. Not organizing my exterior and interior self for the approval of men—which I had done a lot of before. It's not a bad thing to please a husband or a lover, but I couldn't do that. It took up time and thought.

There's a lot of sexual violation in your fiction. Why?

Because when I began to write, it was an unmentionable. It is so dangerous, it is so awful, so wicked, that I think in connection with vulnerable black women it was never talked about. I wanted to write books that ran the whole gamut of women's sexual experiences. I didn't like the imposition that had been placed on black women's sexuality in literature. They were either mothers, mammies or whores. And they were not vulnerable people. They were not people who were supposed to enjoy sex, either. That was forbidden in literature—to enjoy your body, be in your body, defend your body. But at the same time I wanted to say, "You still can be prey." Right now, I've been writing a page or two in my new book, trying to evoke out-of-door safety for women. How it feels. How it is perceived when you feel perfectly safe a long way from home. This new book, "Paradise," has taken over my imagination completely and I'm having the best time ever. I wrote thirteen pages in three days. I've never done that in my life.

When you relax, what do you read?

Well, I don't read much fiction when I'm writing, as I am right now.

If I read fiction, I want to be in the author's head, and I have to be in mine. I did have some time off recently and I read Marguerite Duras and Leslie Marmon Silko and Jean Genet's biography. When I'm on tour or traveling, I generally read mystery stories—Ruth Rendell, John le Carre, P. D. James and this man called Carl Hiaasen. He has a wonderful ear for dialogue.

Have you been following the O. J. Simpson case?

Yes, and I find it very sinister. It's a carnival. Sometimes you think it's about men beating women, sometimes about athletes and their being made into things. Sometimes you think it's about white/black, Hollywood, but it's not. This is just one big national spectacle, and they get to kill him. We get to watch. We get to focus on the detritus, not the victim.

Beloved *is the story of an escaped slave, Sethe, who kills her daughter rather than see the child live in slavery. Were you frightened while writing it?*

I had never been so frightened. I could imagine slavery in an intellectual way, but to feel it viscerally was terrifying. I had to go inside. Like an actor does. I had to feel what it might feel like for my own children to be enslaved. At the time, I was no longer working at an office, and that permitted me to go deep.

With *Beloved*, I wanted to say, "Let's get rid of these words like 'the slave woman' and 'the slave child,' and talk about people with names, like you and like me, who were there." Now, what does slavery feel like? What can you do? How can you be? Clearly, it is a situation in which you have practically no power. And if you decide you are not going to be a victim, then it's a major risk. And you end up doing some terrible things. And some not-so-terrible things. But the risk of being your own person, or trying to have something to do with your destiny, is one of the major battles in life.

Do you ever get writer's block?

I disavow that term. There are times when you don't know what you're doing or when you don't have access to the language or the event. So if you're sensitive, you can't do it. When I wrote *Beloved*, I thought about it for three years. I started writing the manuscript after thinking about it, and getting to know the people and getting over the fear of entering that arena, and it took me three more years to write it. But those other three years I was still at work, though I hadn't put a word down.

Several of your friends told me you were surprised when you won the Nobel Prize. Why?

Because I never thought I had that many supporters. I never thought that the Swedish Academy either knew about my work or took it seriously. The reason it didn't occur to me is not because I didn't think my work eminently worthy. But I was aware of the cautions and the caveats and the misunderstandings that seemed to lie around the criticisms of my work. My books are frequently read as representative of what the black condition is. Actually, the books are about very specific circumstances, and in them are people who do very specific things. But more importantly, the plot and characters are part of my effort to create a language in which I can posit philosophical questions. I want the reader to ponder those questions not because I put them in an essay, but because they are part of a narrative.

Let me put it another way. I think of jazz music as very complicated, very sophisticated and very difficult. It is also very popular. And it has the characteristic of being sensual and illegal. And its sensuality and its illegality may prevent people from seeing how sophisticated it is. Now, that to me says something about the culture in which I live and about my work. I would like my work to do two things: be as demanding and sophisticated as I want it to be, and at the same time be accessible in a sort of emotional way to lots of people, just like jazz. That's a hard task. But that's what I want to do.

•••

Recommended Reading

Brady, John. *The Craft of Interviewing*. New York: Vintage Books, 1976. An old book, but the absolute horse's mouth, on the nuts and bolts of interviewing. Nothing has ever been produced that's better.

Fallaci, Oriana. *Interview With History*. New York: Liveright, 1976. The Queen of the Q and A collects fourteen of her "oldies but goodies."

Fallaci, Oriana. *The Egoists: Sixteen Amazing Interviews*. Chicago: Henry Regnery, 1968. And they are.

Golson, G. Barry, editor. *The Playboy Interview*. New York: Playboy Press, 1981. Golson, the smart, smart editor who brought the *Playboy* Interview to its heights, collects some of his favorite pieces and adds a dynamite introduction full of marvelous ideas on the craft.

Golson, G. Barry, editor. *The Playboy Interview II*. New York: Putnam, 1983. More great stuff.

Groebel, Lawrence. *Conversations with Capote*. New York: New American Library, 1985. *Playboy's* best interviewer shows how he does his thing. What he elicits from Capote is delicious.

Kent, Eileen, editor. *The Playboy Interview: Three Decades—A Multimedia Mirror of Contemporary Culture*. Chicago: Playboy-IBM, 1994. The complete text of 352 *Playboy* Interviews, with background information on one CD-ROM.

Sylvester, Christopher, editor. *The Norton Book of Interviews*. New York: Norton, 1996. An absolutely mindboggling collection including Horace Greeley Q and A-ing Brigham Young, Joseph Stalin interrogated by H. G. Wells, Vladimir Nabokov questioned by Penelope Gilliatt, and Bette Davis interviewed by Rex Reed.

Photo Credits

THE DALAI LAMA WITH CLAUDIA DREIFUS. © Mike O'Neill.

ANDREW YOUNG. © Susan J. Ross. Courtesy of HarperCollins.

AUNG SAN SUU KYI. © Steve McCurry/Magnum Photos, Inc.

ARTHUR CAPLAN. © Tommy Leonard. Courtesy of University of Pennsylvania Medical Center, Center for Bioethics.

KAREEM ABDUL-JABBAR. © Wen Roberts. Courtesy of William Morrow.

ALVIN AND HEIDI TOFFLER. © Bonnie Schiffman.

BARNEY FRANK. Courtesy of Barney Frank.

BENAZIR BHUTTO. From the author's collection.

HANAN M. ASHWARI. © Ed Kashi.

MYRLIE EVERS. Courtesy of Home Box Office.

JOHN SHALIKASHVILI. Courtesy of the office of the Chairman of the Joint Chiefs of Staff.

NADINE STROSSEN. Courtesy of Nadine Strossen.

RICHARD DREYFUSS. From the author's collection.

ESTHER DYSON. Courtesy of Esther Dyson.

NINA TOTENBERG, LINDA WERTHEIMER, COKIE ROBERTS. © Neil Selkirk.

JOHN SAYLES. From the author's collection.

DAN RATHER. Courtesy of CBS News.

SAMUEL L. JACKSON. Courtesy of Wolf Kasteler Inc.

ARTHUR MILLER. Courtesy of Twentieth Century Fox.

TONI MORRISON. © Kate Kunz. Courtesy of Alfred A. Knopf, Inc.

About the Author

In 1975, **Claudia Dreifus** received a grant from the Fund for Investigative Journalism to study coercive sterilizations performed on Mexican-American women at Los Angeles County Medical Center. Her exposé, published in *The Progressive*, helped lead to enforcement of federal regulations against the practice. A 1987 *Mother Jones* story on the murder of a young American in Chile, "Rodrigo's Last Trip Home," was named Best Feature Article of the Year by the American Society of Journalists and Authors. That same year, "How Rural Women Are Saving Their Families' Farms," which appeared in *Glamour*, received the American Values Award. Her 1988 memoir on her parents' and grandparents' immigration to America, "Why I Write," was published in *Present Tense* and received Brandeis University's Simon Rockower Prize for Distinguished Commentary.

From 1981 through 1992, Dreifus was one of the regular *Playboy* interviewers, producing Q and A's with such figures as Gabriel García Márquez, James Woods, Donald Sutherland, Susan Sarandon, Daniel Ortega, Gregory Hines, and Arthur Schlesinger. (As *Playboy's* most frequently published female interviewer, she holds the honor of having been misquoted by then-President Reagan in one of his State of the Union addresses.) More than three hundred of her interviews have appeared in publications ranging from *TV Guide* to *The Nation*, and including all of New York City's major newspapers.

Today, Dreifus is considered to be the leading interviewer in American journalism. Since 1993, her interviews have appeared regularly in *The New York Times Magazine*, where she is a Contributing Writer. Dreifus is also a Distinguished Visiting Professor in the Graduate Creative Writing Program of the City College of New York. She lives in New York City.

Clyde Haberman writes a column for *The New York Times* called "NYC," about life in New York. A longtime foreign correspondent working extensively in East Asia, Europe and the Middle East, he has been the *Times's* bureau chief in Tokyo, Rome, and Jerusalem.